THE YOUNG HUSSAR

THE YOUNG HUSSAR

The Peninsular War Journal of
Colonel Thomas Wildman of Newstead Abbey

Edited by Michael Birks

Book Guild Publishing
Sussex, England

First published in Great Britain in 2007 by
The Book Guild Ltd,
Pavilion View,
19 New Road,
Brighton, BN1 1UF

.

Typesetting in Times by
IML Typographers, Birkenhead, Merseyside

Printed in Great Britain by
Athenaeum Press Ltd, Gateshead

A catalogue record for this book is available from
The British Library.

ISBN 978 1 84624 111 6

Contents

Preface

During the final campaign of the Peninsular War, Colonel Thomas Wildman, then a captain in the 7th Hussars kept a journal giving a day-to-day account of his life and his regiment's movements and, to a large extent, those of the Hussar Brigade. When the colonel died in 1859 the journal passed to his widow, and upon her death in 1879 it came into the possession of his brother Edward's daughter, Elizabeth Darling. She had no surviving children, and it remained in the family of her husband, Colonel Augustine Darling, until it was acquired on behalf of Wildman's old home, Newstead Abbey, in 1963. So far as I have been able to ascertain the journal had never been transcribed. My interest was aroused because I too had served in horsed cavalry during the early days of the Second World War, so I decided to transcribe and edit the journal myself.

The journal is contained in a slim volume bound in dark-red leather measuring just over seven inches by four inches – a convenient size to slip into his sabretache. Wildman evidently ruled the pages himself, dividing the left-hand pages into the days of the week, in which he recorded daily events. He kept the right-hand pages blank for any comments he wished to record. (In editing the journal I have placed the weekly comments on the left-hand page immediately following each week's daily entries, thus avoiding any blank spaces on the right-hand pages.) Wildman's writing is very small and neat, but often difficult to read without a magnifying glass, especially where the paper has been affected by damp. This is hardly surprising in view of the appalling weather in the Pyrenees during the winter of 1813–14.

The Peninsular War produced a vast number of diaries and reminiscences. The latter, written with hindsight and sometimes with memory fading, lack the immediacy of a diary, while many of the diaries are incomplete or have gaps. Perhaps the chief interest of Wildman's journal is that he began it a few days after the 7th Hussars set out from

London in August 1813 and continued it without a break until after the regiment returned to England in August 1814.

In editing the journal I have tried to paint a picture of the everyday life of a young cavalry officer. I have drawn on regimental records and the letters and recollections of Wildman's brother officers in the Hussar Brigade. I have tried to confine the narrative to matters which would have been within his own perspective and have concentrated on the everyday aspects of army life – marches, care of the horses, food, uniforms, postal services and so forth. All matters which play a not insignificant part in the conduct of a campaign.

All stories should have a beginning and an end as well as a middle. I have included a sketch of the Wildman family's humble origins in North Lancashire, the questionable way in which they acquired their wealth, and Thomas Wildman's life at Harrow, his friendship with Lord Byron and early military career. I have included a short account of his experiences at Waterloo and his later life at Newstead Abbey which he bought from Byron in 1818.

Wildman had no children to whom he could pass on family history and anecdotes, and nearly all his his papers were destroyed. In tracing Wildman's later life I have had to rely largely upon what his friends had to say about him. Moreover I doubt whether he or his cousin James Beckford Wildman knew much about their family origins. Until Dr Coope and Mrs Haidee Jackson discovered Barkin Yate, their grandfather's little farm, I had assumed it was a grand property – James Beckford Wildman was my great-great-grandfather.

In my efforts to trace Wildman's family history I have received help from many people too numerous to mention each one individually. However, I am particularly grateful to Dr Rosalys Coope whose own researches have been invaluable, and to Mrs Haidee Jackson, the curator of Newstead Abbey, who supplied me with a copy of the journal and much other original material. I wish to express my thanks to the following persons: to Mrs Melinda Elder to Dr Dalziel of the Lancaster Maritime Museum, Mrs Woodhouse, whose family own the old Wildman home, now called Barkin Gate, Mr Jim Murray, Miss J.T. Smith, principal archivist at Essex County Council, Mr Terry Knight, principal librarian of Cornish Studies, Falmouth, Miss Hammond, librarian at Chiswick Library, Mr J.R. Elliott, Dr I.D.K. Hawkyard, archivist of Harrow School, and Mr I. MacKenzie of the Lancaster Maritime Museum. With regard to Wildman's military career I am greatly indebted to Major J.S. Knight, regimental secretary of The Queen's Own Hussars, to the staff of the

National Army Museum, and in particular to Dr Peter Boyden, Mrs Marion Harding, Mrs Lesley Smurthwaite and Mrs S.K. Hopkins. Finally I am most grateful to Dr Noel Hopkinson of Trinity College, Cambridge for kindly translating Wildman's quotation from Albius Tibullus, to my friend Hilary Sweet-Escott for allowing me to include verse from Caroline Preisig's album and to my friend Mr Ron Hoare for putting the whole book onto my computer.

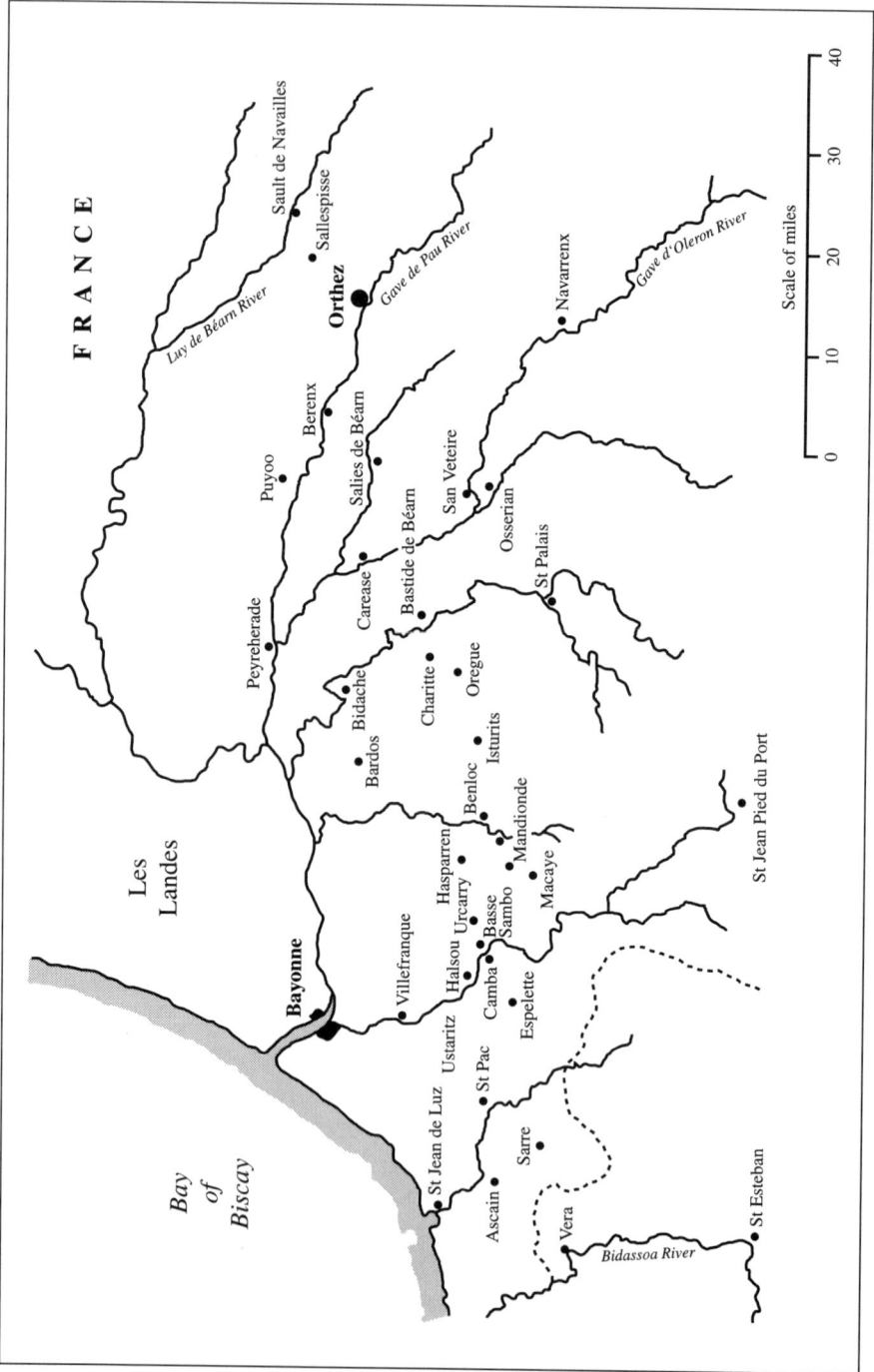

FRANCE

Les
Landes

Bay
of
Biscay

Luy de Béarn River

Sault de Navailles

Sallespisse

Orthez

Gave de Pau River

Puyoo

Berenx

Salies de Béarn

San Veteire

Navarrenx

Gave d'Oleron River

Peyreherade

Bastide de Béarn

Carease

Osserian

St Palais

Bidache

Charitte

Oregue

Bardos

Benloc

Isturits

Mandionde

Hasparren

Macaye

Villefranque

Bayonne

Halsou Urcarry

Basse
Sambo

Camba

Espelette

Ustaritz

St Pac

St Jean de Luz

Sarre

Ascain

Vera

St Jean Pied du Port

St Esteban

Bidassoa River

| Scale of miles |
| 0   10   20   30   40 |

x

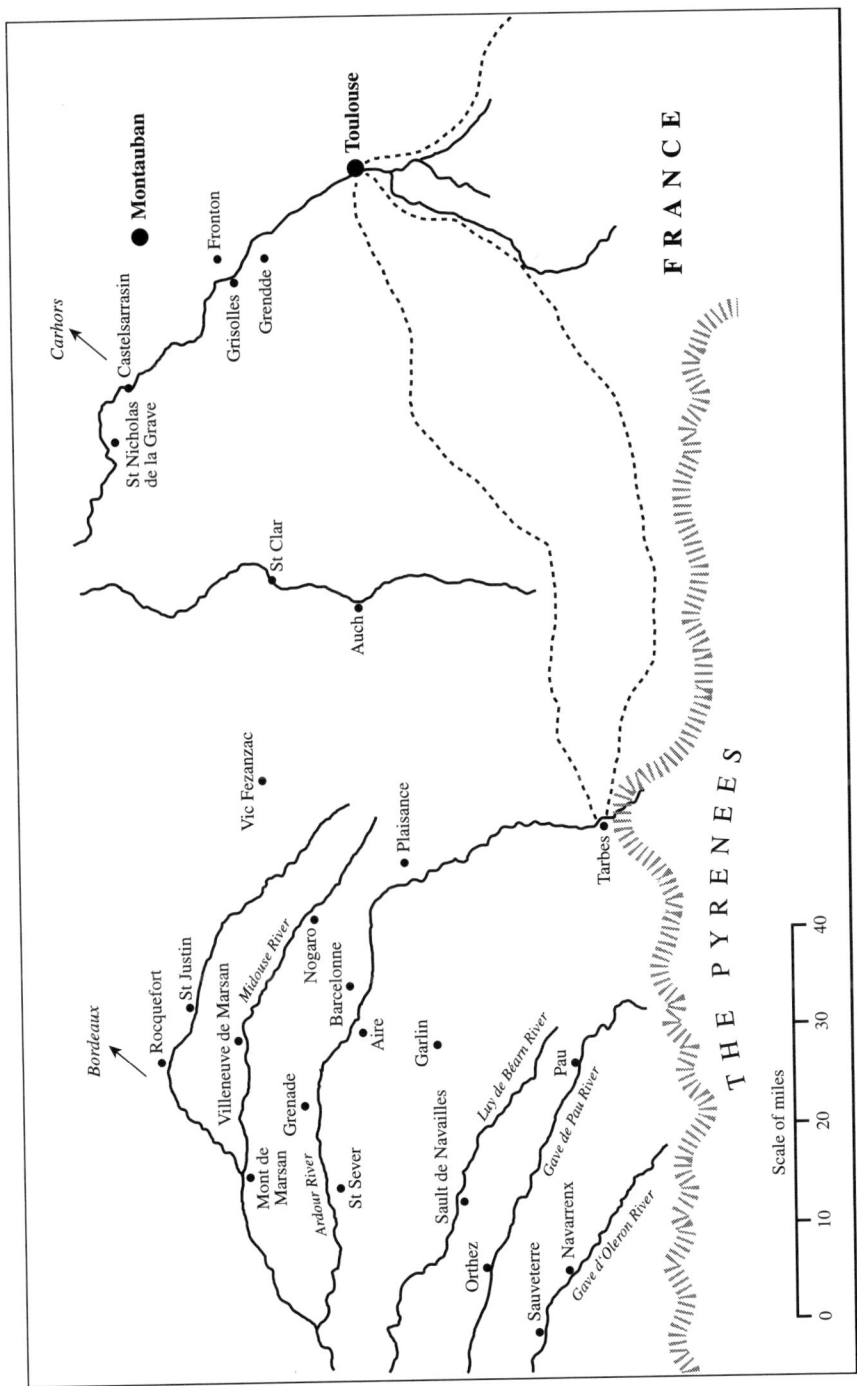

Maps of France showing locations mentioned in the Journal

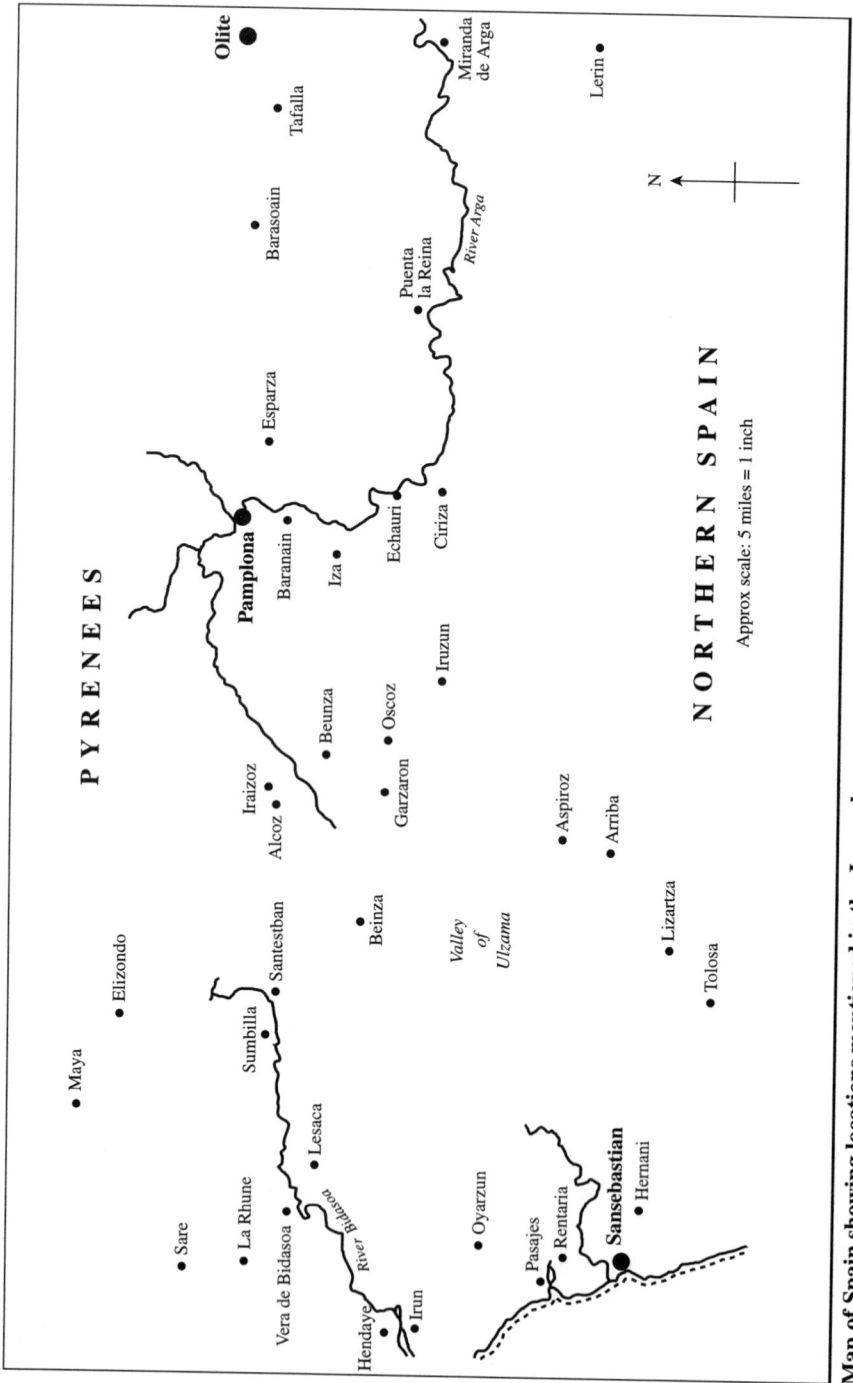

PYRENEES

- Olite
- Tafalla
- Miranda de Arga
- Lerin
- Barasoain
- Puenta la Reina
- *River Arga*
- Esparza
- Echauri
- Ciriza
- Pamplona
- Baranain
- Iza
- Iruzun
- Beunza
- Garzaron
- Oscoz
- Iraizoz
- Alcoz
- Aspiroz
- Arriba
- Beinza
- *Valley of Ulzama*
- Lizartza
- Santestban
- Tolosa
- Elizondo
- Sumbilla
- Maya
- Sare
- La Rhune
- Lesaca
- Vera de Bidasoa
- *River Bidasoa*
- Hendaye
- Irun
- Oyarzun
- Pasajes
- Rentaria
- **Sansebastian**
- Hernani

N ←

NORTHERN SPAIN

Approx scale: 5 miles = 1 inch

Map of Spain showing locations mentioned in the Journal

xii

PROLOGUE

The Wildman Family

In 1813 Tom Wildman was rich and was a captain in the 7th Hussars, a crack cavalry regiment whose dandified colonel, the Earl of Uxbridge, was a close friend of the Prince Regent. The Colonel and his brother officers might have been rather surprised if they had known that Tom's grandfather Edward Wildman who died in 1786, a year before he was born, was only a small hill farmer in a remote part of North Lancashire. Indeed it seems likely that Tom himself might have been surprised to know this.

In the seventeenth century there were scores of Wildmans in this part of Lancashire, but the earliest one who can be identified as an ancestor of Tom was Edward Wildman, his great-great-grandfather, who died in 1706. The family, including sons and daughters and their spouses and children, all lived in an isolated farmhouse upon the fells in Roeburndale, in the parish of Melling some miles from the little village of Wray. The property was then called Barkin Great or Barkin Yeat; it is now called Barkin Gate and is still a working farm. The house lies in an exposed position, though sheltered to some extent by Claughton Moor and Whit Moor which rise above it on the west side. On the east side the ground drops away into a steep little valley with a stream running through it. Beyond the valley the moors stretch eastward into North Yorkshire. It is a lonely place even today, but in the eighteenth century it would have seemed very cut off from the outside world, although the port of Lancaster is less than ten miles away. With so many children and their husbands and wives, conditions in the farm must have been cramped.

Three years after Edward died his son and heir, Richard, rebuilt the house, placing his initials and the date – 1709 – above the door. It is a sturdy stone house with a slate roof, and despite some alterations and additions the house must look much the same as it did all those years ago. Richard died in 1733 and his eldest son, Edward, inherited the farm. During Edward's long life – he was born in 1695 – the family fortunes improved somewhat. He married a Lancaster girl named Elizabeth Bagott and they acquired another little house in Wray. A stone set in the wall bears the date 1746 and their initials, E & E W. By this time they had been married for some years and the fact that both their initials appear may suggest that the property was jointly owned, or at any rate that she had a financial interest in it. Edward was now referred to in deeds as 'gent' rather than 'yeoman', but it is doubtful if his social status had really altered very much. His son James was almost illiterate and Ann, his son Richard's wife, could not write.

Edward's eldest son, George, died in 1780. During his lifetime he had acquired some land of his own in the area, including a house in Wray called Greystones. At the date of his death Mary, his wife, was pregnant. When Edward died in 1786 he left all his property in trust for his grandson George, subject to a life interest in favour of Richard, his second son, who died in 1800, leaving two sons. When young George grew up he went to live in Littledale near Lancaster where he married and had nine children. He died in 1841, but Barkin Yeat must have passed out of the family some years after Richard's death.

The fortunes of Edward's other sons, Thomas, Henry and James, were very different. Thomas went up to London where he entered the law and was admitted as a solicitor and attorney in 1764. It is possible that he was related to another attorney named Thomas Wildman whose name appears on the Solicitors' Roll some years earlier. He then went into partnership with a solicitor named James Coulthard who came from Cumberland, which may point to a family connection. Mr Coulthard had a fashionable practice in Lincoln's Inn where 'he had the superintendance of the affairs of several of the nobility and gentry in the kingdom'. Shortly before he died Mr Coulthard took his nephews Thomas and James Graham into the partnership. They, too, came from Cumberland.

There is a further possibility that Thomas Wildman was related to a London wine merchant also named Thomas Wildman. The wine merchant had married a sister of a notorious political agitator, John Horne Tooke, and they were both friends of John Wilkes, who achieved fame as a champion of popular rights against the encroaching power of the executive. Three times Wilkes was elected as Member of Parliment for Middlesex, and each time his election was annulled by the Commons. In his challenge to the government, one of his supporters was his fellow City alderman, the millionaire William Beckford, twice Lord Mayor of London. The evidence for linking the attorney with Alderman Beckford is contained in a letter written by a descendant of his brother Henry. She states that her great-grandfather had emigrated to Australia in 1845, and she recalled that her grandfather had spoken of 'a colonel who made a lot of money in the West Indies, of John Horne Tooke, a member of Parliament who married a Wildman'. Making allowances for family traditions becoming distorted as one generation succeeds another, this story seems sufficiently close to the truth to support a link between the two Thomas Wildmans. It would certainly explain how an obscure North Country attorney came to the attention of the millionaire alderman.

The turning point in Thomas Wildman's fortunes came with the death of Alderman Beckford. He owned vast sugar plantations in Jamaica and boasted that he was the richest man in England. When he died in 1770, William, his only legitimate son, was ten years old. However, the alderman had a large number of bastards for whom he had made provision. His widow then became involved in a dispute with the executors, and it was at this point that Thomas Wildman was called in to advise her. He became a member of the family council set up by the late alderman to manage his estate during William's minority. In view of the dispute with the executors, the estate was administered by the Court of Chancery until young William came of age. During the intervening period Thomas Wildman's influence over William and his mother steadily increased, and he advised on every aspect of William's life including his religion, though the young man found the solicitor too pious for his taste. In September 1781 Beckford came of age and obtained control of his vast fortune.

From the age of seventeen Beckford had spent much of his time abroad and was more interested in art and literature than he was in business matters, which bored him. He is best remembered as the author of an Oriental tale, *Vathek*, and as one of the great English eccentrics. He was wildly extravagant and was to become a prey to a succession of predators. Thomas Wildman did little to encourage him in the management of his fortune, and the young man left his affairs entirely in the hands of his solicitor. Now that Thomas Wildman's management was no longer subject to the restraint of the Court of Chancery, he was able to run the estate to his own advantage. Thomas lost no time in bringing his brothers James and Henry into the management of the Beckford properties. James became agent in Jamaica and Henry became the London agent responsible for ordering stores for the plantations and selling the annual sugar crop.

Nothing is known about the careers of James and Henry up to this time. However, it seems inconceivable that Thomas would have dared to entrust Beckford's vast estates to the management of two young and inexperienced men from a remote Lancashire farming community, notwithstanding the ties of nepotism. The most likely explanation is to be found in the proximity of Barkin Yeat to the city of Lancaster.

Lancaster was then an important trading port and provided many opportunities for landless younger sons who had to make their own way in the world. The local merchants usually preferred to employ sons of friends or relatives, as this gave them an opportunity to satisfy themselves that they were honest and reliable. Once overseas, supervision of their employees was well-nigh impossible and dishonesty was rife. They preferred also to employ young men as they were more likely to survive tropical diseases and the harsh conditions aboard the ships.

The name Wildman crops up regularly in relation to the port's commercial activity, though none of these men can be positively identified with this family. In such a close-knit community it is possible, and even probable, that they were related. Richard Wildman and his father both had brothers about whom nothing is known. For example, in 1747 a James Wildman of Tunstall, which is about five miles north of Barkin Yeat, apprenticed himself to a Liverpool firm to sail in the ship *Vine*. The ship *Tartar*, commanded by a Captain Thomas Wildman, was sailing to Africa and the West Indies in 1761–2. In 1766 a James Wildman was sharing a house in Lancaster with a Robert Rawlinson, who may have been a member of a prosperous local family of that name, who were West India merchants. This James could have been Thomas and Henry's brother, who was then nineteen years old.

Assuming that James and Henry did gain experience in the West Indian plantations, they could have been employed as factors or overseers, or they could have been actively employed in the slave trade. Factors were responsible for obtaining supplies and provisions which came from England and arranging for the shipping home of the sugar crop. Most of these transactions were conducted not for cash but by bartering with the ships' captains. The overseers were employed to run the plantations. Supervising the slaves who cut the cane, they were responsible for the highly skilled process of boiling and skimming it to produce molasses to be distilled into rum, and the brown muskovado which was shipped home to England for refining. In the absence of the plantation owners, such men could do more or less what they pleased to the slaves, both male and female. Opinion in England was that the majority were ill-treated. William Hickey who visited Jamaica in 1775 found most of the slaves he saw 'dejected and miserable'.

During the eighteenth century Lancaster was the fourth most important slave port after Liverpool, London and Bristol, although its volume of the West African slave trade was modest in comparison with the other three. Many of the Lancaster slave merchants were ambitious young men with little prospect of inheriting any property, who were prepared to sign on as deck-hands in the slave ships, and work their way up to become mates or even skippers. Such men organised trading partnerships, of usually six to eight members, among men with money to invest. They chartered ships, enlisted crews and arranged for the purchase of cargoes from the manufacturing towns of Yorkshire and Lancashire. The Lancaster slavers were usually small ships, not requiring large crews, which could work their way up the estuaries of West Africa. Most of the crews were recruited locally. Some of the provisions too, such as beans for feeding the slaves, were often obtainable from local farms.

The slavers followed the well-established triangular route. Arriving on the west coast of Africa, their trading stock of muskets, knives, tobacco, beads and a wide assortment of manufactured goods would be bartered for slaves. The ships then set off as speedily as possible on the Middle Passage. A fast voyage was essential to keep losses through sickness among their human cargoes to a minimum. Arriving in the West Indies the slaves were sold for cash, or preferably bartered for sugar, rum and mahogany through resident merchants, many of whom had also come from Lancashire. On arrival home the slave traders disposed of their return cargoes and shared the profits or reinvested the money in a fresh venture. The harsh life of a slave trader would have certainly turned James and Henry into tough men of business well qualified for their new employment, and none too scrupulous.

No doubt James was ruthlessly efficient and increased the productivity and the profitability of Beckford's estates. He was a tough determined-looking man who wore his hair in a short queue throughout his life. He soon made his mark on the plantations, for on 21 August 1782, Thomas Thistlewood, an overseer on a neighbouring estate recorded in his diary: 'In the evening when I got home found Mr. Francis Scott here. He has left Ackendown. Mr Wildman discharges everyone.' In the same year he became a magistrate and in 1786 he was made a member of the Jamaican Legislative Council and had a street in Kingston named after him.

For the next twenty years the three brothers had virtually unfettered control of Beckford's properties. They increased their hold over him by letting him become deeply indebted to them. For much of this period Beckford was abroad, and so long as Thomas supplied him with money to buy antiquities and works of art or pay for the building of his Gothic pile, Fonthill Abbey, he did not question their activities. In the Wildmans' defence it could be said that they were no more dishonest than many of the other West Indian agents who fleeced their employers; they were just rather better at it!

During these years Thomas Wildman prospered in his legal practice and

7

was improving his social status so far as he was able at a time when attorneys were not generally held in high esteem. In 1773 he became a member of Lincoln's Inn, although the Bar was beginning to exclude attorneys from the Inns of Court. Three years later he took out a grant of arms, an essential requirement for anyone with aspirations to gentility and fairly easy to obtain if one had money. He was also on the Committee of the Society of Gentleman Practisers, the forerunner of the present Law Society.

In 1785 Thomas, who was now forty-five years of age, married a lady of thirty-five named Sarah Hardinge, the daughter of Henry Hardinge of Bacton Hall in Suffolk. There is no record of the Hardinges owning the property, a pleasant house but hardly up to the appellation of 'Hall', and they probably held it on lease. Nevertheless the lady was said to be worth £30,000.

They set up home at 16 Bedford Square in Holborn within easy reach of the office of Messrs Wildman Coulthard and Graham.* Five years later his increasing wealth enabled Thomas to adopt the lifestyle of a country gentleman, and they acquired another large house on Twickenham Green named Gifford Lodge, since demolished.

It is possible that they retained Bacton Hall, for in the Waterloo Roll Tom Wildman gave this as his home address, unless, of course, he gave it because he wanted an address that sounded substantial and was not his mother's.

During these years William Beckford was becoming more and more in debt to the Wildmans. Thomas now further increased his hold over him by buying up the mortgage on one of Beckford's English estates. By 1795 Beckford's indebtedness was so great that Thomas was in a position to compel his feckless client to let him have his parliamentary seat at Hindon, one of the pocket boroughs he owned. However, Thomas's parliamentary career was short-lived, for in the following December he died of 'gout of the stomach' – probably cancer or a perforated ulcer.

After his brother's death, James took his seat in Parliament, and he and Henry continued to act as Beckford's agents until 1802 when they presented him with an extortionate bill of £86,000 for their services. When he could not pay, they took over his Esher estate in Jamaica in satisfaction of the debt. There was certainly a good deal of truth in the assertion Beckford later made in his *Liber Veritas* that 'between this harpy and his two brothers who played in concert at proper time half my substance has

---

* This firm still exists under the name of Payne Hicks Beach.

been devoured'. Rogues they may have been, but in fairness to Thomas, he appears to have protected Beckford's interests in other matters, and so far as the rest of the world was concerned he was a God-fearing and respected citizen.

Thomas and Sarah had five children: Thomas, born in 1787, followed by Maria, Edward, George and John. When her husband died, Sarah was forty-five years old and Tom was eight. Thomas made ample provision for his widow, who, of course, had her own fortune, and left each of his younger children £10,000. The rest of his estate, his Jamaican plantations and his English property, he left to his eldest son. It is difficult to estimate how much he was worth, but as regards his Jamaican property the *Slave Register* in 1810 recorded that his Quebec plantation had 800 slaves. Henry owned the Esher estate with 273 slaves, while James owned Salt Savannah and Low Ground with a total of 480 slaves. James was reputed to have had an income of £20,000 a year when he died in 1816. During Tom's minority the income from his father's estate would have been accumulated, so that by the time that he received it the income alone would have amounted to a substantial fortune!

Schooldays and Early Army Life

Mrs Wildman's few surviving letters show her to have been an intelligent and educated woman. She took an interest in current affairs and was well versed in the Classics and literature. While Tom was at school she had no inhibitions about displaying her knowledge. For example, in 1804, she writes:

> I will give you an observation of Lord Bacon – taken from one of the papers in the World – that the fame of Cicero, Seneca, and the younger Pliny, had scarce lasted to this Day, at least not so <u>fresh</u> if it had not been joined with some vanity and boasting in themselves for boasting (continues that great writer) seems to be like varnish, that not only makes wood shine, but last – this may be very just, but I do not think it a very liberal observation of Lord Bacon; for were it not for this <u>varnish</u>, or in other words, which I think a man's giving a <u>fair</u> account of himself and his actions, – much pleasurable and useful knowledge would be lost to the World.

Even when he was grown up her letters to her 'beloved son' indicate a quiet but firm influence over him, even though she was apt to talk about her 'silly nerves'. However, that may have been no more than an affectation to hide her abilities at a time when ladies were expected to play a subordinate role in life. For, as Jane Austen observed in *Northanger Abbey*, 'A woman, especially if she have the misfortune of knowing any thing, should conceal it as well as she can.' But it was as an artist that Mrs Wildman excelled. Both Tom and Maria inherited this talent. A number of Tom's drawings have survived, but Maria was by far the most talented. Fortunately her album has not been lost and contains some exquisite flower paintings by her mother as well as her own meticulous drawings and some charming paintings in gouache and watercolour.

How much Tom knew about his father's early life and business activities it is impossible to say. He was only eight years old when his father died. Mrs Wildman certainly had the utmost faith in her husband's integrity. In one of her letters to Tom she says:

I well know your ambition as well as mine, looks forward to the dear idea of your being a perfect Representitive of your Father – shall I repeat to you my beloved Child – his mode of conduct whenever he was about to engage in any persuit whether in the acquirement of Education (for I can <u>confidently</u> go back as far as that), Knowledge of his profession or in the very many undertakings since those? It was this, first to consider it to be <u>right</u>, that determined, no <u>suppresion of pleasures</u>, no inconvenience to himself whatever could check his resolution in his progress to the attainment of it ...

How little she knew about her husband! Whether she changed her mind when Beckford sued her for the recovery of his Quebec estate we do not know. Beckford was a strange man, for he seems to have remained on friendly terms with those who had defrauded him. His godson James Beckford Wildman used to go and stay with him at Fonthill, although Beckford had sacked his father James Wildman. James Pedley, the Wildmans' successor as agent, was still regarded as a friend even after he had relieved his employer of three of his English estates. Beckford was a lonely man despite, or perhaps because of, his wealth, who wanted above all things to be loved. So Mrs Wildman may have had little difficulty in convincing herself that that allegations against her husband were without substance, especially as the proceedings were dropped before they came to trial.

It is likely that she was little better informed about her husband's family. She seems to have had no contact with her Lancashire in-laws, though she did execute a conveyance of a small plot of land held in her late husband's name to these relations. Having left Lancashire, the three Wildman brothers appear to have had little desire to be reminded of their humble origins. When Thomas died the only provision he made for his brother Richard was a gift of 'whatever sums of money he may have due and rent due for the land called Martine and the farm at Cragg'. Richard seems to have been forever in debt and his widow died in poverty in 1824.

It is quite possible that Sarah never met her father-in-law, who was eighty-nine at the date of her marriage and died a year later. She would have had nothing in common with these poor relations, for she was a lady who liked to mix in the best circles. Tom came to realise this, for in a letter written to his mother from Harrow in 1805 regarding arrangements for Speech Day he says, 'I think you will like my Harrow friends this time. I assure you our party contains all the great men – I have asked Lord Byron, Long, Franks, Annesley and Peel ...' What little evidence there is suggests that Tom and his cousin James were totally ignorant of their grandfather's background. When Thomas Wildman joined Lincoln's Inn in 1773 he gave his father's address as Scambler House, Melling. In nineteenth-century editions of *Burke's Landed Gentry* this address is given, but with the added words 'near Ormskirk', which is many miles south of Roeburndale. Local records do not reveal any trace of the family in the area of Ormskirk, nor is there any record of a Scambler House. In a deed of 1806 Edward is described as 'late of Barkin Yeat in the Parish of Melling'. It would seem that Tom's father was trying to enhance the family's status for his own ends. His sons, knowing little or nothing of their grandfather, wrongly assumed that he lived in the better-known Melling near Ormskirk!

With five small children to bring up, Mrs Wildman decided to dispose of the Twickenham property and bought Heathfield House overlooking the green at Turnham Green on the other side of the Thames. She lost no time in doing so for the records of the Westminster Fire Office show that she took out a fire insurance policy on the new property in May 1796. The house, which she renamed Turnham Green Hall, was a pleasant Queen Anne house, double-fronted with a classical portico and steps leading up to the front door and stabling for a fair number of horses. A drive led up to the south side of the property with extensive formal gardens on either side.*

Mrs Wildman now decided to send the boys to Harrow. Tom, now aged nine, entered the school in 1796. His brothers followed as soon as they were old enough; in the meantime they were taught by a tutor, Mr Clarke. Maria appears to have had a governess. Tom settled down well at Harrow, judging from his first surviving letter written on 1 April 1799:

> My very dear Mama, I am very much obliged to you for sending Coachman over and I was very glad to hear that you was not the worse for coming out on Thursday last, I ashure you I am quite well and happy. I now get up at six o'clock and go to bed at eight and I ashure you that I do not speak a word after I am in bed but go to sleep immediately ...
>
> P.S.
> Mrs Drury Desires her love, and says that if she does not soon hear a

---

* The present Heathfield Gardens runs through the site of the property, which was demolished in about 1840.

12

good accoumpt of you, she shall go to Turnham Green and bring you here to make you well … I hope you will excuse the seal for it is but a marble with W cut out upon it …

The teaching, if it can be called that, was confined to Latin and Greek, transcribing and learning passages from Classical authors and reciting them. Other subjects were 'extras', a matter of private arrangement with the masters. The only extra we can be sure that Tom had was French, taught by a Monsieur Butticaz, a middle-aged Swiss. His journal shows that he knew the language in 1813, although he had never been to France before. However, we can be sure he took other subjects as well, for his later life leaves the impression that he was a man of intellectual pursuits.

In 1801, when Tom had been at Harrow for four years, Lord Byron entered the school. Some months younger than Tom, they had little to do with one another until their last year in 1804–5. By then they were classmates and monitors. Byron, who was very conscious of his title, gathered round him a number of other younger titled boys. Years later Tom told the poet Thomas Moore that he thought that Byron's passion for these boys was influenced by their being fellow nobles. In this regard Tom, in common with other boys at Harrow, was no respecter of titles. Indeed the American ambassador had recently sent his son to the school, 'because it was the only school in which no special favour was attached to rank'. Moore's note of his conversation with Tom continues, '*W[ildman] being a monitor, one day put Delawarr on his list for punishment. B[yron] coming up to him said, "W-I find you have got D on your list, Pray don't lick him". "Why not" "Why, I don't know except that he is a brother peer; but pray don't do it."*' Moore added '*W did.*'

Tom and Byron may not have been close friends, but Byron appears to have respected him. In 1817, during the negotiations for the sale of Newstead Abbey, Byron's solicitor, John Hanson, queried Tom's means and Byron replied, 'I recollect him as my old school fellow and a man of honour and would rather as far as my personal feelings are concerned that he should be the purchaser than another.' In Tom's last year the headmaster, old Dr Drury, retired and the boys expected his younger brother, Mark, to succeed him. Instead, a young and able mathematician, Dr Butler, was appointed, and there was much opposition among the boys led by Tom. He wanted Byron to join them, but one of the others told him that Byron would only do so if he were the leader. Tom promptly stepped down.

The resistance came to nothing. Dr Butler took up his appointment and soon afterwards Tom was writing to his mother: 'I like Butler more and more as I have had a good deal to do with him lately, and have been to him very frequently both alone and with Lord Byron about different things from the school, and he has always behaved in the most handsome manner...' He goes on to describe the arrangements he has made for Speech Day, at which he and Byron were to recite:

> I have arranged most capitally for Speech Day having procured a room in Mr. Page's. The Woman who takes care of the house says Old Hemmings will have no objection to her letting us have one, only I must not talk too much about it, lest she should have more applications than would be agreeable. We must bring a Table Cloth & everything, as there is nothing in the house to be had but tables & chairs; though Mr. Drury says he hoped you would not think of sending so much as you did last time, as he can help us out...

Notwithstanding that Byron had been asked to join Tom's party, he had invited his half-sister Augusta to come along too. 'I beg you madam,' Byron wrote to her, 'you may make your appearance in one of His Lordship's most dashing carriages, as our Harrow etiquette admits of nothing but the most superb vehicles on our grand Festivals.' Mrs Wildman, who was a frequent visitor to the school, would have needed no such encouragement to arrive in a spanking turnout for this occasion.

George and John were boarders by now, being about eleven or twelve years old, and another of Tom's letters written the same month provides a glimpse of them. 'George and John are now with a large party driving their hoops up the Town, to the annoyance of everyone they meet ...'

Both Tom and Byron left Harrow that summer, and the latter went up to Cambridge in October. Tom must have been undecided about his future for he spent six months with the Reverend Robert Afleck in Retford in Nottinghamshire. Byron must have talked about Newstead to Tom while they were at school and it seems more than likely that he would have taken this opportunity to visit the abbey. At a time when the Romantic movement was gaining ground and Gothic architecture was fashionable, Newstead was calculated to make a lasting impression on a young man who was himself a talented artist. The opportunity to acquire this ancient abbey some ten years later, coupled with its association with his friend whose verse he admired, was to prove irresistible.

In 1806 Tom went up to Christ Church, Oxford. Although he seems to have had a cultivated mind he had no enthusiasm for the academic life.

Nothing is known about his life at Oxford. Unlike his friend Byron and so many of his contemporaries, he seems to have had little interest in women or the bottle. His education was probably limited to some desultory reading and sporting activities.

While at Oxford he started to keep a register of the horses he bought, the sellers' names, the prices paid and what happened to them. He bought the first one in April 1807, but within a month he sold it in favour of an eight-year-old mare, Miss Peggy, which he kept until 1816. He bought four more horses while he was at Oxford, only one of which he kept for more than a few months. Thereafter he continued to buy and sell them as frequently during the next twenty years. Occasionally he sold horses to his brothers, but more often he gave them horses as presents.

While Tom was still at Harrow, his brother Edward had indicated that he wanted to go into the Army. In 1805 a friend of the family, Colonel Lemon, had tried unsuccessfully to procure a commission for Edward, and he had to wait another two years before he obtained one. One suspects that Mrs Wildman may not have been in favour of a military career for Tom. Until he came of age he was financially dependent on her and had little choice in the matter. As soon as he came into his fortune, he left Oxford without taking a degree in order to join the Army. Whether he obtained a commission in the 7th Hussars through the good offices of Colonel Lemon one cannot say. But it may be that Harrow helped, for the commanding officer, Lieutenant-Colonel Vivian, was an Old Harrovian, and at least two of Tom's future brother officers were also his contemporaries at Harrow.*

Before joining the Army, Tom met Byron again. After coming down from Cambridge in 1808, Byron began to renew contact with his Harrow friends while living a rather dissipated life in London. Thomas Moore records that when Tom met him Byron was running 'two Nymphs', one of whom he met while he was having breakfast with him in Brompton. He was surprised when Byron called the girl, a Miss Cameron, to come downstairs. This resumption of contact was short-lived. By September, Byron left London and went down to Newstead to supervise repairs before entering into occupation when he came of age. On the 28th of that month Tom received his commission as a cornet in the 7th Hussars. The following day he was gazetted lieutenant.† However, he had already joined the regiment in Guildford some weeks before and attended a

---

* The Hon. C. Lowther and James Fraser.
† Army commissions were published in the *London Gazette*.

review. Mrs Wildman was somewhat startled to learn that he had done so. In a letter dated 23rd September she wrote:

> I must say I think it was tolerably saucy in you to show yourself and Miss Peggy in a review, at such early Days, tho' I really rejoice in this laudable piece of vanity, now it is over at the same time notwithstanding your kind wish to have given me and your sister the pleasure of being present at so fine a sight as a review of your Regt. yet upon the whole, it is as well perhaps for my silly nerves we were not. It is indeed a matter of great comfort to hear you speak so highly of your most respectable associates not that I ever doubted your naturally good heart and disposition would ensure you friends…

He was a pleasant young man and later on in the same letter she mentions visiting a friend in Putney: 'when we talked you over pretty well, she told me she liked all my children but that always loved you and always should for she thought you a delightful young man.' In later years he was described as kindly and courteous. His cousin James's daughter Matilda recalled his tact when she was staying at Newstead in the 1850s and Tom had taken a party for a walk. When he spotted that she was embarrassed at the prospect of climbing over a stile he immediately turned back home.

Physically he was a small man. His contemporaries often made a point of mentioning this, and there are many references to 'the little Colonel'. He had fair hair and a round boyish face, and probably lost no time in cultivating the drooping moustache that was almost de rigeur among hussars of every nationality and which appears in all his portraits.

Tom had little time in which to settle into the routine of regimental life, let alone learn the elements of cavalry drill, for on 30 October the regiment set sail for Corunna to join Sir John Moore's army in Spain. Only one letter from Tom survives from this disastrous campaign, written at Astorga on 29 November 1808:

> I am in excellent quarters thanks to Coln. Vivian, who has taken me in with himself in the house of a Grandee who is absent: our squadron are in the Convent of St. Domingo, The Horses in the Cloisters and the men in the Galleries above. The Friars and I are great Cronies, but they brought a sad complaint to me this morning of the loss of a Saint from the Gallery which some of our Hussars had used for fire-wood; however as I made a great bustle about him, They were entirely pacified, and even begg'd that no more might be said about it.

Although Tom had seen no action during the advance through the mountains of Galicia, he had been able to do some sketching: '... but there are not many scenes as yet suited to my scale, for the Country is more Grand than pretty, and would generally require an oil painting on a very large scale to do it justice.' Not long afterwards they came up with the French, and on 21 December the 15th Hussars, in a brilliant charge, delivered at full gallop routed the 1st Provisional Chasseurs à Cheval and the 8th Dragoons who received the onset while stationary. Two days later Sir John learned that Napoleon was approaching from the south aiming to encircle him. The army was ordered to retreat back across the mountains with the Emperor hard on their heels.

The Hussar Brigade covered the rearguard during the first part of the retreat to the mountain passes, keeping at bay the massed squadrons of French dragoons. Although the French ability to manoeuvre large bodies of cavalry was superior to that of the British, they were no match for them in close combat. The hussars were then replaced, and the half-starved men and horses continued their march through the mountains with occasional brushes with the enemy at the outposts.

Edward, who had been commissioned in the 4th Dragoons a year before, was not so lucky as his brother. His regiment was covering the infantry rearguard during the retreat through the mountains when he was wounded and taken prisoner during a cavalry skirmish:

He was very soon relieved of all his small clothes, which were I believe of leather, particularly his boots, were in great request. He was marched prisoner with the party who were pursuing us, and occasionally got a bump from the butt end of a musket, because from his wounds he could not keep up. He had not as he thought anything worth stripping him of, but it appeared he was mistaken. He saw a soldier eyeing him for some time, and at last he was asked to release himself of his culottes; the order was soon obeyed and he was left 'en chemise'. He was suffering so much from his wound that he was unable to proceed further and lay down by the roadside expecting to be put to immediate death. However perceiving that he was unable to walk he received the prod of a bayonet and was left on the road, as they no doubt expected, to die.

Edward was made of sterner stuff, and as soon as his captors had gone he made his escape. All this in bitterly cold and wet weather!

The cavalry arrived in Corunna on 11 January 1809 in a terrible state, with most of the horses lame or unfit, and they now had to wait for transports. Hundreds of horses were shot in scenes of appalling carnage to prevent them falling into the hands of the French. Tom managed to embark his horse, one that Colonel Kerrison* had given him three weeks earlier, but the transport was lost during the voyage home, along with all his baggage.

When the 7th Hussars arrived back in England they returned to Guildford, remaining there until May the following year when they were posted to Ireland. Tom was now able to enjoy for the first time the rather leisurely routine of peacetime regimental life. The daily routine at this period is described in a letter written by another young subaltern:

About 9 o'c the trumpet sounded for foot parade, when the different troops formed before the stable doors, marched toward the centre of the barrack square, and after formed in line are examined by the major (viz. their dress and arms are inspected; then the sergeant major exercises the regiment with which we have nothing to do. At 10 o'c I breakfast with some officers in the mess room, many officers preferring to breakfast in their own rooms.

At 11 o'c all the subalterns are to go to the riding school, but if you don't go, no notice is taken of it, excepting you were to stay away for weeks to-gether, and at 12 the same subalterns have to attend foot drill, and then your business is done for the day.

During these months Tom bought eight more horses, most of which were resold within weeks or months. Many of these transactions were with officers of the regiment. He was probably buying and selling no more horses than most of his wealthy brother officers. They needed a couple of chargers for regimental duties; they hunted, and they kept carriage horses for their phaetons, tilburys or curricles or whatever kind of vehicle happened to be fashionable.

Apart from Tom's register of horses, all that survives from his time in Ireland are a few sketches he made. The regiment was stationed in Dublin for the best part of a year. For an officer of a cavalry regiment the gaiety and wit of Dublin society, centred on the Lord Lieutenant and his entourage at the castle, provided a most agreeable mode of life. The following year, 1811, found Tom posted to Dundalk further up the coast. In peacetime, light cavalry were usually employed in keeping public order

---

* Second-in-command of the 7th Hussars.

or helping the revenue officers to combat smugglers. Towards the latter part of his time in Ireland, Tom, along with a a number of the other officers, must have spent long periods away from the regiment, for in August 1812 a respite for their pay and allowances, imposed for absence of more than three months, was removed.

In November 1812 the regiment received orders to return to England. They arrived back in London the following January, where they took up public order and escort duties, replacing the Life Guards who had been sent out to Spain. In February, Tom obtained his promotion by purchase from an officer named Crauford who was retiring. Although we do not know what Tom's regimental duties were, surviving regimental records provide a few examples. On 31 January a captain, two subalterns and seventy-three privates were detailed for duty at Carlton House, 'to preserve good order and regularity in the passing of carriages to and from Carlton House'. On other occasions detachments were ordered to patrol the coach road and garden wall of Carlton House to prevent people climbing over.

At the end of March, the old Duchess of Brunswick died. She was the Prince Regent's mother-in-law as well as being his aunt. She had been living in lodgings in Hanover Square, lonely and neglected by her family, 'a melancholy spectecle of decayed Royalty'. However much the Regent detested his wife, he felt compelled to give the old duchess a suitable funeral. On the 28th an escort of the 7th Hussars attended in full dress uniform with pelisses buttoned, at 6 a.m. to accompany the coffin from Hanover Square to Windsor. The escort was replaced at Hounslow by another, which in turn was replaced at Egham by one to complete the final stages of the journey to St Georges Chapel. On other occasions the regiment provided escorts for the Prince Regent himself. He did not often show his face in the streets, for when he did, he was usually booed, so unpopular had he become.

Carrying out these duties in connection with the royal household would have introduced Tom into London society. During that season Beau Brummel, Lord Alvanley, Henry Pierrepoint and Sir Henry Mildmay gave the famous 'Dandy Ball'; Byron was enjoying the company of the dandies at Watier's Club and being generally lionised by society, while at the same time trying to extricate himself from his affair with Lady Caroline Lamb. Whether or not Tom and Byron met during these months, hussar officers were a familiar sight at London balls.

Hail, nimble nymph! to whom the young hussar,
The whisker'd votary of waltz and war,

His night devotes, despite of spur and boots;
A sight unmatch'd since Orpheus and his brutes ... *

Tom's diary suggests that he was well used to society life. Indeed he would have been a catch for any hostess with eligible daughters. And yet he does not appear to have been attracted to the worldly and sophisticated young ladies he would have met in the London ballrooms.

Meanwhile regimental life went on, though leisurely by today's standards. Parades were held at various places including Turnham Green. Mrs Wildman and Maria had a splendid view from their windows of the green and Acton Common beyond. As the green was no larger than it is today most of the exercises probably took place on the common. On 8 June there was a review on Wimbledon Common. Mrs Wildman and Maria would certainly have driven over for such a special occasion. Up by the windmill they would have sat in their carriage along with scores of other carriages, carts and riders, surrounded by swarms of sightseers, children, hawkers and orange sellers held in check by dismounted hussars.

After being submitted to an inspection, the regiment went on to perform a series of complicated manoeuvres. These movements might include extending from close column of squadrons into line, retiring in double column of divisions, countermarching in column of divisions and so on. The commanding officer, squadron officers and troop leaders all had their allotted words of command for these movements, which were executed with the utmost precision. Completion of each movement was followed by the command 'Halt – Dress – March', before they moved off again. This may have slowed up the proceedings, but ensured that not a man nor horse was out of place! This obsession with mechanical precision has often been criticised, and no doubt the commanding officers, who had little better to do in peacetime, carried it to extremes. On the other hand, it has to be remembered that battles were fought at close quarters, and the shock effect of cavalry could only be maintained by keeping rigidly in formation. This is difficult enough on foot, but with excited men and frightened horses half blinded by smoke and deafened by volleys of musket fire, constant practice for men and horses was essential to enable officers to maintain control over their units.

This, the last full-dress occasion before the regiment's departure for Spain would have been a colourful spectacle. At this time a bluebell-shaped shako with a peak had been adopted for active service

---

* Byron, 'The Waltz'.

instead of the tall fur cap or busby with its scarlet bag. A tall red-and-white feather plume was worn on both types of headdress on full-dress parades. (The cloth-covered shako was more practical, though less popular with officers, than the fur cap, which was liable to fall off and, because it was lined with cardboard, lost its shape in wet weather.) On this occasion they might have worn either, though one suspects the fur cap was the more likely choice. The uniform was a blue jacket with white facings, frogged and embroidered with silver lace (white cord for other ranks), a blue pelisse, also frogged and embroidered and trimmed with white fur, worn slung over the left shoulder, and white buckskin breeches and black boots. With flashing sabres and silver laced sabretaches, the hussars presented a superb sight.

Tom's brother John was commissioned and joined the regiment that month, being attached to Tom's troop. He had to attend the sergeant major every day for drill at twelve o'clock and he also had to receive instruction from the riding master. He was directed to attend the orderly officer on Tuesdays and Fridays and all regimental courts martial. Along with all other officers he was not allowed to absent himself from midday stables without permission, or evening stables unless he had good reason. Fortunately he had a little more time to settle into regimental routine than his brother before embarking overseas.

Preparations for Spain

As early as April 1813 the 7th Hussars knew they would be returning to Spain. Before considering the preparations for embarkation, it may be helpful to say something about the organisation of a light cavalry regiment. At this period the regiment was not the tightly knit unit to which we are accustomed today. From the point of view of organisation, a cavalry regiment was based on the troop commanded by a captain, who was subordinate only to the commanding officer. In time of war there were theoretically eight troops. What with losses in action, sickness and the problem of maintaining an adequate supply of recruits, numbers varied. However, the 7th Hussars does not appear to have had recruiting difficulties. Within two months of embarkation, Major Hodge told the adjutant that two additional troops were being formed and twenty-five recruits had been enlisted. When they embarked for Spain, the regiment mustered some six to seven hundred men.

As a formation the regiment was organised in four squadrons, each comprising two troops. In this context a troop was often referred to as a 'half squadron'. The squadrons were named as if the regiment were drawn up in line: Right, Right Centre, Left Centre and Left. When acting in squadron the senior captain normally took command. The 7th Hussars were still commanded by Lieutenant Colonel Richard Hussey Vivian. His second-in-command was Lieutenant Colonel Edward Kerrison, who was also assigned to lead the Right Squadron. There were two majors: Edward Hodge, who remained in England in charge of the Headquarters Squadron, and William Thornhill, who led the Left Squadron. The latter had been promoted to major in April that year.

As so many names crop up in the diary, it may be useful to name the troop leaders. In order of seniority they were Thomas Pipon, William Verner, Thomas Robbins, Edward Keane, Peter Heyliger, the Hon. C. Lowther, Baron Robeck and Thomas Wildman. In fact three other captains accompanied the regiment: James Hamlyn, James Fraser and Charles O'Hegaty. Then there was the adjutant, Lieutenant Myer, seven other lieutenants and one cornet, John Wildman. There was also Dr Irwin, the surgeon, Robert Chermside and James Moffit, assistant surgeons, and Richard Darville, the vetinary officer.

The various troops were stationed in barracks in and around London. The Right Squadron with Colonel Kerrison, Captain Heyliger and Captain Robeck were in Hyde Park Barracks, on the site of the present Household Cavalry Barracks. Captain Pipon commanding the Right Centre Squadron was also at Hyde Park with his troop.

Tom was fortunate for his troop was stationed at Hounslow Barracks, only a short ride from Turnham Green. The Left Centre Squadron with Captain Verner and Captain Robbins were also at Hyde Park, and the Left Squadron with Major Thornhill and Captains Keane and Lowther were at Hampton Court. The Regimental Depot in the charge of Major Hodge with Captains Hamlyn and Fraser was at Hounslow, but when the regiment began to prepare for active service Hodge was told to remain at Hyde Park. This arrangement no doubt suited Hodge who was living at 41 Craven Street, one of a modest row of terraced houses running down from the Strand to a timberyard by the river and not far from Northumberland House. Colonel Kerrison was wealthier and more conveniently placed in a fairly new house in Hertford Street leading out of Park Lane, then called Tyburn Lane.

On 13 July, Colonel Vivian received orders to prepare eight troops for service in Spain. The men were all eager to go. Despite the dangers and hardships, active service relieved the harsh discipline and monotony of their lives. Moreover, it opened up the only prospect they ever had of making any money, whether by way of loot or prize money. Whatever the state of their health – one man was incurably deaf – they all clamoured to go. Detailed orders now appeared dealing with all aspects of these preparations. Officers were told to pay the utmost attention to their men, who were to be well disciplined and well disposed. No drunken or bad soldiers were to be taken.

Troop officers were required to obtain a return of all the wives and children of their men and provide certificates for returning them to their parishes. There were no marriage allowances for these poor souls, who at best could look forward to being maintained by the parish under the Poor Laws, unless they could find work or had relatives who could care for them. These women were provided with papers entitling them to a government allowance of two pence a mile to 'take them home'. Non-commissioned officers and farriers, on the other hand, who wished to make an allowance to their wives and families were directed to give their names to the orderly room. Normally four or five wives per troop were allowed to accompany their husbands overseas, and there are astonishing accounts of these hardy women who trudged around Spain in the wake of their menfolk. Regimental orders called for a return of women in each troop 'who wish to embark with the regiment'.

Following infantry was one thing, but keeping up with cavalry would have been well-nigh impossible without a mount of some kind.* Although there may have been some wives who decided to go, Tom's embarkation return shows that no women went out with his troop. However the wives of two men among a contingent of the 74th Foot, who were attached to Tom for the voyage, sailed in his transport.

Five days later, on 19 July, leave passes were stopped and officers attending the fête at Vauxhall Pleasure Gardens the following day were ordered to go in regimentals. As for the men, the 'indulgence' of allowing them to stay out until 11 p.m. was stopped, since it was 'productive of venereal complaints'. The wives, meanwhile, saw little point in keeping the officers' barracks and men's rooms and passages clean. Colonel Vivian eventually threatened to withhold pass certificates home from any woman who refused to scour her part!

Orders relating to arms equipment and uniforms followed. All carbines and pistols were to be inspected by ordnance inspectors and all carbines and pistols were to be flinted, which suggests that firearms were not kept ready for use in normal peacetime conditions. Sabres had to be taken to the farrier to be sharpened. Although the curved steel scabbard tended to take the edge off the blade, swords were always kept blunted when not on active service. The farrier was also instructed to make the rowels of the men's spurs very sharp. Cruel as this may seem, the need for a horse to respond instantly in action was vital.

No horse less than four years old was to be taken. Each man was to have a set of horseshoes and forty nails to be carried on the peak of his saddle. The state of Spanish roads during the Corunna campaign had taught the hussars the need to be able to replace shoes without calling up the farrier. (As a result of his experiences, Captain Verner always carried spare nails in the top of his cap.) Strong horses were to be chosen for the forge carts 'in place of the blind horses that were before chosen for this purpose'.

Officers were supposed to have two chargers, which were inspected by the commanding officer. Officers whose chargers were approved 'but not properly broke will send them to the riding school at ten o'clock until perfectly steady. Those at outquarters will be worked by the rough riders. The officers whose chargers were not approved will immediately provide

---

* At least one wife accompanied her husband (Serjeant Major Edwards of Captain Fraser's troop) during the Waterloo campaign until ordered to the rear by an officer.

themselves with others.' Of course, they had pay for their horses out of their own pockets, but a cavalry officer's pay was slightly more than that of the infantry. The need to bring horses to military standards may, to some extent, explain the number of horses Tom disposed of within a few months of purchase. However, between January and July he purchased fourteen, six of them in July, though only two of these were sold before he embarked for Spain. One, 'a bright brown mare' named Vittoria, he gave to John in July.

Much attention was paid to clothing. Leather breeches or pantaloons had now been discarded in favour of grey overalls or trousers with a white stripe down the outside leg. However, the men were to wear pantaloons until orders were received to march. Each man had to take three shirts, two pairs of flannel drawers, two pairs of trousers, two flannel jackets and three pairs of stockings. They had two towels, three shoe brushes, one clothes brush, a brush and comb, a pair of braces, one stock and clasp, a mane comb and sponge, a pair of scissors and case, one razor and case, one lock case, one hair comb, one button brush, one foraging cap, a corn bag, one large feather,* a turn screw and horse picker, two stable jackets, a pair of 'high lows' (i.e. boots) and one pair of low shoes. All this will have a familiar ring to a modern soldier; indeed, the hussars were better equipped in some respects. In addition every man was provided with a quarter of a yard of grey cloth and half a 'quarter of a yard' of blue cloth for mending his uniform. The men's best uniforms were to be put in store to be sent out later. Finally in view of the filthy conditions on board the transports, the men were ordered to wear old stable jackets and their worst pair of trousers while at sea.

Officers' baggage was also restricted, and they were told to take as little as possible. Subalterns were limited to 180 pounds and field officers could take proportionately more. Whether Tom took much notice of this seems doubtful, for, as will be seen, on arrival in Spain he required two mules to carry his effects.

An insight into the kind of clothing Tom and his brother officers took is provided by a letter written from Spain by Benjamin Badcock of the 14th Light Dragoons, to his father in September 1813, asking him to send out six shirts, six pairs of stockings, six pocket handkerchiefs, three pairs of flannel drawers, three flannel waistcoats and a 'red morocco dressing case compleat ... one that rolls up'. He also needed soap and tooth powder.

---

* 'The feathers are not to be worn without orders.' An example of this feather can be seen in the 7th Hussar museum in Warwick.

Tom would have taken two or more uniforms, two or three pairs of boots, a cloak and, probably, some civilian clothes. Vivian advised them to leave some summer and winter clothing in a small portmanteau to be sent out later with the men's baggage. He himself favoured 'nankeen overalls and white trowsers for summer wear'.

While awaiting marching orders all troop officers were 'to give their whole time and attention to their troops ...' They were all to have 'a book of instructions for hussars.' Finally Colonel Vivian issued a memorandum regarding behaviour on active service to be read out to the men on the first Monday in every month. This included care of his horse: 'a good dragoon loves his horse as himself.' Attention must be given to cleanliness and health. A change of wet clothes should be made immediately after a march if possible. With regard to rations, 'a careful soldier always takes care and keeps a little in haversack and canteen. A crust of bread will often contribute to preserve health, and a spoonful even of spirits will support a man under great fatigue.' 'Arms and appointments must be kept in perfect order,' and the men were reminded that any damaged equipment was to be taken immediately to a tradesman for repair. (Each troop had eleven different tradesmen.) On the battlefield they were exhorted to 'charge with resolution ... to move by word of command and to halt and form when ordered and not to scramble or race in such a manner as to expose themselves and the whole regiment to be attacked with advantage ...' If they suffer the extreme disgrace of being surprised on outposts and surrounded, 'there is almost always some part where they may cut their way through'. But this is only as a last resort!

They were to be 'kind, civil and obliging' to the people of the country, for that reflected on the credit of the regiment and the British name. Finally they were to avoid drunkenness, be careful of themselves and their horses, and 'the character of the Regiment will be such as to reflect credit on it and we shall hereafter be proud in having belonged to the 7th'.

On 2 August the carts carrying the heavy baggage set off, and the following day the routes for the march were received. At this point, Tom's journal takes up the story. Meanwhile, the European powers were at last joining forces to take the offensive against Napoleon. England had entered into an alliance with Russia and Prussia. On 11 August Austria declared war on France, and despite a victory over the combined armies of Russia, Prussia and Austria on 26 and 27 August the Emperor's star was now on the wane.

THE JOURNAL

August–September 1813

There was a continual movement of ships sailing to and from the Peninsular during the war years. Troops were returning home, while others were awaiting transports to take them out to the front, and quarters had to be made available between London and Portsmouth. During the course of the war many new barracks, mostly wooden buildings of a temporary nature, had been constructed to accommodate the regular forces as well as the militia regiments for home defence.

Organising troop movements was a daunting task. Until the transports actually arrived there was no knowing what ships would be available. In favourable conditions the passage from Spain might take no more than ten days; if the weather was bad it could take a month or more. Likewise departures from Portsmouth were at the mercy of the wind. Without an easterly wind the ships could not get down the Channel and, of course, the prevailing wind was westerly. Long delays were inevitable, and in the meantime accommodation had to be made available for those awaiting embarkation.

It was not surprising that the 7th Hussars were unable to embark as one unit. The Left, Left Centre and Right squadrons were fortunate: ships were available and on 14 August the *Hampshire Telegraph* reported: 'Sabrina, 20, Capt. Alex McKenzie goes to Lisbon. Three squadrons of the 7th. Hussars will embark on Tuesday and Wednesday next for the peninsular.' On the 25th the paper reported:

> 7th Hussars (500 men) commanded by Col. Vivian sailed yesterday for St. Andero [Santander] under convoy of the Sabrina. During the last 2 months not fewer than 5000 men have embarked from hence in numbers from 10 to 100 to join Lord Wellington. They were men who had recovered from sickness, recruits and volenteers from the Militia.

We do not know why the Right Centre remained behind, but the most likely explanation is the unavailability of ships. The first day's march on the 7 August from Hounslow Barracks to Kingston, where Tom Wildman and his troop were to rendezvous with Captain Pipon, his squadron leader, was only a few miles. When marching orders were issued, officers received a written description of the route. Although there are no surviving instructions for this march, here is one for a similar march:

> From Croydon to Staines is 22 miles. First 3 miles is open and level the Road upon an average 20 feet wide, for the next 9 miles and the last few miles rather hilly. At Kingston cross the river Thames by a good wood bridge, the remainder of the road open and tolerable level. At Staines cross the Thames by a good stone bridge to Egham – The Routes leading to Richmond etc. are sufficiently passable for Horses and Carriages, the County in general open and tolerable level.

The width of the road was important, for this determined how many men could ride abreast, and consequently the length of the column. Apart from private coaches and carriages, the roads leading into and out of London were thronged with waggons bringing farm produce and drovers with cattle, sheep and geese to feed the population.

On 7 August the trumpets would have sounded before 3 a.m. calling the troop to water and feed their horses and, an hour or so later, to saddle up. The men were then ordered to form up on parade, standing to the nearside of their horses. As soon as the troop leader appeared the sergeant gave the command, 'Troop! Stand – to your *horses!*' The men sprang to attention, right hand grasping the reins close to the bit with arm outstretched in line with the shoulder. An inspection followed, each man's equipment, his horse bridle, saddle and girth straps checked. Unfortunately British soldiers did not look after their horses well, and this regiment had previously had trouble with ill-fitting saddles which caused sores. Admittedly the French showed even less concern for their mounts. The Germans of The Kings German Legion, on the other hand, had the highest reputation for the way they looked after their horses.

As the troop moved off men and horses were well burdened. Haversacks and canteens were carried on the right shoulder (with the mess tin in the haversack), forage cords fastened to the rear peak of the saddle on the offside, the horse's nosebag on the rear peak on the nearside, and corn sacks carried on both sides. As the weather was warm, pelisses were strapped to the saddlebags and cloaks carried on the pistol holsters. In addition to sabre and sabretache, the men carried a carbine suspended by a swivel from a bandolier over the left shoulder as well as two pistols. Thus encumbered, the march would have been fairly slow, mainly at a walk, for trotting any distance would have been tiring. The cavalry rode with their legs almost fully extended – sometimes called the 'tuning fork' seat – and did not rise on the trot. Senior officers, more concerned with appearances than with the comfort of soldiers, felt it was unsightly on parade to see heads bobbing up and down out of unison. However, the discomforts of jogging were cushioned to some extent by sheepskins placed over the saddles.

The roads through the countryside of Surrey and Sussex were all turnpikes made of stone macadam, and reasonably well maintained. According to William Cobbett, the turnpike from Godalming to Petworth was one of the best he ever saw. Here they would have passed a man cracking great lumps of stone into small pieces with a sledgehammer, and pounding them into any broken surface with a heavy wooden tamper. Riding through Godalming they could see one of the twenty-four semaphore stations stretching from Portsmouth to the Admiralty with their six large rotating letter-boards. The countryside was now fully enclosed except for a stretch of heathland between Emsworth and Chichester.

They passed fields of wheat, barley, swedes and turnips. Writing some years later, Cobbett thought Petworth:

> a nice market town but solid and clean. The great abundance of stone in the land hereabouts has caused a corresponding liberality in paving and wall building so that everything of the building has an air of great strength and produces the agreable idea of durability. Lord Egrement's House is close to the town, nearly as big as the town; though the town is not a small one.

Although no trace remains, there was probably a camp of some sort here where the squadron spent the night of 10 August. The tithe map indicates a cottage and garden called The Barracks.

Each day's march was little more than twenty miles and would have taken no more than three or four hours. On a long march, cavalry aimed to reach each day's destination by about midday. This enabled the horses to be rubbed down, watered and fed, and properly rested. On arrival at Chichester the squadron was permitted to stop only one night. This must have been due to lack of available quarters. Cavalry barracks for fifteen hundred men had been erected in 1802. Three hundred carpenters had been employed and timber brought down from London in twenty vessels. By 1813 the barracks could accommodate three hundred and forty horses and three hundred and twenty-eight men and a thousand infantry. These barracks were about a mile to the north of the city walls and were on the site of the present Royal Military Police barracks.

Redirected to Arundel on 12 August, the squadron spent upwards of a fortnight in a camp at Crossbush, east of the town by the turning to Littlehampton. Major Thornhill and the Right Squadron arrived the following day and remained until the 17th when they marched to Portsmouth.

Mrs Wildman and Maria had come down to stay at Littlehampton, no doubt to see as much as possible of Tom and John before they embarked. Little Hampton, as it was then called, was a small village about three-quarters of a mile from the sea consisting of a couple of streets and a novel chain ferry that could take a carriage across the River Arun. Fortunately for Mrs Wildman there was 'nothing to alarm the most spirited horse or the most timid lady'. Over the previous twenty years the village had been developed as a watering place:

> Eastward of the town, within about a furlong of the Coast, are the lodging-houses, consisting of a very respectable line of buildings dominated by Beach Terrace. The sands extending to Worthing, are excellent; and the terrace walk, on the margin of the Sea, is truly delightful, commanding fine Sea and extensive land views ... There are also very commodious hot and cold baths.

The enforced wait at Arundel must have been an unexpected pleasure for the Wildman family, who were able to spend much time together. We have no means of knowing why or when Tom decided to keep a diary. One might suppose that he would have started it when they set off from Hounslow, but the first entry was not made until 30 August, the last day he spent with his mother and Maria. This rather suggests that it was they who put the idea into his head. Of course it would be a useful way of storing up material for letters home. During the course of the ensuing campaign he wrote twenty-one letters, each one numbered, to his mother and his sister, the first written within two days of landing in Spain, and the last on 18 May 1814 a fortnight before setting off on the long march home. In addition he wrote about four more to Maria alone. Sadly none of them have survived.*

Leaving Arundel at 5 a.m. on the 30th, the squadron passed through Chichester and took the turnpike to Emsworth – a distance of about twenty

---

* References to names in the diary indicate the recipients of Tom's letters.

miles, which took them six hours marching at a walking pace. Retracing his steps to Littlehampton, Tom would have shortened his stirrups and set off at a brisk trot, anticipating the advice of the Victorian author of the Queen's Regulations: 'Our officers look upon the military seat with the bumping, as part of their equipment, put it on when they fall in on parade, but wisely discard it afterwards.'

Leaving Emsworth, they continued along the turnpike as far as Cosham. They had to ford numerous streams running down to the marshy shoreline on their left. At Cosham they turned south onto Portsea Island to Portsea, which had grown up around the naval dockyard during the previous century and was now a suburb of Portsmouth. Entering the town up Lion Gate Road, crossing the ravelins, they passed through the fortifications, and clattered up Queen Street to the dockyard. Here three transports awaited them: the *Duchess of Richmond* (240 tons), *Canada* (296 tons) and *John Bushman* (387 tons). These vessels may be compared to Captain Cook's *Endeavour* (368 tons) and Captain Bligh's *Bounty* (228 tons), and like them the three transports would have the same square sterns and bluff bows of a typical east-coast collier. These ships had been converted to horse transports for the duration of the war. Fortunately Tom entered a copy of his embarkation return in his diary, and we know that he sailed in the *Duchess of Richmond*. Captain Pipon and his troop probably sailed in the *John Bushman* as she was the largest of the three vessels.

The first task on arrival at the quayside was to lift the horses on board. A hoist with a block and tackle was suspended from the mainyard; another was attached halfway down the mainmast forestay. The horse waiting on the quayside was then brought alongside the ship where a canvas sheet was passed under its belly. Battens were stitched to either end of the canvas with loops attached which were drawn up and hooked onto the two hoists. Several men hauling on the hoist suspended from the yard lifted the horse, while others hauling on the tackle attached to the forestay guided the animal towards the open hatch, where it was lowered into the hold. A line of stalls ran down either side into which the horse was led and where they faced the centre of the ship. The canvas sling under the horse was then hooked onto the crossbeams above and poles fitted into slots on either side to separate it from the next horse. The unfortunate beast could barely move and certainly could not lie down; not that this mattered much for many horses seldom, if ever, lie down. In front of these stalls ran a trough into which their fodder was placed. The planks in the deck immediately above the horses' heads were removed to provide access to the animals and ventilation. Here they remained for the duration of the

33

voyage. Cruel as this arrangement may seem, it was necessary if serious injury was to be avoided when the ship pitched and rolled in heavy seas. Even so, there were frequent losses caused by sickness and injury on these ships. Fortunately Tom's troop suffered no casualties, but Arthur Myers, the adjutant, writing to Major Hodge on 13 September reported that fourteen or fifteen horses died during their voyage in the earlier convoy, adding, 'I will state the others that may occur when I make out our next monthly return.'

Well might Tom complain about the filthy stinking cabin. The stench from the stalls below decks would have been appalling unless they were constantly hosed down and the bilges pumped out. Add to this a hundred or more rank and file and a ship's crew of twenty or thirty men all crammed into a vessel some ninety feet long, conditions were very unpleasant indeed. Colonel Vivian's order prior to leaving London that on board ship old stable jackets and the 'worst pair' of overalls were to be worn indicates the squalid conditions to be found on troop-ships. Tom, John, Lieutenant Black, the doctor and the commissary would have had tiny cabins – probably shared and where they slept in hammocks. These cabins had very little headroom and no ventilation apart from louvres in the doors.

With the horses on board, the baggage was loaded and the men followed, slinging their hammocks on the lower deck forward of the officers' quarters. A couple of longboats then towed the ship out to an anchorage in the main harbour. The men had to remain but the officers wisely took themselves ashore. If Tom had allowed his men shore leave, they would have promptly disappeared into the taverns and brothels of the old town, where an excitement and boisterousness reigned like that depicted by Thomas Rowlandson thirteen years before in his drawing *Portsmouth Point*. The likelihood of getting them all back would have been fairly slim.

Accommodation for Tom and his brother officers was provided in barracks in the old town, possibly Canbrowe Barracks, a few steps away from the Crown Inn in the High Street. It was now just a question of waiting for a favourable wind. Being rich, Tom could afford not to dine in the mess. With a mixed bag of officers arriving and departing, there would have little incentive to do so. So for the next seven days he took his meals at the Crown, except for one day when he dined at the George. The Crown was a fashionable inn built in 1805 by a Mr Herman on the site of the old gaol. Mainly frequented by naval officers it was known as the Navy Inn. The week after Tom sailed, Lord Melville, the First Lord of the Admiralty, stayed there, and the following summer Field Marshal von Blucher was a guest.

Apart from visiting the transports and holding a court martial with Lieutenant Black on Sergeant Hardy of the 74th Foot, Tom spent his time looking round Portsmouth. The town had a population of over 33,000 at this time and, in the words of a contemporary, 'Few places are at present more flourishing than this: the great sums of prize money spent by the sailors, added to the wages constantly laid out by the number of hands employed in the dockyard cause a greater circulation of cash than is to be found in most parts of the Kingdom.' The old town with its narrow streets and clapboard houses, cookshops, trinket shops, tailors' and pawnbrokers' would have had little to offer the Wildman brothers.

Most visitors to Portsmouth made a tour of the dockyard, and Tom was no exception. The yard was open from 10 a.m. to 3 p.m. Visitors had to attend at the gate and sign a book. A warder then took them on a conducted tour. Apart from the mast, rope houses, the store houses and anchor forge, the most fascinating spectacle for those as yet unfamiliar with the wonders of the industrial revolution was the block house constructed in 1802. The machinery for making rigging blocks had been invented by Marc Brunel, the father of the great engineer Isambard Kingdom Brunel. Forty-four machines driven by steam engines, installed by Bolton and Watt (the firm founded by James Watt), sawed the wood, chiselled out the cavity for the sheaves, turned and polished the blocks, and fashioned the sheaves. The machinery was able to turn out upwards of 1,400 blocks a day.

On the day that Tom visited the yard, the convoy bringing General Farmer arrived from Bilbao with 2,500 prisoners and wounded men. Carried by a south-westerly wind, they made the trip in ten days; Tom's somewhat shorter voyage was to take twice as long. As the days passed with no change of wind, they became more and more impatient. Apart from John, Tom makes little mention of the other officers in his regiment. One might have expected some reference to Thomas Pipon, his squadron leader. Pipon was some years older than Tom, having joined the regiment in 1803, and was now senior captain. In fact, throughout the campaign Tom only mentions associating with Pipon on half a dozen occasions, though they would been thrown together constantly, which makes one wonder whether they liked one another. So instead of spending his time with his brother officers, he entertained Captain Saurin of the sloop *Hope*, Lieutenant Black of the 74th Foot, Captain Payless of the 52nd Foot and others.

Five days after his arrival in Portsmouth, with a fresh sou'westerly blowing, Tom lounged about the ramparts which stretched from the harbour entrance in the south to Waterside on the Landport side of Portsea. According to the *Portsmouth Guide* of 1822, 'The Ramparts are pleasingly shaded with fine rows of trees and are the resort of genteel company; commanding beautiful views of the Harbour, Porchester Castle, Portsdown and the surrounding country.' At the northern end of the harbour, beyond the forest of masts of the waiting convoy, lines of hulks could be seen, in which over 20,000 French prisoners of war were incarcerated.

By Tuesday the 8th the wind began to shift round to the north, and the following day it had moved to north north-east which would enable the convoy to leave the harbour. We do not know how many ships made up the convoy, but the column entitled 'numbers or letters' recorded on Tom's embarkation return may provide a clue. Each ship carried a number fore and aft as a means of keeping some sort of tally and enabling the ships to be recognised. The convoy was escorted by two frigates, *Cydnus* and *Cossac*, as well as the sloop *Hope*. Even at this late stage of the war, when the French fleet had been confined to port for eight years, it was still not safe for ships to sail unescorted.

French privateers were operating out of the Channel ports, and now American privateers were lurking in the Western Approaches, for England had been at war with the United States since the previous year. Four days after the convoy sailed, the *Hampshire Telegraph* reported that a French lugger had captured a merchantman two miles off Dover. Fortunately an English schooner recaptured her. The following month HM bombship *Thunder* sailing up the Channel saw a sixteen-gun French lugger to windward. The captain of the bombship immediately began to steer wildly, yawing his ship to make the Frenchman think he had panicked. The lugger's skipper took the bait, gave chase and just as he was about to board *Thunder*, the bombship turned across his bows and raked the lugger with grape and cannister and then boarded her instead!

The north-easterly lasted just long enough to enable the fleet to clear the Isle of Wight. By the following day the fleet was becoming strung out and the wind backed to the south-west again. Having weathered Portland Bill, the *Duchess of Richmond* found herself in Lyme Bay and was forced to beat out into the Channel in order to clear Start Point and Salcombe. (The references to Tynemouth and Lymington are obviously errors, and refer to Teignmouth and Lyme Regis.) With the wind now backing south the Master, Mr Read, was faced with the choice of making Plymouth or beating out into the Channel with no protection in order to reach Falmouth.

At midday on the 13th they arrived at Plymouth where they remained for two days until they could pick up an escort. This gave Tom and his companions an opportunity to replenish their food stocks now, rather than wait until they reached Falmouth. Officers, whether at sea or on land, were expected to provide and pay for their own food (for which they received a 'bat' allowance), unless they were content to eat the same rations as their men. And one can hardly imagine the Wildman brothers being prepared to do this. They went ashore and dined at the King's Head, which still exists and is believed to be the oldest inn in Plymouth. Tom, and no doubt the others too, went to the New Theatre Royal, which had only opened three weeks earlier on 23 August.

No play bills survive, but the opening production was *As You Like It*, or part of it, followed by *Catherine and Petruchio* based on Shakespeare's *Taming of the Shrew*. The doors opened at six o'clock and the curtain went up at seven. There were separate entrances for different classes of patron, so Tom would not have had to rub shoulders with those in the 'upper regions' to which he refers. It was a large neo-classical building, far too large for the town as it turned out, and the most expensive box cost four shillings. The New Hotel, which along with a ballroom formed part of the same complex, was functioning, although it was not completed until some years later.

Plymouth audiences could be rowdy. This is confirmed by Tom's quotation from Albius Tibullus describing the Elysian Fields:

Here disport themselves a band of young men
in the company of tender girls, and Love wages
his battle continuously ...

Little is known of Tom's actor friend Sandford, who appears to have gone to the United States at a later date. There are references to a Sandford appearing in New York in the early 1840s, but one cannot be sure that this was the same man.

Two days later they set sail again for Falmouth escorted by the schooner *Sea Lark*. After battling against head winds followed by a calm, they finally made Falmouth on the afternoon of the 17th. There must have been a pre-arranged plan to rendezvous here, for this was the last haven before venturing out into the Atlantic. The diary shows how difficult it was for the escorts to keep a convoy together in the days of sail. The leading ships set sail from Portsmouth at 4 p.m. on 9 September, but the *Duchess of Richmond* did not weigh anchor until three and a half hours later. By noon the following day she had dropped four or five miles behind the fleet. Not withstanding the two days in Plymouth, they still managed to arrive in Falmouth ahead of the rest of the fleet. *Cydnus* and part of the convoy came in the next day and the rest on the day after.

The first fleet with Colonel Vivian and the main body of the 7th Hussars had arrived in Spain before Tom had even arrived in Portsmouth. Writing to Major Hodge on 13 September, Arthur Myer, the adjutant said:

> We disembarked at Algarta about 8 miles from here on 31st. ult. and 1st and 2nd. – all but the 2 ships which Capt. Robeck and Lieut. Uniacke are on board of which have not yet arrived nor have we had any account of them – if they are not taken or lost they must have put into some port and we daily hope for some good account of them.

In fact their ships had been in Falmouth for three weeks, waiting for the second convoy to turn up before venturing into the Bay of Biscay.

Captain Pipon and Captain Hamlyn and Lieutenant Shirley went off to spend the weekend with Mrs Daniel. Why Tom and John elected to stay in the town is puzzling. Mrs Daniell was the wife of Ralph Allen Daniell, who had been MP for West Looe until the previous year when he lost his seat at the general election. Politically he was listed as 'doubtful' by both Whigs and Tories. The Daniells lived at Trelissick, a neo-Greek mansion overlooking Falmouth harbour. Mr Daniell owned tin mines and was said to be the richest man in Cornwall. It seems likely that Mrs Daniell extended the invitation to the officers of the 7th Hussars because the Daniells had known Colonel Vivian all his life. Both families came from Truro, and Hussey Vivian's father still lived there. He was older than Ralph Daniell and was Vice-Warden of the Stanneries.

Hussey was born in 1775 and, like Tom, was educated at Harrow. After coming down from Exeter College, Oxford he was articled to an attorney in Devonport. His father was obviously a practical man, for at that period the social status of attorneys hardly measured up to that of the Vivians. Anyway young Hussey did not care for the law, and his great-uncle got him a commission in the 20th Foot in 1793. By the following year he had been promoted to captain – probably by purchase. After exchanging into the 7th Light Dragoons and serving in Flanders and Holland, he had attained the rank of lieutenant colonel by 1804 and commanded the regiment during the Corunna campaign in 1808–9. His portrait shows a tall man with bushy side-whiskers and the drooping moustache fashionable among both French and English hussars at this period in acknowledgment of their Hungarian origins. He was a strong, determined-looking man, irascible, but not perhaps without humour.

Tom's opinion that praying was the only amusement in Falmouth is borne out by the *Falmouth Guide* published in 1827:

> It has been observed that Falmouth contains a greater proportion of persons adhering to different religious sects, than any other place of the same population in the Kingdom. The degree of emulation that is consequently excited among them, to surpass each other in moral excellence, excludes such enjoyment as may be derived from public entertainments.

Methodism was very strong among the tin miners as a result of John Wesley's visits. The Fox family who had extensive engineering and shipping interests in Falmouth accounted for the prominence of the Quakers.

Back on board the *Duchess of Richmond*, Tom and his companions had to endure once again the verminous conditions that were endemic on ships of this period. Writing twenty years earlier, Tom's father's erstwhile client William Beckford, on a voyage to Portugal in one of his own ships, was disgusted by the cockroaches 'who amuse themselves with parading up and down the varnished paper of the cabin, like fashionable gentlemen who have no employment'. Confined to a stuffy little cabin at night, they all had to share an ill-lit 'great cabin' that belied its name during the daytime. There were no washing facilities other than a bucket. There was no lavatory, unless like Captain Cook's *Endeavour* there were minute 'heads' in the corners of the great cabin. Otherwise there would only have been the heads situated on either side of the bowsprit. Tom's comment that 'Tout effet augmente par son contraste' seems an understatement! No wonder he longed for activity. He sums up his feelings in the quotation from Byron's long poem *The Giaour*. He must have purchased *The Giaour* shortly before leaving England. First advertised in the *Morning Chronicle* in June that year, a second edition had been issued in July. There is no means of knowing if Tom had any contact with Byron during the winter and summer of 1813 when they were both in London. Byron was still being lionised by society and his affair with Lady Caroline Lamb was causing him problems. With the 7th Hussars employed on ceremonial duties in the capital, a rich young bachelor in a fashionable regiment would be a tempting catch for London hostesses seeking husbands for their daughters. From later comments, it is clear that Tom was no stranger to routs and balls in London. Byron himself had planned to sail to the Mediterranean and had secured a passage in HMS *Boyne*, but cancelled it when the captain declined to accommodate his half-sister Augusta and a bevy of servants. HMS *Boyne* sailed from Portsmouth with a convoy for Santander a week before the main body of the 7th Hussars set off.

For the first two days after leaving Falmouth, the *Duchess of Richmond* had favourable winds and was surging along at six or seven knots, which would have been just about her maximum speed. With a following wind from the north-east, land was sighted around Santander, and the convoy then altered course to sail close-hauled along the northern coast towards Bilbao, standing well out from the land to avoid being caught on a lee shore. The wind then dropped and progress was slow for the next three days. Tom and the others whiled away the time practising with carbines. One wonders whether they even hit a bottle, let alone a seagull. Light cavalry regiments were armed with carbines, which were similar to the infantry musket, the Brown Bess, but with a much shorter barrel. This made it even less accurate. An infantryman had to be a good shot to hit a man with a musket at a hundred yards.

The last night on board was marked with a celebration dinner. After they landed, neither Dr McKenzie nor Mr Acum the commissary are mentioned again and were presumably posted elsewhere. These two were good company and would have provided a rather different perspective on life than that to which the two young hussars were accustomed. Surgeons and commissaries attached to regiments were in a difficult position, being neither civilians nor soldiers, save in so far as they both wore cocked hats. The surgeon was usually regarded by regimental officers as someone quite different from themselves, hardly a gentleman. Some regiments would not allow the surgeon to dine in the mess and even the most junior officer took precedence over him. This does not appear to have been the case in the 7th Hussars, for Tom frequently mentions the surgeon Dr Irwin and assistant surgeon dining with the other officers.

On the whole, army commissaries did not enjoy a reputation for honesty, and there were ample opportunities for peculation. A commissary's only qualification was the ability to pass a simple examination in English and arithmetic. Their social status was even lower than that of the surgeon, many being former non-commissioned officers. A commissary received a commission, and some wore a red coat and a cocked hat and were sometimes taken for staff officers!* Mr Schauman, a commissary who had

---

* The correct uniform was a blue coat with black facings.

been in Spain for some time wrote that he was 'aware of the ridiculous pretentions of English cavalry regiments in general and cordially detested them'. When the 18th Hussars arrived in Spain in the summer of 1813, Schauman was attached to the regiment. At first he complained, 'The whole crowd were like fledglings; they only knew how to open their mouths to be fed. If anything was lacking the officers knew no other remedy than to exclaim to one's face in a cold and stately fashion, "I shall report it.' How different things were in the 1st German Hussars.' Later on when they found that he could from time to time provide their mess with delicacies (at a price no doubt) they accepted him as an equal, or so he thought. However, the tone of Tom's diary does not suggest such snobbery on the part of the Wildman brothers.

As Wellington advanced toward the French frontier, the supply bases were moved from Santander to Bilbao, and then to Pasajes (needless to say called 'Passages' by the British soldier!) While the ships waited off San Sebastián to enter harbour, Tom was able to visit the city, which had fallen a month earlier. The first attempt to storm San Sebastián had taken place on 25 July and had failed, largely because the trenches were not near enough to the walls and the attackers were subjected to a heavy barrage from the French guns. The second and final assault took place on 31 August and succeeded, but with a loss of two thousand men killed or wounded. Such was the slaughter that the maddened soldiers went on a drunken orgy and sacked and burned the city. As one observer wrote: 'With the exception of ten or twelve fortunate buildings there is nothing left ... but the blackened walls of the houses and these are falling every instant... How the fire started is uncertain ... In a town so constructed as this there is little chance of its being got under control when kindled.' The destruction caused a great deal of ill-feeling among the Spanish population and some members of their government went so far as to accuse Wellington of burning the city deliberately to damage the country's commerce.

The day after Tom's visit, the *Duchess of Richmond* entered Pasajes. Because of the narrow entrance, she would have been towed in by the ship's longboats. Once inside, the river opens out to form a basin. The villages of Pasajes de San Juan and Pasajes de San Pedro lie just inside the entrance on either side of the river, each with a single street of houses with balconies and steep wooded hills rising up on either side. It was considered the finest harbour in the north-west of Spain, but concern had already been expressed that it was becoming overcrowded. Captain William Bragge of the 3rd Dragoons wrote home to his father, 'The most Hazardous thing that I ever adventured was bringing the Two Horses in an

41

open boat through 500 sail of shipping over and under twice as many Ropes and Cables.' A fortnight after the arrival of the *Duchess of Richmond*, the Adjutant General was complaining to the Spanish governor that access to the port 'is very dangerous and difficult; and that if a vessel has not room to anchor when she enters she must inevitably be lost.' It is not surprising that Tom complained that the squadron's disembarkation was badly conducted. Fortunately they had lost no horses on the voyage.

The Journal

Mon 30th   *Marched from Arundel to Emsworth & Havant. Turn'd out at 4. March'd off a little before 5 – Arrived at Emsworth about 11 – Return'd by Arundel to Little Hampton. Din'd with my mother & sister – Set out at 8 – Saw Mr & Mrs Smith in Arundel – Rode back to Emsworth by 12 o'clock –*

Tue 31st   *Went round the Troop in quarters – Rode over to Havant – My mother and Maria came to Emsworth but did not stay above a few minutes. All officers Din'd except Pipon who went to see his friends –*

Wed Sep 1st *March'd from Emsworth at half past 4, Join'd the Troop at Havant at 5 – Arrived in the dockyard at Portsmouth at 8 precisely. Embar'd the squadron without accident – Officers remain'd on shore. Din'd at the Crown.*

Thu 2nd   *Wind fair – The Cydnus Frigate appointed to take the Convoy – Capt. Langford detain'd on a Court Martial. Went on board the Transports – Return'd to dinner – Din'd at the Crown. Capt. Saurin din'd with me.*

Fri 3rd   *Wind SW Capt Saurin recieved Orders for sea, went on board The Hope Sloop of war – visited the transports – return'd to dinner – din'd at the Crown. Mr Black of the 74th Ft din'd with me*

Sat 4th   *Wind SW went over the Dock Yard, Block house &c – Din'd at the George – Gen Farmer, Major Barrington & Mr Rolls landed from Bilbao & Major Godfrey 61st Fusiliers. Passage 10 days*

Sun 5th	*Wind S & SW – Visited the Transports – Din'd at the Crown. Capt'n Payless 52nd Ft & Rolls din'd with me. Mr Strutt din'd with John.*

The First Division of the 7th Hussars March'd from Hyde Park Barracks on Thursday the 5th of August 1813 – The 2nd Division on the 6th for Petersfield, Havant, Emsworth & Lee – B Troop marched from Hounslow Barracks on Saturday August 7th to Kingston where they join'd A Troop in Squadron. Halted the Sunday at Kingston; March'd on Sunday 9th to Godalming – 10th to Petworth – 11th to Chichester – Got a fresh route in the evening. March'd to Arundel Friday August 12th 1813.

The left Suadron, Major Thornhill marchd in on saturday 13th Aug, March'd again from Arundel on Wednesday 17th – three squadrons embarked on 17th, 18th, Friday l9th Aug 1813 –

Mon 6th	*Wind SW Blowing very fresh – Lounged about Portsmouth & the Ramparts. Din'd at the Crown Mrs Strutt din'd there. Much grumbling –*
Tue 7th	*Wind NNW Blowing hard with rain – went on board the transports – with Mr Black of the 74th to give orders about a Court of Enquiry – Din'd at the Crown. Mr Black din'd with me & Majr. Godfrey .*
Wed 8th	*Wind N went on board: Held a Court of Enquiry on Serj Hardy of the 74th – Retir'd to dinner Din'd at the Crown – Henry Peters arrived & din'd at Mess –*
Thu 9th	*Wind NNE Waited upon Genl. Houston with the Proceedings of the Court – Signal made for Sea. At 2 pm went on board; Convoy sail'd at 4. Our ship under weigh at 1/2 past 7 – Light breeze –*
Fri 10th	*Wind Changed about noon to S W – some swell – but a light Breeze – saw the fleet 4 or 5 miles ahead – wind died away about 2 – a Dead calm off Weymouth –*
Sat 11th	*A breeze sprang up from the West about 10 right against us –*

Lost the Convoy in the night – Beat about all day – just weather'd Portland about 6 in the Evening.

Sun 12th
Wind WSW a fresh breeze; stood into the Bay close to Torbay, Tynemouth Lymington out again to Sea in the Afternoon – Beating about all night, slight swell

Mon 13th
Wind more towards the South; fresh breeze – Made Plymouth about noon – Pilot came on board about 1/2 past 1 – Came to Anchor in Cat Water a little before 4: Went on shore – Din'd at the King's Arms – Went to the Play

Tue 14th
Breakfasted late – Walk'd about the Town. Got some fresh provisions – All din'd at the New Hotel – Went to the Play return'd to the ship to sleep

Wed 15th
Sail'd about 9 AM under the Convoy of The Sea Lark, Schooner – Wind WSW Beating about all Day – and all night –

Thu 16th
Wind SW – Standing off and on the Coast of Cornwall all Day – a Pilot came on board from Falmouth 3 leagues about 6 PM – Wind died away. A Dead Calm all night –

Fri 17th
Dead Calm, drifted close in shore during the night off Falmouth. Still a thick mist Pilot came on board about 8 – Went into Harbour and came to Anchor at 3. Went on shore Din'd at Comins's Hotel

Sat 18th
Remain'd on shore: Wind foul – Pipon, Hamlyn, & Shirley went to Mrs Daniel's. Din'd & slept on shore. Mrs D got me a draft cash'd for £30

Sun 19th
Remain'd on shore: Wind foul. Went to a Methodist meeting – Din'd at the Hotel. John went to hear an Extemy. Sermon by Mr Owen at the Church for The Bible Society

The Shores about Torbay beautiful, but not equal or to be compared with the Entrance to Plymouth. The Town very old, but did not answer my expectations. Poor accommodation, but anything after the ship. The

Theatre very good, and New Hotel adjoining very handsome & well planned, on a most liberal Scale – Performers very fair – my old Friend Sandford the best – The House is intended to be a miniature of Drury Lane, as we were informed. The Audience not very similar, or very numerous except perhaps in the upper Regions.

*'Hic juvenum series teneris immister puellis
Ludet, et assidne pralia miscet Amor '**

The Entrance to the Bay of Falmouth, and the bay itself & Harbour are on a smaller scale than that of Plymouth – I am in doubt which is most picturesque.

The Cydnus Convoy arrived there, some on Saturday, the rest on Tuesday – Found also a store Ship & two Transports of the First Fleet who had lost the Convoy & put in there about 3 weeks before (Robeck's & Uniacke's Ships) –

Falmouth is a good Town – plenty of Red Mullet but very stupid [†] indeed Praying the only Public Amusement – Inhabitants chiefly Quakers, Jews & Methodists –

Mon 20th   *Remain'd on Shore – Pipon &cc return'd from Mrs Daniel's – Din'd & slept at the Hotel –*

Tue 21st   *The Frigate made signal for Sea soon after Day Break. Went on board – Convoy all under weigh about 9 AM Fresh Breeze from the N E –*

Wed 22nd   *Weather very fine, Wind fair, steady light breeze. The Fleet well together making 6 knots per hour*

Thu 23rd   *Fine clear Weather & Fair Wind 6&7 knots per hour all day – Showery towards evening –*

Fri 24th   *Dead calm from 6 AM till Noon – Light breeze from N Saw Land about 2 near 40 miles distant – About 9 the Cydnus*

---

* Albius Tibullus, 1. 3. 63–4.

[†] At this period stupid meant poor or dull.

*made Signal to stand off shore again – A heavy squall with
with Rain about 10 – Rough all night –*

Sat 25th *Light Wind from NE 35 miles from Shore. Hail'd by the
Commodor about 7 PM Spoke Robuk's & Pipon's Ships – All
well Fleet all together, standing in –*

Sun 26th *Light Breeze towards Noon, Calm all night – Land about 40
miles, very mountainous Supposed off San Andero –
Paraded the Ship at 3 Smart breeze from 3 to 6 – Died away
again towards evening. Convoy standing to the Eastward –*

*Enough motion to be very disagreable, Rain occasionally to drive us
below, and a filthy stinking cabin to drive us up again – 'Tout effet
augmente par son contraste'*

> *'As yet in hours of Love or strife
> I've 'scap'd the weariness of Life
> Now leagued vith Friends, now girt by Foes,
> I loath'd the langour of repose'*
>   *Byron*

*Some exertion of patience requisite to bear the loathsome weariness of
Shipboard – Dr Mc Kenzie & John amusing themselves in writing Poetry
en Burlesque on some of our Fellow Sufferers – Practising with Carbines
at Sea Gulls, Bottles &c during the morning –*

Mon 27th *Very little wind and most beautiful weather. The sea as calm
as a Lake, still standing East along the Land – Mr Read (the
Master) went on board a sloop at 1 o'clock. Talking on & off
all Evening & Night. Weather calm & beautiful*

Tue 28th *Lovely weather, a fine light breeze – close into San
Sabastian – Came to Anchor about 11 – Went on Shore
about 12 – Walk'd all over the Trenches out-works,
Breeches & Castle Return'd to the Transport about 7 PM –*

Wed 29th *Weigh'd anchor at Day Break, and sail'd round to
Passages. Anchored in the river about 9 OClock – Went on
Shore – bought a Mule 125 Dollars. Began disembarking*

about 3 – got about 1/3 of the troops on shore before Dusk. Disembarkation badly conducted. Slept on board

Thu 30th   Disembark'd at Day Break the remainder of the Troops & march'd about 12 to Lezo – 2 miles – Got the Troops into wretched Quarters, bought an Ass 24 dollars. Officers din'd together – Pipon, Peters, John myself in the same room

27th   As yet we had supposed that we were to land at Bilbao, but the Master heard from the Sloop that we were close to Passages, and pointed out that place & San Sebastian close abreast of us – Several Grampus's *appeared about the Ship during the morning, got some shots at these – Dress'd a Turkey for Dinner – Got some Port Wine very tolerable, and spent a very jolly evening. The Commissary & Irish Doctor affording inconceivable sport – sat up laughing till 3 o'clock A M. The state of San Sebastian would baffle all description. The Great Church & one House retain any part of a Roof; much of the Town was destroy'd by fire, & the Shot & Shells produced an effect scarcely conceivable – The whole Town is one Mass of Ruin, and the Streets in many places hardly passable from the rubbish; and every where strew'd with innumerable heavy & cannister shot & broken shells – The Bodies buried under the ruins, parts of which are here & there visible, some that have been partly consumed, and several about the Breach which remain as yet unburied and wholly exposed on the shore renders the place and all its environs dreadfully offensive – the French Guns in the advanced Battery of the Castle (El Miradon) which were continually playing upon our people are almost all dismounted & beat to pieces – their touch holes being almost melted. The French, before the Castle surrender'd, lost 100 Men per day in that Battery from our Shells –

29th   The Entrence to Passages very remarkable; the river so narrow that you might throw a feather on shore from either side of the ship – with high rocky mountains, tolerably wooded on either side – an Eagle on top of one of the highest added to the effect.

---

* A species of whale.

47

October 1813

Tom Wildman was now back in Spain exactly five years after he had arrived at Corunna in 1808. During this time the British and Spanish armies had been wearing down the French forces, which were now in any case being depleted as a result of Napoleon's disastrous defeat in Russia. In May 1813 Wellington had advanced out of Portugal for the last time. The French army in Castile was now under the command of Napoleon's brother Joseph, whom he had placed on the Spanish throne five years earlier. He was no soldier but was advised by Marshal Jourdan. The Marshal had no real authority, and the Emperor was contemptuous of his ability. The French army was pushed steadily north, giving up Valladolid, then Burgos and finally standing at bay at Vittoria. Outnumbered and no match for Wellington, Joseph was soundly defeated, though he managed to get the remnants of his army back to France. He lost all his baggage, coaches, treasure chest, paintings and jewellery, most of it pillaged from the Spaniards, and even his silver chamber pot, which was seized by the 14th Light Dragoons. After the battle, the British troops, officers and men, indulged in an orgy of pillaging, in which the 18th Hussars disgraced themselves. Major Hughes found himself confronted by Wellington, who had come upon a number of his men lying dead drunk in the street.

The British army was now able to advance to the French frontier. In the meantime Napoleon ordered Marshal Soult, a veteran of the war in Spain, to go back and try to stem the British advance. He hurried south and within a few weeks he had rallied the army and re-entered Spain through the mountain pass at Roncesvalles, with its evocative memories of Roland and Olivier. However, he hesitated, and Wellington defeated him at Sorauren before he could relieve Pamplona, which was being besieged by the Spaniards. In August, Soult made an attempt to relieve San Sebastian, but the city was stormed before he could cross the Bidassoa. Soult then set about digging defensive works along the line of the river and up into the mountains to La Rhun and St-Jean-de-Pied-de-Port. The front had been stabilised by the time Tom Wildman arrived, and Wellington was preparing to cross the Bidassoa into France.

After disembarkation, the first thing that Tom and John did was to purchase mules. The roads in Spain were so rough that all baggage, provisions and horse fodder had to be carried by pack animals. According to General Orders a captain was allowed one mule, but two subalterns had to share one between them. By 1813 officers were paying little regard to these regulations. In smart regiments like the 7th Hussars the officers were not inclined to allow the rigours of a campaign to interfere with their comforts if they could help it. Tom bought two mules and a donkey. However, he had brought out only two horses, while John had brought only one; most officers had at least two or three. Tom's requirements seem quite modest beside those of Colonel Vivian. He brought out seven horses, though he sold two to pay for all his mules. These were mainly needed for his servants to ride. In addition, he bought a pony for Mrs Jarvis, his cook, but she cannot have been very competent, for she was soon relegated to scullion and washerwoman. Higgins who had been the colonel's steward on board ship – 'really a most useful and excellent servant' – became the cook. In addition, there was Walker, his valet, Williams and Foxlow, who looked after the mules, and a German who took care of his goats – 'a most excellent fellow'. Tom did not equip himself on such a grand scale, but it is apparent from his diary that he had a number of servants during the course of this campaign, two of them, Domingo and Antonio, being Spaniards. Like so many young officers landing in foreign ports, he was clearly overcharged for the animals he bought. In Lisbon the price ranged from fifty to ninety Spanish dollars. In January 1814 the Adjutant General ordered Lieutenant O'Grady to pay fifty dollars to the owner of a mule he had commandeered to convey the regiment's baggage and which had died on the road. Maybe Tom was sharper than his commanding officer, for Vivian was paying a hundred and forty dollars for his mules.

The main body of the army was now encamped between San Sebastián and the frontier at Irun, and Tom comments on the camps up in the mountains behind the coastal plain and extending almost up to the summits. Throughout September the main body of the regiment had remained in Bilbao. It was apparent that the cavalry would have little part to play in the campaign until the army was clear of the Pyrenees. Negotiating stony mountain tracks was going to be hard on the horses, and the farriers would be in constant demand. Despite this it was impossible to take the regimental forge carts up country, and they were ordered to remain on board the transports to be returned to Ordnance. These were heavy two-wheeled vehicles requiring four horses to pull them. Only portable forges were disembarked, and the farriers were told to take all the shoes and nails from the forge carts and lodge them with the heavy baggage along with the fodder and rations. The portable forges would then be carried on mules.

On 2 October, Colonel Vivian and the main body of the regiment set off, their destination being Tafalla and Olite, towns fairly close to the valley of the Ebro, where fodder could be obtained for the horses. Fodder, or rather the lack of it, largely dictated the movements of the cavalry during the first four or five months of this campaign. However, all was well on this score until they advanced over the mountains towards France in November.

Tom's squadron left Passajes on 4 October for Tolosa, some thirty miles south in the foothills of the Pyrenees. John had been taken sick soon after landing, and on the 6th Tom also succumbed. The regimental surgeon was Dr Irwin, who had two assistant doctors, Robert Chermside and James Moffitt, but it was Wildman's shipmate Dr McKenzie who treated him in the absence of the regimental surgeons. Quite a number of officers were taken ill at this time. The health of the men was generally good, and most of those who fell ill were officers and their servants. This suggests that the cause lay in the richer food enjoyed by officers and shared, no doubt, by their servants. Benjamin Badcock of the 14th Light Dragoons cured his upset stomach with regular doses of bark and bitters.

They joined up with the rest of the regiment at Tolosa, a large dirty town according to Vivian, though Tom describes it as a good town. The squadron was quartered at Lizartza, to the south of Tolosa on the road to Pamplona. Here the officers dined together for the first time since leaving England. Lieutenant Arthur Myer was able to pay Tom and his brother officers their bat money (ration allowance), forge money and troop allowance, these payments being in addition to pay which was invariably months in arrear.

Arthur Myer was one of the few officers – usually reckoned at about one in twenty – who were promoted from the ranks. He had been a sergeant in the regiment and was promoted cornet when Tom was promoted to lieutenant, filling this vacancy without purchase. Of course he had no money of his own and had a wife and child in Guildford. Vivian had a high regard for Myer, whom he described 'as gallant a soldier as ever drew sword'. He helped him by providing him with his mounts, which officers were expected to pay for out of their own pockets. Despite the wealth of his brother officers, one can be fairly sure that an experienced and resourceful ex-sergeant would have soon have found ways of augmenting his income! On active service, disparities of means would not have have proved an embarrassment. At home he could probably manage on his pay provided he avoided involvement in too many of the regiment's social activities. At a period when few privates could read or write, Myer's correspondence in the regimental records show that he was a man of some education, and he was certainly well liked.

After five days at Lizartza the regiment was ready to continue its march to Olite. They had now left the mountains of Guspuzcoa and were entering Navarre, crossing a plain which was covered in vineyards and olive groves. According to Vivian, 'The olives are still green, and are as nasty as the grapes are good; but every species of fruit and vegetables, and the wine are delicious.' The countryside was green and dotted with white farmhouses. To their left and north, as they marched through Iruzun to Tafalla they could see the peaks of the Pyrenees in the distance. On their right to the south the land gradually dropped away down to the valley of the Ebro.

The road took them south of Pamplona, which stands on a low plateau with the River Arga flowing at the foot of the walls on the north and north-east sides of the city. Beyond the defences on the other sides there were market gardens and wheat fields, which the Spaniards had failed to burn or dig up at outset of the siege. The Spanish troops under the command of Don Carlos de España had been blockading the city, rather incompetently, for four months. The French had managed to take possession of the Spanish guns and had harvested all the wheat and vegetables in the surrounding countryside, which they had taken into the city. Now the garrison was starving, and Commissary Schauman maintained 'all provisions – aye, even to the last rats, cats and dogs in the place – had been consumed.'

Although the distance travelled was not great, the roads were so bad that the regiment barely covered twelve miles a day. Tom with the right wing of the regiment reached Olite on 14 October. Olite is a pleasant little town in open countryside. It was then a jumble of narrow streets and small squares dominated by the Moorish castle; a complex of crenellated towers and turrets. In earlier times the castle had been the residence of the kings of Navarre, but the year before, General Francisco Espoz y Mina, a farmer turned guerrilla and now a major-general and governor of Navarre, had all but destroyed it. William Bragge remarked: 'They say Mina is very mercival and never kills the Prisoners unless they are badly wounded … They consult the Surgeon if a Prisoner knocks up, who at once passes sentence as we do on a Glandered Horse.' Commissary Schauman, on the other hand, considered he was inflated with pride and 'his behaviour all too frequently betrayed his lowly origin and his total ignorance of decent manners and decorum'.

The regiment was to remain in Olite for the next two weeks. The 7th

51

now joined the 10th and the 15th Hussars in the Hussars Brigade, under Lord Edward Somerset, the older brother of Lord Fitzroy Somerset, who as Lord Raglan gave the fatal order to charge that sent the Light Brigade to destruction forty years later at Balaclava. The 7th Hussars replaced the 18th Hussars, who had not been distinguishing themselves even before their disgrace at Vittoria. The Hussar Brigade was not popular with the heavy cavalry, and William Bragge of the 3rd Dragoons had told his father in July:

> The Hussar Brigade are at Olite about 3 miles off and are to be broken up immediately and brigaded with more experienced regiments, being found to be perfectly unacquainted with their duty as Hussars and having nearly Galloped their Horses to Death. They are very conceited and extremely jealous of our Brigade which has been working with them, and is at present Twice as effective.

Shortly after this he wrote, 'The 18th are sent to the Germans to learn Out Post Duty ...' The commissary attached to the 18th Hussars, Auguste Schauman, shared these sentiments.

The truth of the matter was that Colonel Colquhoun Grant, who then commanded the Hussar Brigade, was incompetent and arrogant. He had been hoping for promotion, saying that the Duke of Cumberland had promised this to him. Wellington thought otherwise and had tried unsuccessfully to have him recalled. However, fate stepped in and on 11 September Vivian had told his wife, 'I am sorry to hear from the army that Colonel Grant is dangerously ill with a liver complaint; so much so that if he recovers it will be necessary for him to go to England. This will, I expect put me in command of a brigade.' Whether the illness was genuine or a face saver one does not know. Tom and his brother officers had a lucky escape, for the tall black-whiskered Grant who, with his adjutant, a little foxy-haired man with red whiskers, were known in the brigade as the Black Giant and the Red Dwarf, was not popular with Peninsular veterans.

All the heavy cavalry (including Edward Wildman's regiment, the 4th Dragoons) had been quartered in this fertile area for several months and were to remain there until the following year. Although the light cavalry were to have a role to play at the outposts, and for pursuit of the enemy, these mountainous and hilly areas of Spain and France precluded any large-scale operations with heavy cavalry. General Hill's corps was also still encamped in the area, for Wellington had to maintain this presence so long as there was any risk of Soult making another attempt to relieve Pamplona.

On the Sunday after their arrival at Olite there was a church parade, or divine service, to use the nineteenth-century army phrase. Wellington had a pragmatic approach to the spiritual welfare of his army.

> It was to my knowledge that Methodism is spreading very fast in the army ... The meeting of soldiers in their cantonements is, in the abstract, perfectly innocent; and it is a better way of spending their time than many others to which they are addicted: but it may become otherwise and yet until the abuse has made some progress the C.O. would have no knowledge of it, nor could he interfere.

The traditional hostility of the upper classes towards dissenters, aggravated by fear of egalitarian notions from revolutionary France, had convinced the military that Methodism could encourage subversive ideas among the ranks. Hence the need to send 'respectable clergymen' to minister to the troops. The Adjutant-General had recently placed the Reverend H. Landon at the disposal of the cavalry commander, Sir Stapleton Cotton, with a request that 'Divine Service should be attended every Sunday by as great a number of troops as can be paraded for that purpose in the quarters of the cavalry.' Admirable as these sentiments may have been, Tom records only three church parades, and they ceased as soon as the regiment moved up to the front.

Having settled into quarters in Olite, the regiment resumed its usual routine of parades in watering order.* A contemporary print shows the men wearing short cotton jackets with forage caps not unlike those worn by French naval ratings today, with a pom-pom on top. Once parades were over there was little else for both officers and men to do. 'The order of the day,' wrote the colonel, 'is for everyone to live as well as he can; and a very wise plan it is.' His men took his advice to heart. 'They get sadly drunk now and then, for which I have tickled a few of them; but in general they have behaved admirably well. Wine is so cheap it really is no wonder they get drunk. It is sixpence a quart only and very strong.' Despite these tolerant sentiments, Vivian was a disciplinarian, but we do not know how many lashes constituted a 'tickle'. In Wellington's army twenty strokes was regarded as a minimum. Whatever the penalties for getting drunk may have been, soldiers who made advances to the girls of Olite risked far worse treatment. The local peasants would walk through the streets at night with carbines concealed under their cloaks. 'They were so jealous

---

* Manner of dress worn by cavalrymen when taking horses to drink.

that no Hussar was safe whom they saw joking with a girl. They actually killed two men of the 10th Hussars, and tore their eyes out. The eyes were found afterwards about twenty feet away from the bodies.'

Tom and the other officers occupied themselves by entertaining one another in their billets. Colonel Vivian gave a dinner for Lord Edward Somerset when he reviewed the regiment on 20 October. He never invited more than six guests, and on this occasion he gave the General a first course of salt fish and potatoes, a choice of roast saddle of mutton, stewed beef, roast potatoes, steak, boiled chicken and ham, followed by a second course of roast partridge, apple stewed, rice pudding, tart, mushrooms and an omelette. A rather curious assortment, but the modern practice of serving consecutive courses rather than having everything on the table at the same time had not yet come into fashion. Vivian's only regret was that his canteen was made of lead, and that he had not brought plated dishes. He was piqued that Kerrison, Lowther, Wildman, Verner and others all had plated dishes. 'It is astonishing besides, how much better a dinner looks on them.'

Tom must have been a good deal better off than his colonel, and we can be sure that his dinners were of an equal standard. Among those who dined with Tom and his brother while in Olite were Captain William Verner, Arthur Myer, the adjutant, James Elphinstone, John Needham, John Breedon, Robert Douglas, Duke A. Descars and Henry Peters who were all junior officers in the regiment, and Robert Chermside, the assistant surgeon, and Richard Darville, the veterinary officer.

Verner's family had settled in Ulster in the early seveenth century, and William had inherited a substantial estate in Armagh from his grandfather. His father had been a member of the Irish Parliament before the Act of Union in 1802. John Elphinstone's father was a director of the East India Company. Two other officers who dined with the Wildmans at other times were James Fraser, whose father was a baronet, and Standish O'Grady, the son of the first Viscount Guillamore, Chief Baron of the Exchequer in Ireland – 'a sharp useful fellow,' according to Lord Uxbridge, who commanded the cavalry at Waterloo. But of all these men, perhaps the most interesting was Richard Darville. Brought up in a racing stable, he had been the servant of an officer in the regiment. When his master left the regiment on account of debt, Darville entered the Veterinary College in 1808. The head of the college was so impressed by the young man that he recommended him to Vivian who accepted him as veterinary officer. Verner recalled that 'his education, except in the stables, had not received much attention'. He could write an intelligible letter if not too long. 'In a regiment like the 7th,' Verner went on, 'in which there were many young men of large fortunes, many opportunities occurred of picking up horses to advantage.' Accordingly Verner used to lend Darville money to buy horses which he then sold, and repaid the loans by instalments. In this way he was able to maintain himself in the regiment.

Everyone was expecting Pamplona to fall at any moment. Major Thornhill took five guineas off Colonel Vivian and agreed to pay him one guinea for every day that the French held out. They held out for another seven days and Thornhill lost two guineas. During this last week Sir Staplton Cotton arrived in Olite. He commanded the Cavalry Division, which comprised four brigades, including both the light and heavy cavalry. Known as 'Lion d'Or', Stapleton Cotton looked impressive in his splendid hussar general's uniform of red and gold, reputed to be worth 500 guineas. He had a special aptitude for inspecting troops, but Wellington was not greatly impressed with his tactical ability, and did not allow him any independent command of the cavalry. Wellington preferred to employ the cavalry for scouting and for covering his front, as evidenced by Tom's diary. The cavalry brigades were kept under his direct orders and moved wherever he needed them. After the war, Wellington wrote:

> I considered our cavalry so inferior to the French from want of order, that although I considered one of our sqaudrons a match for two French, yet I did not care to see four British opposed to two French, and still more as the numbers increased, and order (of course) became more necessary. They could gallop, but could not preserve their order.

This was unfortunate for regimental officers who regarded charging at the head of their men as their primary function. There was to be little opportunity to charge during this campaign.

On 25 October the officers of the brigade gave a ball for Sir Stapleton Cotton. The officers of the other regiments, having been stationed in the area for several months had in all probability made friends among local families. There may not have been many attractive girls in Olite, for Vivian, writing to his 'dearest Eli', told her that 'the quarters I now occupy are most excellent ones, with admirably good civil creatures but <u>no pretty girls</u>, which I lament as it assists me in learning Spanish, in which, however, I have attained great proficiency.' In fairness, one should add that his hostess had two cousins, 'beautiful creatures', who used to come in and chat to him over breakfast. (The Black Giant who had occupied the house before Vivian would never speak to anyone of this household; they disliked him!)

Tom's comment, 'Too late from England to relish the Ball – Did not dance having little or no temptation' seems rather supercilious. Of course a provincial ball in a remote and backward part of Spain might well have been a rather dull affair compared with the ballrooms of Regency London. Tom's attitude calls to mind Mr Darcy when urged to dance at the Meryton Assembly by Mr Bingley in *Pride and Prejudice* (published that same year): 'You know I detest it unless I am perfectly acquainted with my partner. At such an Assembly as this it would be insupportable.' Tom certainly had no aversion to dancing, for years later in 1830 he received a letter from a former admirer reminding him of a regimental ball in Dublin. She wrote:

I am delighted to learn that you remember me, remember me too under the pleasant influence of youth and gaiety when I danced at every ball and flirted with every Beau who came my way – and danced and flirted with you 'pour preference' – I fear we look back with more pleasure on our follies than on our wisdom – and retain more agreeable recollections of those who shared them with us than of more serious friends and important friendships since; bless me! What an important friend I thought you when I saw you enter Lady Clarke's drawing-room with tickets in your hand for the ball given by yr. regiment at the Rotunda and how I blushed and flushed with delight when in addition to the ticket you asked me to dance the 'first sett' (a term now obsolete!) – No, not all the glory ... were worth one such offer of a ticket and dance from a smart gallant young officer of a crack regiment!

Five years earlier he had written to Maria from Astorga during the Corunna campaign:

I rather regret Corunna and Lugo in many respects, for we have no Balls and Routes here, and the Castilians differ very much from the Gallician Damsels, who are all life and spirit, and have more the manners of the Irish; but here we have a little specimen of the old Castilian notions, and no woman of condition is to be seen, or heard of ... I wish you could be present at a party in Galicia, tell Eliza I think she would be highly amused, and have no doubt but she would greatly excell in the waltzes, which are preferable to our Country Dances though the Ladies here say they like them best.

It seems as if the 'damsels' of Navarre did not bear comparison in Tom's eyes with those of Galicia. Those officers who had spent years in Spain deprived of female society probably had less exacting standards.

The fall of Pamplona within days of the ball gave the signal for the hussars to advance into France. Tom received an invitation to dine with Sir Stapleton Cotton on the following Sunday, but as the General left in the afternoon Tom may have missed this dinner. The diary shows that the senior officers were at pains to get to know the officers under their command. Throughout the diary there are many references to such invitations, which must have greatly assisted in promoting cohesion and mutual understanding.

The order had come sooner than expected. Tom received his orders at 4 p.m. on the 31st. The 18th Hussars were not aware of the order until the following day while heir food was cooking; it had to be thrown away. Tom had already sent John forward to arrange billets for the troop.

The Deputy Quartermaster-General was responsible for going ahead of the army and making arrangements with town magistrates, and then parcelling out the town or village between the various units and chalking the unit and the number of men to be accommodated on the doors of the houses. Of course these arrangements could not always be followed, and the fact that John was sent to arrange billets suggests that this was one of those occasions. They were now about to enter sparsely populated country and cross the Pyrenees, albeit the lower end, but the countryside was rocky and the roads mere tracks.

By all accounts their stay in Olite had been pleasant. Colonel Vivian and Major Thornhill had been able to go out shooting game. Apart from the high cost of eggs, sugar, meat and wax candles, the only complaint from some officers was that 'every chair, Bed, Brick and Tile swarms with Bugs'. Although these did not bite William Bragge, his friend Spencer complained that, 'They look so scandalous about one's Clothes!'

Fortunately the men's health had been good, though some of the officers had had the usual bowel trouble. Captain Hamlyn and Verner's servant had both contracted typhus and had to be left behind. Hamlyn was taken back to Vittoria. Ten sick men also had to be sent to the rear along with about fifty-six horses. However seriously ill Hamlyn may have been, Colonel Vivian had little sympathy for him. Writing home a fortnight later, he said:

As to H ..., he is absent sick; he is not quite what he ought to be at bottom in any way, I fear. You know what a fuss he made about coming out, and yesterday I received a letter from him, saying that his fever is gone, but that his <u>constitution</u> <u>was</u> so <u>shattered</u> that it required the care of his friends in England to restore it, begging me to make application for leave. Only conceive that at the moment when the regiment is commencing on active service! If he was half dead he should never have asked such a thing. There are hundreds of officers in the army who are now serving having had similar fever without going home but there is more vapour than anything else about that young man! I said before I left England that he would be he first to return; you see what a prophet I am!

Vivian was not the only officer to have a poor opinion of Hamlyn. In a letter to his father the following January, William Bragge said:

Lucy is very Misterious about Susan Adney and says she is greatly mortified at her Conduct and almost fears she may yet <u>do</u> <u>worse</u>, which I think by no means improbable as I am confident her Husband is a poor, weak jealous Creature and not by any means likely to keep so lively a Lady in order. Her ci-devant Lover, Capt. Hamlyn, is at Vitoria, but as he behaved very improperly to Lucy at Exeter, I shall not be at the Trouble of calling on him.

Journal

Fri
Oct 1st

John bother in the night with Dissentry. Rode over to Passages, bought two Mules, 100 & 130 Dollars – Brought Dr McKenzie back with me to Dinner. John much better towards evening.

Sat 2nd

To Edward

Lt Jones came into Breakfast – Major Stanhope arrived soon after. John & Stanhope rode over to Passages – Return'd to Dinner. Stanhope din'd & slept in our house

Sun 3rd

To my Mother

Blackman of the Guards & Lascelles come over to Breakfast – I rode with Shirly & his Brother to the Camps near Irun, Din'd with G Ramsden Shirly din'd with his Brother – Rode back to Lezo at night

Mon 4th	*Orders to march at 7. The Forage did not arrive till past 11. Mov'd off about 12 – Robek join'd us at Rentaria, arrived at Ernani ½ past 4, where Col Ponsonby & other officers of the 12th Light Dragoons got our horses in had provided for forage 7 c*
Tue 5th	*March'd at 7 through Tolosa to the village of Lizarza, where the squadron was very tolorably put up. Robek's Troop went to another village in the Mountain – Met Myer on the road – Saw Light in Tolosa – Got no Forage till 9 at night*
Wed 6th	*Maj. Hodge*
	Col Vivian arriv'd; Receive'd Bât & Forage money, Troop Allowance &c from Myers – Taken unwell in the night –
Thu 7th	*Bother'd all day – Col Vivian & all the officers din'd with us – Descars* arrived in the Evening –*
Fri 8th	*To Maria*
	Heyliger's Troop March'd in to join Robek's in Squadron under Col Kerrison – Rode out with John – Din'd a large Party with Peters at Pipon's Quarters. Douglass slept in our House
Sat 9th	*Rode out on my Mule about the Mountains – Col Kerrison, Heyliger, Douglass & Peters Din'd with us*
Sun 10th	*Turn'd out at ½ past 7 – March'd at 8 to Arriba, a small village on the Borders of Navarre, only 2 Leagues from Lizarza. Hamlyn, Peters, John & Myself Din'd together at my Quarters*
4th	*Some part of the road almost impassable even for Mules. Weather very hot – Ernarni a tolorable siz'd good Town – The 12th Light Dragoons quarter'd there from whom we received the greatest assistance & civility. Col Ponsonby*

---

* Duke Descars was a lieutenant with the 7th Hussars.

was engag'd to Dine out: But had dinner provided for us in his own Quarters, & room to put up our beds

5th

Left Moffit at Ernani, very ill with Dyssentry – Weather intensely hot – Camino Real the whole way and the country beautiful. Tolosa is a good Town, and the country round very fine, but the village of Lizarza is one of the most picturesque spots I ever beheld

6th

Took a Romantic walk with John in the Evening – Beautiful star light, but clouds resting on the Mountains and continually emitting most brilliant flashes of lightning

Lizarza lies in a deep Valley so completely hemmed in by immence mountains and containing so many natural beauties in itself, that you might imagine it the Valley of Rasselas, if the Buildings were of more elegant construction

7th

Lord Wellington crossed the Bidassoa and drove the French from all their Positions – The British Army in France

10th

March'd through a tract of fine mountain scenery – in some places immencely Grand – About half a mile before you arrive at Arriba are two Large Rocks on either side of the Road and a small Bridge between them through the arches of which the river runs diagonally under the Road – These the Priest at whose House I was billetted informed me, were called the 'Gates of Navarre': But on our March the next day – we were at first told we had not yet seen the real 'Great Gates of Navarre' and when we arrived at them, were no longer in doubt – About a mile from Irurzun, where the Mountains of Bare Rock, the space at their foot being just enough for the width of the Road – and immediately upon passing these, you enter a comparatively Champaign Country bounded by the Mountains we had pass'd – These are the real 'Gates of Navarre'

Mon 11th

Turn'd out at ½ past 5. March'd at 6 to Irurzun. 4 leagues Camino Real – a miserable village, pillaged & destroy'd in the French Retreat; used now as a halting Place for sick & Provost Guard –

Tue 12th	*Turn'd out at ½ past 8. March'd to Esparza de Pamplona a village about a league from Pamplona – 4 leagues from Irurzun, which we contrived by circumambulation to make 7 – John & I din'd with Col Vivian*
Wed 13th	*March'd at 8, 3 leagues to Mendivil, a small miserable village, occupied by some of the 10th Hussars who turn'd out to make room for us on the march – Irwin, John & myself got a very good Clean Billet – The Horses, other troops were at a village about a mile farther –*
Thu 14th	*Turn'd out at 7 – Join'd the Division at Barasoain March'd at 8, pass'd through Tafalla; saw several of the 10th – Lord G. Lennox* rode with us to Olite where we were very well put up – Elphinstone & O'Grady din'd with Us*
Fri 15th	*Watering Order at 9 – The Left wing of the Regiment under Major Thornhill march'd in about 11 – Several Officers Breakfasted with us – Verner, Gordon & Peters din'd with us*
Sat 16th	*Parade with Arms at 8 PM – Watering Order at 10 – Turn'd out at 4 in Marching Order to change Quarters – Edward came over about 12 and remain'd with Us – Din'd at Shirly's Quarters Edward, John, Shirly, Descars & Douglas –*
Sun 17th	*Parade for Divine Service at 9 – Verner & Elphinstone Breakfasted with Us at my Quarters – Edward & John rode over to Lerin about 2 – Rode part of the way with them. Brigstock & Synge rode over from Tafalla & din'd with me; Maddison & Chirmside din'd with Us*

The Country in Navarre is very different from that of Biscay and Gulpascoa, not by any means so picturesque but of a fine soil, and better cultivated than any part of Spain I had before seen! The latter part of our March was through vineyards & olive groves and on our side of the road near Tafalla, a large tract of land had very much the appearance of a market garden in England – On our March to Esparza (12) we pass'd

---

* Son of the Duke of Richmond and Lord Lieutenant of Ireland when Tom was stationed there.

within 2 miles of Pamplona, of which we had a full view from the Hills The Town stands in a vast plain; and seems large & handsome, all appears quiet, but there was a good deal of firing the two following days – No one seems to have an idea how long it will hang out –

Olite is a good siz'd town, tolorably well supplied. In the Plaza are the remains of the palace of the ancient Kings of Navarre; which to prevent the French from occupying & fortifying it Gen. Mina beat to pieces

It was said by some that this was the birth place of Henry 4th of France, but it seems more probable that he was born in French Navarre, than in this, which belong'd to Arragon – The Palace seems to have been handsome and the ruins are of some extent.

Mon 18th   *Major Hodge O'Hagarty*

Parade at 9 to inspect & fit saddles &c Stables at 12 – Rode out into the Country. Met A. Shakespear – Edward & John return'd to dinner. Myer & Chirmside din'd with Us

Tue 19th   *Watering Order at 10 – Stables 12 – Inspection of Appointment & Necessaries at 2 – Rode with Col Kerrison, John & Edward part of the way to Lerin. Edward left us – Din'd with Robbins*

Wed 20th   *To My Mother*

Parade at 8 Pt. Lord Edward Somerset inspected the Regiment in Watering Order at 11 – John taken very unwell. Sat with him & Chirmside all day – Got him into my Billet. Chirmside din'd with me tête à tête –

Thu 21st   *John much better – Rode over to Lerin through Miranda – My Horse fell down a Water Course – had to walk the last 3 miles – Edward sent some men who caught him – Din'd with Edward – Major Hugorn [?] – Capt Porter, Mr Gregory &c &c*

Fri 22nd   *Pour'd with rain all the morning – Set out about 3 – Edward rode part of the way with me. Road wretchedly bad &*

slippery – Pass'd Miranda de Arga about Sunset – Lost my way in the plain: arrived at Olite about ½ past 7 – Found John much better –

Sat 23rd   *Parade at 8 Pt. Inspection of Horses at 9 – Inspection of Arms & Appointments at 2 – Din'd with Needham – Heyliger Shirly & Elphinstone*

Sun 24th   *Rain'd – No Church Parade. Muster at 10 A.M. Edward rode over to Us – Din'd with Col Kerrison, Stanhope, Edward Buckman [?] O'Grady & myself – Stanhope slept in John's Billet*

*   *   *

The Peasantry in this part of Navarre are stronger & better looking than any I have before seen in Spain; there is some appearance of Agriculture and industry in the Country which is very fruitful. Olite is surrounded by Vineyards & Olive groves – and when the corn had been got in the Peasantry were ploughing & seemed to work as if they were in earnest, though their implements afforded no little amusement to our people. – The Town is very well supplied with Meat Bread Eggs &c and Forage tolerably good & plentiful though Provisions of all kinds are extremely dear –

The Country between Olite & Miranda de Arga may be very fertile just near the two Places but is as ugly and uninteresting as can possibly be conceived: there seems to be plenty of Game: Two Covies of Partridges walked across the road within 12 yards of our horses on Monday 25th – Near Miranda a large Bridge has been destroyed, but the Bridge of Miranda remains entire – All the Towns in this part are much alike both within & without – The Track between Olite, Miranda & Lerin for 2 Leagues is a perfect Desert of Sand or Clay Hills overgrown'd with rushes & rank grass, and it is no easy matter to find your way or keep in the track by day. By night I found it impossible – On my return from Lerin on Friday night, after traversing this Desert for some leagues (my horse lame from constant slipping), I with some difficulty gain'd the ridge of hills cover'd with Box, which rise East of Olite – there, having no road to direct me, nor sign to know whereabouts I was I wander'd about some time, and at last determin'd to find a Tree under which I could wait till morning – having tir'd of leading, or dragging a lame horse, when fortunately a flash of lighting discover'd at no great distance a stone Cross – The situation of which respect to Olite I was well acquainted with – and by this means got back into the road

Mon 25th	Marching order from 8 till near 2 P M – Breakfasted – Stanhope return'd to Tafalla. Rode with Edward to Lerin to Dinner – Went to a Ball given by the Officers of the Brigade to Sir Stapleton Cotton
Tue 26th	The 4th Dragoons Review'd in Marching Order by Sir Stapleton Cotton at 11 – return'd at 1 Edward return'd with me to Olite to Dinner. Needham din'd with us
Wed 27th	To Maria 4
	Inspection of Horses at 7 for Captain of Troops. Edward & John rode to Tafalla. Needham & Peters & Breedon din'd with us. Capt. McNiel of the 4th expected but did not come
Thu 28th	Darvill & Chirmside Breakfasted with us – Edward return'd to Lerin – John & I din'd with E.Peters – Hamlyn very ill –
Fri 29th	The Regiment review'd in Marching Order by Sir Sapleton Cotton at 3 P.M. Darniel & Gordon Din'd with Us – The Spanish Commissary came in & some Ladies &c. Singing & Music
Sat 30th	Rode to Tafalla with Robbins: met an Orderly on the Road with a Note (Invitation to Dine with Sir Stapleton Cotton on Sunday) – Edward arrived about 8 Elphinstone & Darville din'd with us –
Sun 31st	To Majr Hughes 18th Hussars
	Church Parade at 10 – About 12 News arrived of the Surrender of Pamplona – At P M got the order to march in the Morning – Sir S. Cotton march'd in the Afternoon – John

64

went forward for Billets. Edward took charge of Hamlyn to Lerin – Lowther Darvill Elphinstone O'Grady & Myself din'd at Gordon's Quarters

25th *Too late from England to relish the Ball – Did not dance, having little or no temptation. Went to bed about 12 Much better pleas'd with the morning's than the evening's Amusement – The Regiment in excellent Order – The clothing old & bad, but Horses fat and in good condition. Arms, Appointments &c in captial order. Their movements quick & correct tho in deep ground. And the Regiment in every respect in a good and effective state for Service –*

29th *The 7th turn'd out very strong & well. Sir S. Cotton was much pleas'd with our Appearance &c*

31st *We had been so often deceived by the Spaniards with reports of the Surrender of Pamplona, that we scarcely believ'd it till we received the Order to march notwithstanding the ringing of Bells & firing from the Windows in Olite – Hamlyn too ill to march with us – Edward took charge of him to Lerin to be placed under the care of the Surgeons of the 4th Dragoons as they were not expected to move for some time*

November 1813

With the surrender of Pamplona, Wellington was able to undertake the next stage of his advance into France. The forces covering Pamplona could now be moved. The French front followed the line of the River Nivelle from St-Jean-de-Luz on the coast, down through Ascain to the heavily fortified hill of La Petite Rhun, some seven hundred yards from La Grande Rhune, captured when the army crossed the Bidassoa. The line then continued past Sare to Ainhoa and through the mountains to St-Jean-de-Pied-de-Port. Wellington's point of attack was between La Petite Rhun and Ainhoa. This line ran more or less south-east from St-Jean-de-Luz, a distance of about twenty miles. The Hussar Brigade marching up from Olite past Pamplona to Santesteban and Vera de Bidassoa were travelling due north. Vera lies on the river about four miles from La Petite Rhun on the other side of the mountains.

The first day's march took them to Esparza de Pamplona just south of the city. One can understand the hussars' desire to inspect the city. The fortifications had been constructed by Louis XIV's great military architect Sébastien Vauben (1633–1707). Despite the expansion of the city, part of these fortifications can still be seen. Notwithstanding the siege, little damage seems to have been done to the city, and the cathedral, churches and other historic buildings were unscathed. Whether this was due to a natural reluctance to destroy their city or because the French had captured all their guns is a matter of conjecture. Both the Spanish and French commanders were well aware that there was no possibility of the city being relieved, and it was only a matter of time before the garrison would be starved into submission.

At the outset William Bragge thought a siege would cost two thousand men. 'They have a Regiment of Dragoons and about 3000 men within the walls, which are too extensive for the Garrison.' The French casualties must have been light for three thousand surrendered. Nevertheless the French commander, realising that his defence was holding up the British advance and thus gaining time for Marshal Soult, hung on for as long as possible. When he finally surrendered, his men were in a pitiful condition. Even if Tom paid no tribute to their gallantry, Corporal Wheeler of the 51st Foot was full of praise:

when they marched out with the honours of war, so ghastly was the appearance of the men that one would have supposed that they had all risen from their graves. I was told, by some who had witnessed the sight that the men could scarcely stand, they had held out until completely starved. What more could be expected from them. They are an honour to the Imperial Army and to their country.

After the officers had visited the city, the regiment skirted the western side and turned into the mountains and followed the River Ulzama up into the fertile valley of that name. Here the regiment was quartered in a number of villages. Four days later they moved off again higher up into the mountains. Colonel Vivian described the first stage of he march in a letter to his wife written on 3 November from Buenza.

> After making two forced marches which has nearly knocked up all our horses and almost killed my mules, &c, I reached this place last night, and was preparing to proceed this morning to St. Estevan, when, thank God, I received an order to halt; so here I am, in the clouds, with Edward's and Robins' troops.
>
> I say 'thank God' we halted, because another such a day's march as we had yesterday and the regiment would have been <u>hors de combat</u>. No description that I can give you, nor can the worst roads that you ever heard of or saw, at all enable you to form an idea of the mountain paths we climbed yesterday. The worst goat path in all Wales is a garden walk compared to it; and they tell me that we have eight leagues more into France of still worse roads!

The colonel and about half the regiment appear to have set off ahead of Pipon's squadron. On 2 November he had arrived at Buenza with Captain Thomas Robbins and Captain Edward Keane. Keane was a relative of Mrs Vivian, and Robbins appears to have been a close friend. The other troops were quartered in a cluster of villages to the south. While they were in the valley Tom went out foraging with Commissary Woods and his assistant Augustin Diaz, of whom he later wrote, 'I really believe him to be an exception to his Nation in general.' Tom was greatly impressed by the beauty of this valley, as was Vivian, but provisions were hard to obtain.

> We are now in a village situated most romantically in country which is beautiful, and which in happier times must be a delightful

residence. The villages are exceedingly good, and the peasantry admirable people; but alas! the men and the houses are all that are left.

We are almost in a state of starvation. What little our horses have to eat is the wheat taken from these poor creatures; and when you imagine that this has been going on by the French first, in their retreat; then by ourselves; then by the French again, in their advance; then by us; and since, constantly by British cavalry and infantry marching to and fro, you will not suppose much is to be had here.

On the 6th, after two days' rest, Tom and Pipon's troops moved to another village a few miles further on, while Vivian pushed on over the next range of mountains and down to Sanesteban on the upper reaches of the Bidassoa. Unfortunately an order instructing the brigade to remain in Olite had only reached Vivian while we was in Buenza.

The attack on the French positions on the Nivelle had been timed to take place as soon as Pamplona fell, but snow in the area of Roncevalles was delaying General Hill's advance on the right flank of the army. Rain followed, which further delayed matters, and it was not until 10 November that Wellington attacked the French defences on the Nivelle. Nevertheless the Hussar Brigade continued to advance.

On the 7th the regiment continued their march, although there was no likelihood of their having any part to play in the battle. The road was even worse than it was before. That evening Vivian described the march:

After having scrambled for six hours over mountains and roads, if possible ten thousands worse than when I last wrote I attempted to describe, I arrived here half an hour since, with about half of my regiment. You may guess what the roads were when I tell you that in one troop alone upwards of twenty horses lost their shoes; and so full of rocks and loose stones are they that without a shoe it is impossible to move an inch; so the farriers are hard at work in the rear, and the road from here to Arraiz is full of the 7th, and I am here with about half the regiment.

Tom was with the half of the regiment who arrived in Sanesteban, and his description of the road as 'wretchedly bad' hardly measures up to that of his colonel. He seems to have been more interested in the spectacular scenery. Commissary Schauman provides an even more lyrical description of this march.

The roar of the mountain streams, mingled with the cry of the eagles, the sound of our horses' hoofs and the singing of the hussars, made a curious melody. Now and again we would meet a Biscay peasant, looking blooming and robust, with his blue beretta on the side of his head, and his cloak carried on his mountaineer's stick; and as he leapt lightly and boldly past us across the rocks in his sandals, he would greet us affably. Higher up we came on a number of peasants employed and paid by Lord Wellington's general staff, who were levelling some of the more dangerous portions of the road with bundles of wood and logs and making them practicable for artillery. Very often the road ran along a precipice, down which, if a horse slipped or shied, both horse and rider plunged and perished. Here and there we came across some snow. When we came to a sudden sharp turning on the ridge of the mountains, a magnificent panorama presented itself to our view, reaching as far as the Bay of Biscay, and we even fancied we could discern the fields of France.

The march to Sanesteban, a distance of some nine to ten miles, had taken seven hours. The following day Tom and Pipon found Colonel Kerrison in Sumbilla, a village a mile or so further down the Bidassoa from Sanestaban on the opposite side, in a steep valley. The regiment played no part in the Battle of Nivelle which took place on 10 November. The front line was several miles away, the ground was unsuitable for cavalry, and in any case the horses would have been in no condition for action. The attack on the French lines along the Nivelle was decisive, and by the evening of the 10th the French were in retreat towards Bayonne. Two days later Tom and his squadron moved up to Vera further down the river.

Here the regiment was occupied bringing in the wounded and burying the dead. The following week he had an opportunity to study the battlefield. The terrain is described by Schauman:

The country between St. Jean de Luz and Ainhoa, which is broken by innumerable hills, and, particularly in the neighbourhood of the Nivelle, by rocky heights and ravines, bore a strange and terrible aspect. At the cost of considerable pains and much treasure the French had fortified every height, and blocked every gorge with felled timber. The number of redoubts, trenches and earthworks was incalculable, not to mention the isolated peasant farms that had been surrounded by moats and supplied with drawbridges. For miles around every copse and every tree had been cut down to form barricades.

69

Once the lines had been breached the French had no alternative but to retreat or risk being cut off. Tom seemed surprised that they had not been able to hold their positions. If Soult had had sufficient reserves to plug the gaps he might have been able to do so.

Tom also comments on the behaviour of the Spanish troops. On the night after the battle General Longa's Spanish division plundered Ascain, halfway between Sare and St-Jean-de-Luz. According to Schauman, 'Their eyes were aflame. Every Frenchman who fell into their hands was ill-treated or secretly murdered. Before leaving a village they always plundered it and set it on fire.' He then goes on to relate how General Pakenham, in charge of the military police and supported by a powerful guard, began to ride up and down the columns 'like a raving lion seeking whom he might devour. His command, "Let that scoundrel be hanged instantly!" was executed in a twinkling.'

Now that the army was in France, Wellington was anxious to secure the cooperation of the people. Writing to Lord Bathurst a few days later, he said:

> I must tell Your Lordship, however, that our success, and everything depends upon our moderation and justice, and upon the good conduct and discipline of our troops. I despair of the Spaniards. They are in so miserable a state, that it is really hardly fair to expect that they will refrain from plundering a beautiful country, into which they enter as conquerors; particularly adverting to the miseries which their own country has suffered from its invaders. Without pay and food, they must plunder, and if they plunder they will ruin us all.

All the Spanish troops, with the exception of General Morillo's division, were then packed off back to Spain. As a result, Tom, in common with many other soldiers, commented on the friendly welcome they received from the French.

As a relief from tending to the wounded, Tom was invited to dinner by Colonel Vivian. He was impressed by the wines but does not mention the food. Vivian may have been having some difficulties on this score. Back in September he had written home asking for four hams and eight tongues to be sent out, together with butter, cheese and wine. Shortly after this dinner party he wrote to his wife:

> Thanks for the articles you have sent me. They have not yet arrived – at least I have not yet heard of it. You like a stupid woman, do not

mention the name of the man or the ship; so I must send to Passages on a wild goose chase. Oh Eliza, after having been married to me for nine years and a half, to be so very thick!

Poor Eliza. One hopes she was able to hold her own against her forceful spouse!

Regular communications for letters and parcels had been established at Passajes as early as September, and English newspapers were arriving regularly. A few of the letters Mrs Wildman wrote to Tom during the Corunna campaign have survived. At that time she arranged for him to be sent 'through the medium of Messrs Greenwood and Cox the paper called the Examiner, it is weekly, and is considered one of the best in use at present – rather too great a tendency to abuse the government – but that you may pass,' Mrs Wildman sometimes addressed her letters to Tom at regimental headquarters where mail for officers and men would be forwarded in bulk. On other occasions she sent her letters under cover to Messrs Greenwood and Cox who arranged for them to go via the next packet boat. The dates when the packets sailed for the Peninsular were published. Of course the post was not always reliable. At the beginning of the following January, Benjamin Badcock of the 14th Light Dragoons wrote home:

I am sorry to say all my things have been sent to Santander. They might do better in England. I shall soon not have a shirt to my back. I wish my bootmaker to send out 2 pairs of short boots to Passages which I shall then get. There is a commissary stationed at Passages who will forward anything for the regiment to us.

The weather had been cold for some time. Captain Kincaid of the 95th had been bivouacked on the slopes of La Rhune for a month and wrote of their

dearly longing for the day that should afford us an opportunity of penetrating into the more hospitable-looking low country beyond them; for the weather had become excessively cold, and our camp stood exposed to the utmost fury of the almost nightly tempest. Oft have I in the middle of the night awoke from a sound sleep and found my tent on the point of disappearing in the air like a balloon, and leaving my warm blankets, been obliged to snatch the mallet and rush out in the midst of a hailstorm to peg it down.

The cavalry quartered behind the lines in billets were not exposed to such hardships. However, the lack of forage was causing problems. When the regiment arrived in Spain, daily allowances for the horses were 10 pounds of straw and 10 pounds of barley. A pack mule carried 200 pounds and an additional 30 pounds of fodder to feed the mule for three days. If the journey took longer, it would have to start eating its load. (German tanker lorries supplying the Russian front during the Second World War were up against a similar problem with petrol.) Cavalry needed more mules for a brigade than an infantry division. The continuous convoys bringing up fodder and returning to the depot at Passajes were a picturesque sight. 'I have never seen such fine and powerful beasts,' wrote one assistant commissary:

When they are on the road they are decked with numbers of bells which tinkle melodiously in the distance. If they have not got these bells, the leading mule at the head of the column has a bell, or rather a cylinder, slung round its neck, the constant clanging of which makes the rest follow … I have often travelled as many as 45 miles with them in one day, and they carry the largest loads along day after day on long marches and patiently and unwearingly subsist on the most exiguous supplies of food and water. The muleteers form a large and hardy class of men. They seldom change their clothes or sleep in shelter throughout the year; they are constantly on the road, and very merry and constantly singing. They wear large black felt hats with tassels, short jackets, a mantle, a blanket with a hole in the middle for their heads, blue plush breeches and spats or sandals.

On 18 November the Hussar Brigade was ordered back to Spain. Picking their way up the mountain tracks again in pouring rain, closely wrapped in their cloaks, their caps becoming sodden and shapeless, they must have presented a sorry sight. Arriving back in the valley of the Ulzama, Colonel Kerrison and the Right Squadron was at Alcoz, and Tom was now billeted in Iraizoz less than a mile away. After two days' rest they continued their march, stopping a night just outside Pamploma, and finally reaching Echauri, close to the River Arga, a tributary of the Ebro, about ten miles west of Pamploma. There the troop was put up in Ciriza, a tiny village just beyond Echauri. Regimental headquarters were at Echauri and little time was lost in returning to the normal routine of parades and inspections. Scrambling over rough country in wet weather would have caused wear and chafing to saddles and bridles.

Tom carried out the inspection of saddles and bridles himself and does not appear to have delegated this task to his junior officers. On the last day of November the regiment learned that Vivian had been given a brigade. He had been expecting this for sometime, and while at Olite he had written to his 'dearest Eliza': 'If Victor Alten returns to England I shall certainly have his brigade...' In fact he was given Colonel Grant's (the Black Giant's) brigade, the 13th and 14th Light Dragoons on 14 November.

Journal

Mon 1st   *Assembled in full Marching Order at ½ past 5. Parade 1st March'd thro' Tafalla Barasoain & Mendivil to Esparza de Pamplona. Rain'd hard all the afternoon. The French Garrison march'd out of Pamplona at 4 with the Honours of War – Prisoners*

Tue 2nd   *March'd at ½ past 7 to join the Troops at Salinas – The Regiment assembled on the high Road a league from Pamplona – halted at the Gate – Officers went in – Turn'd off about 2 miles further into the Mountains. Rain'd hard all the evening – Arrived at Baranain about 5 in the evening – Pipon's Troop at Ciganda –*

Wed 3rd   *At ½ past 12 AM Got Orders to March at 8 to Yzena de Argu – At ½ past 3 arrived a counter order to remain till further orders – Employ'd all day in foraging & collecting provisions Mr Wood the Commissary & Senr. Augustin Diaz with us*

Thu 4th   *Maj. Hodge*

Darville & Irwin breakfasted with us – Several Officers over the morning at our Village – John rode with Peters –

To my Mother 5

Fraser din'd with us –

Fri 5th   *Rode out with the Troop in Watering Order over the Hills – Went to Verner's Village – Shirly John & I din'd alone –*

73

Sat 6th	*To George*
	At 5 O'Clock a m got the Route – March'd at 9 to Alcoz another small village in the Valley of Ulzama – The Squadron together – Lowther came over & din'd with us
Sun 7th	*Got the route at 7 – March'd at 9 – Wretchedly bad mountain Road, 5 or 6 Leagues: arrived about 4 P M at Sanesteban, a Small Town 3 or 4 Leagues from the French Frontier – Shirly, John & I din'd together –*
2nd	*The Regiment being assembled on the Camino Real about a league in the rear of Pamplona – Col. Vivian sent to ask Don Carlos's permission to march thro' that Town. He return'd a very polite Answer, but it was not possible. Only one of the gates had as yet been undone since the surrender. The Regiment however march'd round & halted at the Main Entrance, when the officers went in by turns to see the Place – The Town is very fine, the Cathedral & some of the buildings beautiful and the whole very clean, and by far the best Town I ever saw in Spain – We had little time for observation: – The Fortifications & works are the strongest and most beautiful I can conceive. It is call'd the Key of the Northern Pyrenees, and was reckon'd a Chef d'oevre of Mons. Vauban – Several of the French who got drunk on marching out, were left behind on the road, and stript & murder'd by the Guerrillas & Peasantry during the night – We saw 36 English who had been prisoners in the Town, they did not appear in general so lean as might have been expected – They said they had had the same rations as the French i.e. 4 Ounces of Bread & 5 Ounces of Horse Flesh per day – Saw some murder'd French on the Road – Nothing can exceed the Romantic Beauty of the Northern Pyrenees – They are not in those immense Barren Masses of Rock, like the Mountains of Galicia and most others I have seen; But exhibit a perpetual variety of Ground. The summits much broken, and cover'd with magnificent Forests of Oak, and the Valleys beautiful and well cultivated, interspers'd with Villages and Farm Houses. The Peasantry are better looking and appear to possess more of*

*the primitive simplicity than those of the other Provinces –
Very few of them speak or understand Spanish or French.
The Basque Language which they speak and all over Biscay
has no resemblance to either, unless that is somewhat
between both in the pronunciation – The Valley of Ulzama
which is of considerable extent, its beauty & grandeur
surpasses anything that pen or pencil can describe*

Mon 8th   *Halted all day at Sanesteban – Lord E. Somerset & his Staff
came in. Synge arrived just as we were sitting down to
Dinner – Din'd with us – went to Robbins's Quarters to play
Cards in the evening –*

Tue 9th   *Pipon's Squadron March'd at 9 o'clock to Sumbilla one
league in advance to join the Right Wing under Col
Kerrison – the Left Squadron march'd into Santesteban –
Col Vivian went with Lord Edward Somerset to the Frontier*

Wed 10th   *Lord Wellington attack'd and Drove the Enemy from their
Positions in front, took Sare and St Jean de Luz, and
pursued them towards Bayonne – We remain'd in readiness
expecting Orders to advance – every hour –*

Thu 11th   *Some skirmishing and small affairs in front. We collected
what information we could from wounded Spaniards who
were coming in all day – No ground for Cavalry!*

Fri 12th   *March'd at ½ past 6. The right squadron, to Sara, the three
Left to Vera, late Head Quarters. Met a great number of
wounded – Vera full of wounded – Saw Brigade Major Alix
who was wounded on the 10th & doing well –*

Sat 13th   *Rode out in the Morning to see the Lines in front – Rain'd
hard all day – No Orders to advance! Call'd on Alix & found
him much better – The wound doing well –*

Sun 14th   *March'd at 8 – (The Right & Left Centre Squadrons to join
the Right Squadron at Sare in France) Rain'd hard all day –
Saw several Bodies on the road – Hospitals full of wounded*

Santesteban is a good Town or larger sort of Village. The French were in possession for a considerable time, and the People seem to like them very well; It is situated in a valley on the Bidassoa about four Leagues from the Frontier –

Vera had been Lord Wellington's Head Quarters since the advance from Lesaca across the Bidassoa on the 7th of October – He left this Town on the 10th – After which the Head Quarters were at St. Pée about three Leagues in front of Sare – Vera was like other Towns pillaged by the French on their retreat, and nothing left but Bare Walls – Some English Settlers had however followed the Head Quarters from whom we procured Butter, Brandy and some few luxuries we had long be strangers to – The Road from Santesteban along the Banks of the Bidassoa is beautiful –

Mon 15th	*Major Hodge To Maria No 6*

Pour'd with rain all day – Parties sent out to bring in the Wounded and bury the Dead – A guard form'd to protect the Inhabitants from Spaniards

Tue 16th	*To Edward*

Rode with John to look for wounded – Brought three Germans of the 60th – Got them into Hospital – Din'd with Col Vivian by a capital fire – Constantia & Claret

Wed 17th	*Thos. Luke To Mr Afflick To Mr Peters*

Weather still bad & stormy – Rode with Robuk & Pipon over the field of Battle. Visited all the Positions of the Enemy. Went very near St. Pee – and saw St. Jean de Luz from the Battery on the right –

Thu 18th	*Got Orders to March at 3 A.M. March'd at 9 – The same wretched track over the Mountains to Vera – Pour'd with rain. The Brigade being order'd to repass the Pyrenees on account of Forage – Took up our old Quarters*

Fri 19th	*Rain'd hard all day – March'd at 9 to Sanestaban took up our old Quarters – Bad Weather, Bad Living, Bad Country – France much better –*
Sat 20th	*Weather something better – Roads as bad as we left them – March'd at ½ past 7. The Regiment nearly in its old Cantonments in the Valley of Ulzama. The Right Squadron to Alcoz – My Troop with Lowther's at Iraizoz –*

The French had so little expectation of holding their position that on the first advance of our Army they drove the Peasantry from their Houses with the Bayonette – They however return'd as fast as they could and seem'd happy to see the English, as they said if the French had remain'd they must have starved, for they took every thing and paid for nothing – They were greatly afraid of the Spaniards, who plunder'd & destroy'd when they could, all that their own army had not time to destroy before – exercising every cruelty upon the Inhabitants –

The Strength of the French Positions is inconceivable, and any one would suppose that Twenty Thousand men might have held them for ever. One Height near the Center cover'd by a double Abatti, which cost our Troops much to carry, ought never to have been Abandon'd – I met with a Burying Party of our Regiment on this hill who had interr'd above 70 that morning – The top of the hill was as thick with graves as a Church yard, and above an hundred & fifty more were then lying about us – One Battery on the Top of an inaccessible Mountain on the right of their Line, and the Works extremely strong, was full of French Arms, 900 having surrender'd without a Shot. There were not above a Dozen Bodies about it, and only two inside – But the French Army is completely cow'd, and tired of an unprofitable War

Mon 22nd	*March'd at 8 to Irza, a miserable village about 2 Leagues from Pamplona which would scarcely hold the Troop – John & I in the Priest's House –*
Tue 23rd	*Receiv'd Orders at 11 to move my Troop upon Echauri Head Quarters – March'd to Zereza [Ciriza] a very good village about a mile & ½ beyond where we were very well put up –*

77

Wed 24th	*To Maria No. 7*
	Inspected the Cloaks & Blankets – Wrote letters – Had the Troop out in Watering Order – Wanted more to do and was glad of Dinner time – Chirmside din'd with Us
Thu 25th	*John & E Peters rode over to Pamplona – Inspected the Saddles & horse Appointments – Peters & John return'd to Dinner –*
Fri 26th	*Pipon, Descass & Shirly went to Pamplona. I remain'd at home to complete my inspection. Din'd with Peters (John Pipon Shirly Descass & myself), return'd to our village at mid-night*
Sat 27th	*Inspection in full Marching Order by the Commanding Officer at ½ past 10 – Took a long walk Shirly & John Din'd with Douglas – Pipon din'd with me*
Sun 28th	*Parade for Divine Service at 11 – Din'd with Lowther at Echauri. John's Mule tumbled down the Hill with him & got away*
23rd	*Saved me the trouble of applying to be moved*
24th	*The Horses appointments &c a good knock'd about by the late Marching in the Pyrenees – but on the whole looking better than would have been expected*
27th	*The Appearance of my Troop commended*
28th	*The Mule found again at 6 next morning – Saddle, Bridle & all complete –*
Mon 29th	*To Edward*
	John went out shooting with the Priest – brought nothing home – I bought a Hare in the absence of a Peasant – Rode over with Shirly & John to Dine with Heyliger. Shirly & I return'd –

Tue 30th   *To Hamlyn*

> *Intelligence receiv'd at Head Quarters of Col Vivian having got a Brigade – Report of Buonaparte being at Bayonne in person – Shirly John & I din'd together*

December 1813

The first fortnight of December was a quiet time. Tom and John were billeted with the local priest, an affable fellow, it seems, who took John out shooting, though without any success. Tom and his brother usually dined at other officers' quarters or else entertained them in theirs. The first evening they spent alone with the priest, he got drunk, encouraged no doubt by the brothers.

Tom's troop was quartered a mile and a half beyond the regimental headquarters at Echauri. He exercised the troop in watering order what in modern times would have been called stable order or fatigues), but this would not have involved musketry practice, let alone any tactical training, which was practically unknown at this period. Lord Edward Somerset inspected the regiment on the 4th. There was an inspection of arms and accoutrements on the 6th. Colonel Kerrison inspected Robek's and Pipon's squadrons on the 8th and there was a final inspection of the whole regiment in marching order on the 13th prior to returning to France. Apart from these duties Tom had little to do and was bored.

There was little contact between officers and men when not on parade. The social gulf was too wide. The sort of contact among junior officers and their men that is a normal part of military life today would have been quite alien to Tom and probably embarrassing to, and even resented by, his men. He makes few references to his men or even NCOs by name. Yet he does show concern that they have proper quarters. That there was a general lack of interest in the soldiers' living quarters at this time is evident from a General Order issued (or more probably reissued) on 18 December 1813 directing that every building inhabited by troops is to

> be visited constantly by the officers of the Company to which they belong and care should be taken that all wet straw and other dirt is removed, and that the Perce or other material which the soldiers have collected to lie upon is rolled up and the floor swept, and that whenever the weather is dry the blankets are put out to dry.

Tom would have delegated this duty to one of his subalterns. His own administrative duties were minimal. There was a brigade order requiring troop leaders to 'send a morning and daily state of their troop accounting for every man and horse which is absent'. He mentions dealing with troop accounts relating to the men's pay, but as this was usually months in arrear it would not have involved much work.

What the men looked for in their officers was not daily contact so much as example. Physical courage was the quality most admired; not necessarily the sight of them engaged in hand-to-hand combat, but their ability to remain cool and fearless under fire. The diary makes it apparent that Tom was greatly concerned about courage. He singles out a number of instances of bravery among his fellow officers, and particularly their ability to endure painful wounds with cheerful fortitude. Indeed one is tempted to think that he rather envied those who wore the 'red badge of courage'. Although he came under fire at the outposts and during the final offensive when 'shot and shells flew pretty thick' and the 'firing was very sharp', he makes no reference to having been involved in any charge or hand-to-hand fighting.

On 3 December there was a meeting of the officers at regimental headquarters at Echauri. In view of Vivian's promotion the regiment was now under the command of Edward Kerrison. He was a year older than Vivian who was then thirty-seven. Having expressed a wish to join the Army, Kerrison's father had bought him a cornetcy in the Inniskillin Dragoons after he served for six months in the ranks of another regiment. Like Vivian he later transferred to the 7th. They both attained the rank of major in the same year. Having purchased a lieutenant-colonelcy in the 25th Dragoons in 1804, Kerrison exchanged back into the 7th without joining the 25th. (These 'paper transactions' were quite common under the purchase system and were negotiated by Army agents on behalf of their clients.) Kerrison was not promoted to lieutenant colonel until a year after Vivian. They both served in the Corunna campaign where Kerrison was seriously wounded, his arm being broken in two places. Although their careers had followed an almost identical course they were very different in character. Vivian was a disciplinarian, whereas Kerrison was more easygoing, influenced, possibly, by his experience in the ranks at the outset of his career. Vivian had a very successful career, retiring with the rank of lieutenant general. Kerrison's military career came to an end as a result of wounds he received at Waterloo, and he retired as a major general in 1819. Which of them was the more able is hard to say, but the likelihood is that Vivian was the superior commander.

After leaving the regiment upon his promotion, Vivian wrote a farewell letter to an officer who is unnamed but who one would assume to be his successor, Edward Kerrison. Feelings toward Vivian among the officers must have been mixed to say the least. In all likelihood Vivian's letter was read out at the meeting. We do not know what was said in the reply, but it caused Vivian great distress. In a letter to his wife dated 23 December he wrote:

> You have no conception of any thing so abominably cold as the letter I received from—* in answer to one I wrote him taking leave of the regiment. My letter was dictated from the heart, and I spoke my feelings toward the regiment. I know not what dictated the answer, but I should feel excessivly sorry if I thought any officer of the regiment approved of it.

The day after the meeting at Echauri, Lord Edward Somerset came to inspect the regiment. He was probably less concerned with appearances than with the men's bearing and the condition of the horses, for they paraded in watering order and not in marching order. A consignment of bullion arrived with him and Tom received back pay to 24 November. It was not until 1813 that the army in Spain was paid in guineas; before that the local population would only accept Spanish or Portuguese currency. An officer who wanted Spanish doubloons or dollars had to hand over a draft or bill of exchange drawn on a London bank, on which he had to pay a substantial percentage. Rich as he was, Tom would have been pleased to receive cash without the trouble of making arrangements through his bank. What is surprising is that his pay was up to date, since the Paymaster General's department was usually months in arrears. What is puzzling is the large amount he was paid. A cavalry captain's pay was about 12 shillings a day. When Vivian got his brigade, he told his mother that his pay was now 20 shillings and 9 pence a day plus 9 shillings and 6 pence 'batalian and forage'.†

Major Thornhill now took over Colonel Kerrison's squadron. Thornhill was a close friend of Vivian; he had stayed with him in Truro, and in their spare time they went out together shooting. Although Thornhill entered the army after Vivian, he may well have been older than the other officers, for in his letters Vivian usually referred to him as 'old Thornhill'. Keane and Lowther, who had previously been troop leaders in Thornhill's squadron, now joined Verner's and Robbins's squadrons respectively.

The weather had now improved, and Wellington was ready to take the

---

* When Vivian's son published his father's letters in 1897 he omitted the writer's name.
† Ration allowances.

offensive again and advance on Bayonne. Marshal Soult had retired behind the west bank of the Nive with his front extending from Cambo to Bayonne. On the other side of the river he had a substantial force between the Nive and the sea in an entrenched camp below Bayonne. Wellington split his army into three corps under General Hill, Marshal Beresford and General Hope. The latter advanced on the east bank of the river and engaged the French below Bayonne; Hill crossed to the west bank of the river by Cambo; while Beresford crossed further north. Hill now pushed forward on a line between the Nive and the Adour. Three days of fighting followed. Soult first turned on Hope but was halted after a fierce engagement. He then attacked Hill and after a desperate struggle round St-Pierre on the outskirts of Bayonne, Beresford's 6th Division came to his support, and Soult was forced to withdraw half his force behind the Adour. This now became the right wing of his army, and he deployed the remainder south of the river and to the east of the Joyeuse, a tributary of the Adour, which flows more or less south to north. His extreme left was at St-Jean-de-Pied-de-Port, which was defended by a garrison of 1,600 men, increased a month later to 2400.

The British army now went into winter quarters in the valley of the Nive. The outposts were established on the west side of the Joyeuse. The decision to halt operations until the weather improved was explained in a letter from Wellington to Lord Bathurst, the war minister: 'In military operations there are some things which <u>can</u> <u>not</u> <u>be</u> <u>done</u>; one of them is to move troops in the country during or immediately after a violent fall of rain … I should be guilty of a useless waste of men if I were to attempt an operation here during these violent falls of rain.'

On 14 December the Hussar Brigade was ordered once more to advance into France. This time they did not cross over the Pyrenees but retraced their steps along the route they had taken in October from Passajes, namely through Iruzun and Tolosa, and then to the frontier at Irun. An 'exceedingly gloomy, dirty and melancholy looking place,' according to Commissary Schauman, and now occupied by the Spanish troops Wellington had sent back home, and none too friendly as a result.

The order to march seems to have come at an awkward moment for Mr Wood, the 7th's commissary, and would account for the delay in setting off that Tom mentions on the 14th. He set out the difficulty he had in providing rations for the regiment in a letter dated 24 December:

> In consequence of the length of time which my Transport was delayed waiting for forage corn at the depot at Passages, I was

necessitated to send the greater part of it out to collect that article from the country – from the distance I had to send the consumption being so great, I could not keep with the Regiment in reserve a sufficient number of mules to convey the supplies necessary upon so sudden and unexpected a march.

On the 14th at an early hour in the morning an order arrived to have the regiment march immediately from their Cantonments at Echauri, preceed to their marching I issued to them Rations of Provisions and Forage for 3 days; at this period the entire of my mules were out: I had them called in with as little delay as possible and left my Storekeeper and Issuer (the only assistance I have) to see the supplies loaded and bring them to the Regiment without loss of time; I accordingly on the 15th arrived at Tolosa and arranged with the Depot Assistant Commissarey Ibbetson for the further supply of the Regiment here.

I stated to the commanding officer the necessity of his taking forward as much provisions as he could for the rapid marches of the Regiment, and the Transport not being up; they however took with them only 2 days Bread and one days forage; meat, rice and spirits were to be issued but the Regiment would not take them on the 16th. I went to Rentaria where I met one of my mule Brigades returning from Passages loaded with Forage Corn; this I took with me to Orazun and on my arrival had it delivered to the Troops after which I sent the Brigade back to Rentaria to reload with the articles.

In view of the difficulties that Tom records in obtaining supplies it seems surprising that Colonel Kerrison did not take Mr Wood's advice, but it is possible that the regiment did not have enough mules of their own to carry them.

On their arrival in France the weather deteriorated. Tom speaks of 'weather raining and bad'; Schauman's description is more colourful:

Rain sleet or hail was the order of the day. Our boots even if we had several pairs in use, were never dry. We always had cold and wet feet. The very sight of stone floors in the house here made one shiver; while the smoking chimneys drove one to desperation. In the evening we used to console ourselves with grog and cigars by the kitchen fire; but alas, cigars began to run short – none were to be had for miles!

84

Tom's squadron, and no doubt the other squadrons too, had to move their quarters several times during these last weeks of December. Having arrived in France, the regiment crossed the Nive at Cambo and halted at Bas Cambo, a small village on the opposite bank, where Lord Edward Somerset had his brigade headquarters. The accommodation they were given was so overcrowded and bad that Pipon and Tom moved their troops two miles down the river to Halsou where the accommodation was good and the forage plentiful. Needless to say they were moved on almost immediately to Urcuray about five miles to the east toward Hasparren. Tom relates that his mules all fell in the river and one was drowned. They would have been following behind the regiment with the baggage, and the river must have been the Nive. The squadron remained at Urcuray until 31st December when they returned to Halsou. Here their old quarters had now become very crowded. However, Tom and his brother officers appear to have been put up fairly comfortably in a house.

At Urcuray, Tom had found Major Hughes of the 18th Hussars, the officer who had borne the brunt of Wellington's anger at Vittoria and who had been severely wounded. Hughes described the result of General Morillo's marauding expedition. On 18 December the Spanish general, whose division was on the right flank of the army, went on an unauthorised expedition down a valley between Mendionde and Helette, driving in the French outposts, and pillaging the country as far as the Joyeuse. For this purpose he had borrowed two squadrons of hussars from Von Alten's brigade. Morillo then found himself attacked by French cavalry and quickly turned back. He suffered considerable losses and the 18th were badly mauled covering his retreat.

Morillo's division, as a punishment for plundering, was ordered to be kept under arms for five days in bitter weather. The general received a stinging rebuke from Wellington. In a letter, written four days later, from the Adjutant-General to Sir Stapleton Cotton, the general commanding the cavalry, he said:

The Field Marshal has directed me to request you will acquaint Major General Morillo that when he shall think fit to send out two squadrons of the cavalry to reconnoitre the enemy without any instruction to that effect it will be but prudent that he should superintend the duty in person; more particularly should it happen that the senior officer to be employed did not possess the advantages of experience.

The General was very angry, so Wellington wrote him a private letter saying:

> If the measures which I am obliged to adopt to enforce obedience and good order occasion the loss of men, and the reduction of my force, it is totally indifferent to me. I prefer to have a small army that will preserve discipline, to a larger one that is disobedient and undisciplined.

It is small wonder 'Nosey' had such a formidable reputation!

The Hussar Brigade was face to face with the enemy for the first time in this campaign, and were now called upon to undertake the role for which light cavalry were originally intended: to be the 'eyes and ears' of the army, to carry out reconnaissance and patrols, to take part in skirmishes and to generally protect the main body. Unfortunately cavalry officers found these duties unglamorous and boring. Consequently they gave little attention to such matters, and even Sir Stapleton Cotton was lacking experience in outpost duty before he took command in Spain.

> To attempt giving men or officers any idea in England of outpost duty was considered absurd, and when they came abroad they had all to learn. The fact was there was no one to teach them. Sir Stapleton Cotton ... once tried an experiment with the 14th and 16th Light Dragoons near Woodbridge in Suffolk. In the end he got the supposed enemy vedettes and his own all facing the same way.

There were no proper training manuals, and such as there were did nothing more than to set out the different mounted functions and movements with the appropriate words of command. Tom compiled his own manual, beautifully written with coloured diagrams, in 1810, but it was of no assistance for patrol work.

Fortunately Verner, Lowther, Pipon and Tom had had experience of these duties during the Corunna campaign, but not the other troop leaders and subalterns, who now had to learn. The other two regiments in the Hussar Brigade, the 10th and 15th Hussars, had both served in the earlier campaign and, along with the 18th Hussars, had returned to Spain earlier in 1813. The 1st Hussars, K.G.L., were by far the most experienced of all these troops and were held in high regard by Wellington. So it is likely that Commissary Schauman was right when he wrote:

Major Aly of the 1st German Hussars had the honour of being specially selected by Lord Wellington for the duty of organizing the whole chain of mounted guards, and of posting pickets. This meant that in the whole of the four English Hussar regiments which, with ourselves, discharged these duties, there was no officer that Lord Wellington could have used in this capacity.

Schauman's evident satisfaction was obviously influenced by the fact that his family was Hanoverian!

The front was patrolled from a main piquet, which would have been of about regimental strength including both infantry and cavalry. Further forward there were a number of advanced posts or piquets, manned by a dozen or more men, according to the situation. From these were posted vedettes, usually two in number, who would be within hailing distance of their piquets. The regiments in the brigade appear to have manned these piquets in rotation. Incursions by small parties of French could be contained by these piquets, but if the enemy were seen advancing in strength, the alarm post would be alerted and reinforcements brought up immediately.

Christmas 1813 was marked by a muster followed by a meeting of the officers of the two brigades. Afterwards they all dined together and spent 'a very jolly evening'. It would seem that the officers of the German Hussars may not have attended the dinner for Commissary Schauman was entertaining many of them to a dinner of his own. But the Germans were probably celebrating Christmas in a way that did not become popular in England until the time of Queen Victoria and Prince Albert.

Colonel Vivian had now been appointed to take over Von Alten's brigade, the 1st Hussars K.L.G. and the 18th Hussars. These had now moved into Hasparren, an attractive, clean and breezy town up in the hills above the Joyeuse, which separated the opposing armies. Here on 27 December, Vivian met his friend Thornhill who told him about the unhappy state of affairs in his old regiment. Feeling that he had been vindicated, he told his wife:

He tells me the 7th are going very badly. Kerrison had no management, no arrangement; in short they want me back, so he says; and this is, he tells me, the wish of the majority of the officers. However I suppose the men do not think so; for he lets them do pretty well as they like, and after he had made them a speech on my going, they gave him 3 cheers. He is always courting popularity, you know, I never cared a damn for it.

Tom allows no hint of these differences of opinion to appear in his diary. How serious they were one cannot tell. Perhaps Thornhill exaggerated because Vivian was his friend. About three weeks later Vivian returned to the matter in another letter:

> I wrote to Hodge by this post and have sent him my letter to the regiment on leaving it, and answer, with directions to send it to you. You will see that I have reason to complain. I have never said a syllable to anyone but Thornhill on the subject and I hear from him that several officers disapproved of it, but did not like to speak.

It may be that he was taking it all too much to heart, for it is apparent that Tom got on well with both men, though he was not as intimate with Vivian as some of the others. He is barely mentioned in the colonel's letters. Moreover there is nothing to suggest in the diary that the regiment's discipline suffered or that it performed less well under Kerrison's command.

On the last day of the year Tom noted that he had paid five men to 1 January 1814; four British and one Spaniard, Domingo. In the following May he mentions Spanish and Portuguese servants returning home, including his Spanish boy, Antonio. If he had been in Tom's employment in the previous December, one might have expected him to have been included. Possibly he replaced Domingo.The other four must have been performing services of some sort, which raises the question who they were and what they did. In the Waterloo Roll Call only five men with these names appear in the ranks of the 7th Hussars.* It would be more than a coincidence if these were not the same.

Officers were forbidden to keep men out of the ranks to act as servants, apart, of course, from one batman, to which they were entitled. Officers who disobeyed this order were liable to be court-martialled, and there are a number of such cases recorded. It may be that the four British were employed part-time as footmen, cooks or grooms when their regimental duties permitted. It is hard to see how all these officers were able to entertain on the scale they did without such assistance. It seems most unlikely that their hosts in billets could have provided it; in particular the priest in whose house Tom and John were quartered.

---

* The five men were Thomas Harris, Robert Chandler, John Fisher, Robert Fisher and J. Beach.

Journal

Wed *Dec 1st*	*Wet foggy weather – Rode over to Echauri. Douglas &* *Elphinstone expected to Dinner. Peters din'd with Us*

To My Mother & No. 8 Major Hodge

Thu 2nd	*Wet again – Read & wrote letters. Shirly John & myself* *Din'd together.*
Fri 3rd	*Meeting of the Officers at 12 Echauri. Rode over to see* *Verner. Lowther & Gordon expected – Pipon & Peters din'd* *with us –*
Sat 4th	*Lord Edward Somerset inspected the Regiment at Echauri* *in Watering Order – Received half Months Pay to Nov. 24th* *– 65 guineas*
Sun 5th	*Parade at 11 – Rode over to Head Quarters – Din'd at* *Home – The Priest got Drunk – New Arrangement of* *Squadrons in consequence of Col Vivian's Appointment to a* *Brigade –*

Major Thornhill	*Right*	*(Robek's* *(Heyliger's*
Vernon	*Right Centre*	*(Verner's* *(Keane's*
Robbins	*Left Centre*	*(Robbins* *(Lowther's*
Pipon	*Left*	*(Pipon's* *(Wildman's*

Pipon's Squadron was Right Centre before this
Arrangement

Mon 6th	*Inspection of Uniforms Arms Appointments & cc at 10 –* *Rode over to Head Quarters – Robek & Peters din'd with us* *– Robek slept –*

Tue 7th	*Went with Robek Peters & John after Breakfast to Pamplona – Return'd by 6 – Rode back with Col Campbell. Elphinstone & Fraser din'd with us and return'd at night –*
Wed 8th	*Col Kerrison Inspected the Right & Left Squadrons at Echauri – Col Campbell*was present – Descars rode home & Din'd with us*
Thu 9th	*Remain'd at Home writing &cc Nothing worth remarking To Maria No 9*
Fri 10th	*Much the same – Rode over to Head Quarters – Din'd at Home*
Sat 11th	*Needham din'd & slept at our Quarters*
Sun 12th	*Chermside din'd & slept at our Quarters*

9th Hard Fighting in front (i.e. in France) on the 9th, 10th, 11th & 13th – On the 10th the Enemy attacked the Left near Bayonne with his whole Force, but was gallantly repulsed by Sir John Hope and driven into his entrench'd Camp – Sir John Hope was slightly touch'd by Several Shots during the Action, and received a most flattering message from Lord Wellington requesting him not to expose himself so much – On the 11th they attack'd the Right and met with as a warm a reception from Sir Rowland Hill who drove them at all points with immence Slaughter –

Mon 13th	*The Left Squadron inspected by Col Kerrison in Full Marching Order at Echauri – Shirly John & Myself Din'd with Peters at Echauri – John came home later*
Tue 14th	*Got the Route a 6 A.M. March'd off at 11 – Detain'd in Echauri foraging till 1 – Got on to the Camino Real near the Gates of Navarre, arrived at Azpiroz at 1/4 past 10 pm*
Wed 15th	*March'd at 10 to Lizartza – Troops none the better for the March of 8 Leagues yesterday – Right & Left Squadrons at Lizartza – Two Centre at Tolosa*

---

* Formerly of the 7th Hussars, Colonel Campbell was now attached to the Portuguese army.

Thu 16th	*March'd at 7 – Detain'd foraging at Tolosa, arriv'd at Oyarzun 7 Leagues about 4 P.M. Badly put up*
Fri 17th	*March'd at 7; foraged in the Town & proceded through Irun & over a Bridge of Boats to Ascain in France – Weather beautiful, very hot – Latterly bad road*
Sat 18th	*March'd at 7 over most dreadfully bad roads to Cambo & Bascambo on the River Nive. Shot one of my Mules on the road – A long tedious March Through St. Pee – in all 7 Leagues – Wretched roads*
Sun 19th	*Foraging Parties sent out most of the morning – with Col Kerrison & the Brigade Major. Weather raining & bad – Sir Stapleton Cotton & Staff arrived in the evening – N.B. Had no Bread or Meat these two Days*

On the 14th We receiv'd a Route to move our Brigade to the Front, and the 7th, being the leading Regiment, march'd at 11 the same day: We were order'd to forage for three days in Echauri which detain'd us till past one; when as Pipon's Troop was not ready I march'd mine off – We had about 3 leagues of wretched cross road, and bad rainy weather till we came on the Camino Real a little beyond Izuryan when the night became clear from rain but extremely dark.

Our village (Azpiroz) laying about ½ a mile out of the main road and we missed the turning off, and march'd above a league beyond, and had to return, so that we did not get in till ½ past 10 at night, having been 12 hours on horse back, – most wretchedly put up at last –

A short distance (about a League) before entering upon the Camino Real, are Two immence Rocks, which rise on either side of the Arga and inclose the river for about a quarter of a mile; The approach to them on a heavy dull day had an extraordinary effect; they are call'd 'The Sisters',and there is a Chapel of some Saint in an immence Cavern close to the river about the centre of the Glen which they form

18th On our arrival at Cambo over the most execrable roads, we found it occupied as a Depot for sick & wounded in the late Actions, and a large body of Spanish troops in the Town. I endeavour'd to put my Troop there but found it impossible and mov'd them over the River to Bas Cambo, the Head Quarters of the Brigade; Bad Accommodation & much crowded

Mon 20th   Went out with a Sergeant & six to Reconnoitre & gain Information in Front – Pass'd Urcuray where the 18th were & Hasparren the Quarters of the 1st German Hussars: examined the direction of the Out Posts, & return'd about ½ past 3 – Wretched weather

Tue 21st   The Left Squadron march'd at Day Break to Halsou about 2 miles down the River where we were capitally put up and plenty of Forage & B [?] Got an Order to march in the middle of the night for Urcuray &cc &c –

Wed 22nd   March'd before Day break to Urcuray 1 League. All my Mules & Bagage fell into the River, one Mule Drown'd – Wretchedly put up, much crowded & scattered – Weather very rainy & bad –

Thu 23rd   March'd the whole Regiment before Day break to the Outposts to Forage, Brought away a great quantity from a village close to the French Piquets; Pour'd with Rain. Return'd after Day

Fri 24th   To my Mother No. 10
The Left Squadron march'd to occupy a village on the Left of our Advanced Piquet – General Sir Stapleton Cotton did not think it safe & order'd us in again. the Tenth foraged the out posts – Return'd to our old Quarters at Urcuray –

Sat 25th   Muster at 9 – Meeting of Officers at 12 – Sat with Major Hughes who was doing well. Shirly went some distance with a Roilemet. Din'd together capitally, and spent a very jolly evening –

Sun 26th   March'd before Day break with the Regiment to Forage at the Outposts – Foraged the village of Greciette on the Left, in front of our Main Piquet – March'd to some Farm Houses in front of Hasparren where the Left Squadron put up – Weather beautiful

20th At Urcury found Major Hughes of the 18th severly wounded. Learnt from him that on the 18th General Morillo had asked General Von Alten for two Squadrons of Hussars to make a Reconnaissance – that they had proceeded with his troops (a Squadron of the 18th & 1 of the Germans) and drove in the Enemies Piquets; and charg'd a Party of Cavalry who retired before them; but that on the Advance of the Enemies' Infantry the Spaniards gave way and let them get possession of a wood on the left, which placed the Cavalry under a cross fire and afterwards so block'd up the main Road instead of keeping the inclosures, that they prevented the Cavalry from retreating, by which one Captain was kill'd a Major & a Lieutenant wounded, & several Horses lost – Gain'd a good deal of Information from Major Hughes of the Positions of the Enemy &c – Pour'd with rain all Day –

22nd – A Piquet march'd Forward at Day break to relieve those of the 18th on the Road to St Jean de Pied de Port – The Patrols had a skirmish in the evening – A Ball struck Colonel Kerisson's stirrup – Order'd to remain constantly saddled at night – The People everywhere delight'd to see us and unanimous in their hatred to Buonaparte & his Cause – The Country beautiful and the Farm Houses are excellent, and the style of living more like England – The Climate delightful in general – Some heavy Rains for a day or two, but at other times clear and the Sun very hot –

* * *

Mon 27th   *Edward Maj. Hodge Maria No.11*

Breakfasted together at Pipon's Quarters a l'anglois – Excellent fresh Butter – Wrote several letters. Din'd at Pipon's Quarters & went to bed early – John remain'd to play at Cards –

Tue 28th   *Turn'd out an hour before Day break to the Advance Posts, an Attack expected: waited till 11 O'Clock – Mounted the Main Piquet – The Regiment went home. The Enemy drove in my small Piquet on the left of Greciette between 4 & 5. Skirmishing with them in front –*

Wed 29th   *Enemy's Patrols very troublesome in the night – All quiet in the morning – Reliev'd at nine – The Regiment forag'd at*

the Outposts – The Enemy shew'd himself in the Afternoon;
one Horse shot, and a Man Taken Prisoner of my Troop.
Squadron Din'd all together –

Thu 30th   Pipon & Peters went out on Piquet – Foraged the Squadron
in our own Cantonments – John & I din'd with Colonel
Keane near Hasparren and spent a very pleasant Evening –

Fri 31st   Marc'd at 7 – The 10th Hussars reliev'd us at the Out Posts
– March'd to Halsou & the vicinity – Our old Quarters but
much crowded this time – Irvin Din'd with us

28th: The whole of the Army on the right were under Arms at Day break.
An attack being expected, some Artillary was brought up and were form'd
on the left of the main Piquet till near 11 O'Clock, when the Regiment
went home; We mounted the Main Piquet at 10 – The 10th Hussars cross'd
to Forage from Greciette to Medionde on the right – They had just done
foraging & March'd off when I return'd from Posting a Corporal & two in
an intermediate Station between the Main & Right Piquet – I found my
vedette making signal of the Advance of the Enemy – He advanced with a
Regiment of Tirailleurs upon Greciette supported by some Infantry in the
Valley, and drove in my advanced Piquet on the Left, under a sharp fire –
Some Cavalry at the same time came down the Main Road in front. I met
them with Skirmishers and they retir'd after a few shots – The Infantry
plunder'd Greciette & drove off a large flock of sheep, and left a post there
at night. I patrol'd the village at day break on the 29th; found all quiet and
resumed that Post –

Harriss	

Chandler	Paid everything
Fisher	up to Jan 1st 1814
Beach	

Domingo   Paid to Jan 1st 1814

January 1814

January was a miserable month, wet and cold, with skirmishes taking place almost daily, and the search for fodder becoming desperate. Skirmishing seldom led to close combat, and usually amounted to no more than the exchange of a few shots. Casualties seem to have been minimal – one man of Tom's troop, Hitchen, was captured, and Captain Heyliger walked into an ambush in a village while on a foraging expedition. This should not have happened if he had sent scouts on ahead of his party before entering the village, but then this may have been an example of lack of experience in reconnaissance duties.

These cavalry encounters seldom amounted to more than 'shadow boxing'. Captain Mercer of the Horse Artillery has left a description of French and English light cavalry skirmishing on the day before Waterloo:

> The foremost of each line were within a few yards of each other – constantly in motion, riding backwards and forwards, firing their carbines or pistols, and then reloading [...] both French and English, generally stuck out their carbines or pistols as they continued to move backwards and forwards, and discharged them without taking any particular aim, and mostly in the air. I did not see a man fall on either side. The thing appeared quite ridiculous, and but for hearing the bullets whizzing overhead, one might have fancied it no more than a sham fight.

Although artists usually portrayed cavalry meeting head on at full gallop, this seldom occurred in reality. Mercer describes one such occasion:

> There was no check, no hesitation, on either side; both parties seemed to dash on in a most reckless manner, and we fully expected to have seen a horrid crash – no such thing! Each, as if by mutual consent, opened their files on coming near, and passed rapidly through each other, cutting and pointing, much in the same manner one might pass the fingers of the right hand through those of the left. We saw but few fall. The two corps re-formed afterwards, and in a twinkling both disappeared, I know not where or how.

95

Of course the horses had a vital interest in all this, and would have instinctively shied away to avoid colliding with one another.

Most of these encounters took place during foraging expeditions, and neither side was anxious to provoke a fight with no particular objective in view. There were one or two more serious incidents at the outposts during this month, and in the first week Wellington thought there was a possibility that the French would attack. Soult must have realised that an advance against his positions would not be long delayed. His divisional commanders would have been seeking information as to Wellington's dispositions and probing to find out their strength.

For most of the time the outposts pursued a policy of live and let live, and normally it was considered bad form for piquets to shoot at one another. Before the French attacked on the Nive, they called out to the British sentinels to retire and the 'enemy skirmishers came forward in a careless fashion talking to each other and allowed our sentinals to retire without firing at them'. Wellington approved of this and at a later date said, 'I always encouraged this; the killing of a poor fellow of a vedette or carrying off a post could not influence the battle, and I always when I was going to attack sent to tell them to get out of the way.'

However, life was not always as simple as this at the hussar outposts. Tom describes an incident that occurred on 11 January at Banloc, about two miles south-east of Hasparren. This resulted in five Frenchmen and three Portuguese losing their lives because the day post occupied by the Portuguese was on the French side of the River Joyeuse. Colonel Vivian gives a rather fuller account of this skirmish:

Covering too much ground, we are liable at any moment to be harassed by the enemy; and they daily take advantage of it. A day seldom passes without my being roused out to the outposts, to stand like a crow to be shot at for half an hour! When this is over we are all the best of friends possible, and ride down to the river and talk across it affectionately as if we were sworn allies! I should tell you that the river is precisely such a stream as runs at the bottom of our garden (neither more nor less), fordable at ten thousand places; and such it is understood to be. This morning at half past four I was roused out of my bed by a considerable firing of musketry. I galloped down to the advance post and found that the enemy had attacked a hill on their side of the water, on which I had a sergeant and six, and a sergeant and twelve infantry.

At this time the 7th Hussars were temporarily under Vivian's command, as Tom recorded on 4 January. Vivian continues:

> They came on with about 150 men. Of course they soon drove us beyond the river; but the firing still continued, I went down and holloaed to the French to cease firing and to send an officer to me. In a short time an A.D.C. of D'Armagnac's came to me, and I asked him if his only object had been to carry the post. If so I told him he should have had it by asking for it without loss of two or three poor fellows' lives on each side; to which he replied he had done; it was their only object to gain the bank of the river, and he concluded that I would admit that they had a right to it as the proper line. I assented. The firing ceased; and we talked together for half an hour.

Apart from incidents such as this, the skirmishes generally occurred while the troops on both sides were foraging at the same time. Commissary Schauman recalled:

> We conducted foraging parties almost daily in front of our line. My road led through Hasparren, past our remotest hussar picket, and then along sunken roads to various farms scattered about in the small villages below. We went in search of maize. As however, the French, who were opposite us did the same, these expeditions were very dangerous, for in the thousand and one ramifications of these hill clefts, it was an easy matter to be cut off, attacked, or surprised. Very often I would find on reaching a certain farm that a French commissary and his escort had only just left it.

Losses among foraging parties were causing a good deal of disquiet at army headquarters, and towards the end of the month the Adjutant-General was complaining that too little attention was being paid to General Orders, and he directed that 'neither officers nor soldiers may be allowed to pass the Advanced Pickets either for forage or other supplies.'

Matters did not end there, for although the French population were not unfriendly and many welcomed the advance of the British army into France, the peasantry were sometimes hostile. Foraging parties from both sides constantly descending upon their farms caused resentment and sometimes this erupted into violence. In a letter to Lord Bathurst on 30 January, Wellington wrote: 'I am sorry to have to report, however, that the peasantry of Bidaray have done us a good deal of mischief by their attacks upon our foraging parties ... '

The search for forage gave rise to rivalry between units of the British army. On 11 January, Tom went out on a foraging party, but was forestalled by the infantry and returned empty handed. About a week later his foraging party was again frustrated by the infantry who, through carelessness no doubt, had started a bush fire. Some time before this, complaints had been received at headquarters from the 7th Division about a foraging dispute with the 1st Hussars K.G.L. who had resorted to force; and the Adjutant-General wrote on the 9 January, 'of the many instances of irregularity which occurred in the foraging of the Hussars this appears to be the most inexcuseable; and His Lordship trusts, for the sake of all parties, that it may be the last.'

Foraging was regulated in the General Orders. Parties were to be in the charge of an officer of the Quartermaster-General's department in concert with an officer of the Commissariat to point out where foraging was to be made. The officer in charge was instructed to take care that regular receipts were given to owners, and each regiment had to keep a list of officers sent with foraging parties and the name of the place where they were sent, so that they could be identified in case of complaints. The need for these regulations was exemplified by Colonel Vivian, who had complained during December that General Morillo's troops were exacting food from the inhabitants of Hasparren without payment. Forage collected by the foraging parties had to be taken to the commissary attached to the brigade and issued in rations. Obviously these instructions were not being obeyed. As soon as he entered France, Wellington had been anxious to secure the friendship of the population and took great pains to ensure that all supplies taken were paid for. This policy contrasted favourably with that of the French army, which had always lived off the country and thought nothing of commandeering grain and livestock in their own country without payment.

The Hussar Brigade, and indeed the whole army, were in dire straits for lack of fodder for the horses. As Tom says, 'No Transport for Supplies, and but little Supplies for Transport; i.e. in the way of forage.' They were now reduced to feeding the horses on turnips and gorse. Resort to gorse and thistles appears to have been fairly widespread in poor areas; apart from the local French peasants there was evidence of its use in Ireland, and to this day ponies in the New Forest can be seen eating gorse when there is no grass available. First of all the gorse had to be crushed otherwise the horses would not touch it. According to Schauman, 'our men would lift a barn door off its hinges, lay it on the ground, and then beat the thistles with the clubs until they were flattened out.' It was then mixed with corn and hay.

The cold wet weather resulted in a number of officers falling sick. Robert Chermside, the assistant surgeon, was ill; Captain Pipon had also been very sick, and even though he returned to duty he still looked dreadfully unwell. Lieutenant Robert Uniacke was in hospital at the rear, and Captain the Hon. Charles Lowther was confined to his bed for six days. He was a close friend of Colonel Vivian, who had him to stay in his house as soon as he was well enough. Colonel Kerrison and Major Thornhill were both unwell but they do not appear to have taken to their beds. Meanwhile Captain Hamlyn, who had succumbed to typhoid at Olite, had now returned to duty from Vittoria. Colonel Vivian evidently had not applied for him to return to England. This wily young man must have been able to pull strings, and on 1st January he was appointed A.D.C. to Major General Sir Henry Clinton K.B. who commanded the 6th Division. Although this staff appointment may have ensured his personal comfort, an A.D.C.'s job in battle could be highly dangerous. Whatever Vivian may have thought of Hamlyn, Tom seems to have liked him and wrote to him while he was in hospital, and they spent a good deal of time together after his return from Vittoria. As a footnote to William Bragge's opinion of Hamlyn, he was again off duty sick in October 1814 suffering from the 'mercury disease', a polite way of describing syphilis.

Tom makes no mention of his men's health, though Vivian told a friend that the army was very healthy. The men may have been more used to hardship than their officers, but it is hard to believe that they escaped illness. Tom mentioned that his men's clothing was old and bad while they were still at Olite, and since then it had been subjected to much hard wear. Huddled round campfires in wet clothes, or wrapped in their cloaks and blankets in draughty barns, if not in tents, life must have been very uncomfortable. Wellington did not mind what his soldiers wore. During this winter many men wore trousers made out of army blankets. A depot for army clothing had been established at Plymouth during this month, and lists of clothing in store at Santander were published.

Commanding officers were to report to the Quartermaster General 'without loss of time what of these articles they are desirous should be brought round to the regiments'. Whether they arrived or not was another matter. Looking through these lists, there were quite a number of bales, cases and boxes of equipment for regiments in the Hussar Brigade, but the 7th Hussars had for a long time made their own arrangements for the supply of uniforms and equipment. They employed a firm named William and Charles Prater in Charing Cross as agents for this purpose. In September 1813 we find Adjutant Arthur Myer writing to Major Hodge, 'I shall be obliged by you sending to me under cover and franked, that last order for clothing that was received before we left England.' In March 1814 Praters shipped goods to Myer ranging from forage caps to curry combs to the value of £1,373.

With news arriving of the advance of the Allied forces in the north, it was apparent that as soon as the weather improved the army would be on the move again. Both sides were sick of the war and anxious for any scraps of news. Newspapers were arriving regularly from England, but as the news was usually several weeks old when the papers were published, it was even more out of date by the time they reached the army three or four weeks later. French newspapers, on the other had, were delivered to the French army within days of publication, but the news was usually suspect on account of the strict censorship.

Rumours were flying about. Tom mentions that Napoleon was said to be at Bayonne (30 November), Lord Castlereagh had arrived in France (6 December), and Napoleon had restored King Ferdinand to the Spanish throne (18 January). When some French officers came to the line of trenches and obstacles placed across the road near Bonloc on 25 January and wanted to talk, it was perhaps not surprising that Sir Stapleton Cotton, who was riding round the outposts with Tom, should have sent him to ask them for a newspaper. Tom was instructed to tell the Frenchmen that he was not allowed to enter into conversation with them. There were strict orders forbidding intercourse with the enemy, and only a few days earlier commanding officers had been reminded by the Adjutant-General of the General Order regarding communication with the enemy. This has always been a problem in every war when the front lines have been in close proximity during periods of inactivity. This order was not always being obeyed, as illustrated by Vivian's encounter with the French a fortnight before.

The first of Tom's rumours was certainly untrue, the third was true, while the second was almost true, for Castlereagh arrived in Fribourg, the temporary headquarters of the Alliance, on 18 January. After Napoleon's defeat at Leipzig, his German Confederation of the Rhine broke up, and Castlereagh was at last able to stitch together alliances with Russia, Prussia and Austria backed by British gold. At the beginning of November 1813, the Allies made overtures for peace to the Emperor's representatives at Frankfurt. At the same time they decided upon an immediate invasion of France. The Austrian general Schwarzenberg advanced through Switzerland, and Blucher with a Russo-Prussian army crossed the Rhine on 1 January 1814. Both armies were now advancing into the heart of France with a view to joining forces. In the meantime Napoleon had entered into a treaty with King Ferdinand VII who had been his prisoner for some years, restoring him to his throne on the understanding that Spain would make peace with him. Of course, Ferdinand had no intention of keeping to this agreement, and in any case the Spanish Cortes refused to ratify it. It was all the embattled Emperor could do to try and relieve the pressure on his southern front. By the end of January the Allies, with a combined force of some 200,000 men, had occupied about a third of France.

Despite the reverses Napoleon had suffered, a negotiated peace was still regarded as a possibility at this time. Vivian's opinion was probably fairly representative of the views of the army. In a letter dated 14 January he writes:

We are most anxious to hear the result of Lord Castlereagh's embassy. For my part I think he is principally gone, from an alarm lest the Allies should make a peace and leave us in the lurch.

I am not one of those Quixotes who calculate upon marching to Paris unless well seconded by the French themselves; and therefore I think that the best way will be to make a good peace while we can …

It will not do to screw anyone too tight: the consequence will be a renewal of the war on the first opportunity.

By the end of the month the weather was still bad, the ground waterlogged and the horses starving. There was little possibility that the army would be able to resume its advance until conditions improved. Quite apart from the logistical problems, flintlock muskets were unreliable in rain. Experiments had been made with a waterproof cover for the lock but it was of no practical use. Rain also reduced the effectiveness of artillery because cannon balls would not ricochet on wet ground but merely ploughed into the mud.

Journal

January

Sat 1st   *Employ'd all day in getting the Troop to rights and arranging them in their Quarters – John rode to Ustaritz with Edward Peters – Maddison Din'd with us*

Sun 2nd   *The Mayor in whose house I was, accused of being a Spy in the French Interest; Had a Trial at the Colonel's Quarters – & Deposed him – Peters, Darville & Myers & Fraser din'd with us –*

Mon 3rd   *March'd at Day break to Forage at the Out Posts in front of the Piquet above Macaye – The Enemy shew'd a large force of Cavalry & Infantry in front; some skirmishing with the Germans – Verner's Squadron Detain'd till late. The Enemy Skirmish'd with our People in front, and shew'd some Disposition to Attack in consequence of which an Order was sent out to stop our Regiment on return from Foraging to support the 10th at the Piquet And several Divisions were brought up, and the whole in position before Day break on Tuesday morning – We were form'd with the 15th in support of the Main Piquet, but were afterwards removed to the front in support of the 18th under Colonel Vivian – No Attack was made – On the 6th Lord Wellington came to the right, he pass'd and spoke to Colonel Vivian while I was with him – We all expected a Fight, as the Order was to advance at 11. The Division in front advanced accordingly and the French fell back, after a little firing. The 88th lost some Men kill'd – Our Brigade foraged in front of the Piquet; Some French Infantry came over the hill, and fir'd a few shots, but an Officer and twenty men of the Infantry soon started them and wounded two – During the Advance an Officer was sent from the French, to say that Lord Castlereagh had arrived in France for the purpose of Negotiations – and requesting to be let alone for the present. The same News arrived from England*

Tue 4th   *Turn'd out at 3 A M, march'd off soon after – The whole Army in position at Day break – Call'd on Colonel Vivian en passant – were reserv'd under his Command in support of the 18th – Went into some Quarters for the night –*

Wed 5th   *Form'd in position before Day break & remain'd till 2*

O'Clock – Got some Rations – & turn'd into the Quarters before occupied by the 18th – Remain'd allways saddl'd &c

Thu 6th Form'd on our Old Alarm Post with the 15th in support of the Main Piquet – All the Army still in Position – Lord Wellington advanced & the Enemy retir'd before him immediately. Foraged in front –

Fri 7th Much Difficulty in arranging Quarters. Order'd to remain in front and occupy the Valley near Hasparren Weather Rainy & Bad –

Sat 8th Turn'd out at 9 to arrange the Quarters. Rode to Hasparren with Colonel Kerrison who took his Quarters in our House. Din'd all together – Bad weather

Sun 9th Turn'd out at Day break, Rainy bad Morning. Foraged in Front of Macaye – Got Corn & Rations, and return'd to our Quarters by 3 P M. Din'd with Colonel Kerrison

Mon 10th Received an Order to be in readiness at a moment's Notice Did not turn out, remain'd saddled all night – A large Party 13 Din'd a la Stevens's with the Colonel & me –

Tue 11th Remain'd saddled &c from yesterday till 10 A M, then march'd to Forage – The whole had been previously taken by the Infantry and we return'd empty. About 4 A M the Portuguese Piquet march'd to occupy the Day Post at Banloc which was always left by night; they found the French there and a sharp firing ensued, which cost the French 5 and the Portuguese 3 kill'd – after which the French sent in a Flag of Truce to say that the Post was on their side of the River & requested it might be given up, as they had no intention to make any further attack – This was accordingly granted – This created an Alarm of course, but of no importance

Wed 12th Turn'd out before Day Break to Forage – Got Straw for the Regiment towards Bonloc. Return'd by 2. Wrote some letters –

To Maj. Hodge My Mother No 12
Din'd with Colonel Vivian – Rainy wet Night

Thu 13th *Foraging Party under Verners at 7 brought Straw – Some few shots fired at them near Greciette – Lowther Bourke 18th – Light Din'd with Us –*
To George
with Bills
Note to Mary

Fri 14th *Foraging Party of 20 per Troop under Robbins at 7 – Got Straw – I rode over to Dine with Bourke of the 18th & return'd – very Rainy Wet weather –*

Sat 15th *Nothing extraordinary – Colonel Kerrison Din'd with Colonel Vivian. Darville & Myers Din'd with Us –*

Sun 16th *Foraging Party of 20 per Troop under Heyliger. Report came in about 9 that they had been attack'd & H Wounded. I rode out by Colonel Kerrison's orders to bring off the Party – They had gone home. Heyliger seriously wounded – Din'd with Colonel Vivian*
What we had long expected at last took place. The French had continually fir'd upon our Foragers with impunity – This morning a party laid wait in the Ditches and fir'd upon the Party the moment it appear'd in the village; Captain Heyliger was wounded severely. The Ball pass'd through his Arm, and into his side and lodged in the muscles of his Back. It was extracted about an hour and half after – Two Troop horses were slightly hit – Hamlyn & O'Grady came up from the Rear

Mon 17th *Nothing occurr'd worth mentioning – Heyliger doing well – Lowther & Chirmside very ill, The Colonel rather unwell Rainy dull weather –*

Tue 18th *Rode with Hamlyn to Hasparren – Descars arrived with News from St. Jean de Luz – Denmark join'd the Allies &c &c Colonel Kerrison & I din'd with Sir Stapleton Cotton The French sent a Messenger to General Murillo on the* right, to say That Bounaparte had made peace with Ferdinand 7th and that they had Orders not to fire upon any Spanish Troops – Murillo very properly kick'd & beat the Messenger, and put him in Confinement – And said he would not only fire upon the French, but upon any Spanish who refus'd to fire upon them – He said overtures had been made to the Cortes, who had refused to hear anything except in the presence of Mr Wellesley – The French shew'd themselves and were fir'd upon the same day –

Wed 19th Turn'd out on the Alarm Post at Day break, proceeded to Forage in Front with Infantry. The Infantry brought on a bush fire – <u>Got nothing</u> – Verners Braden & Hamlyn & Robbins Din'd with us Foraging at the out Posts found to be vanity and vexation of spirit – Nothing but Shots to be got by it – No Transport for Supplies, and but little Supplies for Transport; i.e. in the way of Forage – The Horses looking wretchedly bad indeed. Weather rainy and bad without interruption since the 7th January –

Thu 20th Rain'd all Day – Nothing Extraordinary – All the Forage exhausted. Orders to feed on Fern & Turnips. No Corn –

Fri 21st To Maria No 13

 Rainy bad weather; Court Martial of which I was President at 11 No Meal No Corn – Robbins & Hamlyn Din'd with us

Sat 22nd Parade at 10 in Watering Order – Horses starving – No Corn – employ'd in cutting Furze during the morning Bad weather Peters, Bryer & Darville Din'd with us

Sun 23rd Nothing Extraordinary – Bourke Call'd – John went on Piquet – Cold Frosty Weather – Walk'd out to see Lowther &c Gordon Din'd with Us

Mon 24th Thompson call'd – Gave him a Draft for £100 for Dobloons – Nothing extraordinary – Hard Frost. Descars & Gordon Din'd with us – Got a Mail to the 4th January –

Tue 25th	Mounted the Main Piquet – Lord Edward Somerset visited it in the Morning – and Sir Stapleton Cotton & Colonel Palmer came about 3 – Rode round with Sir Stapleton by Mendionde &cc – Heavy firing on the left during the night The Piquets have been reinforced by Infantry and the Posts considerably strengthen'd since our last turn of Duty – Two Trenches have been cut across the road with Abattis – While Sir Stapleton was there Two French Officers came down, and wish'd to have some conversation. Sir Stapleton sent me to them to ask for a Newspaper and tell them we were forbidden to converse – They were extremely civil, and wish'd me to drink some Claret with them which they had brought down – Heavy fire of Artillery and Small Arms on the left between ten & 11 at night – At 8 French attack'd the Spanish Infantry Piquet on the ridge on our Right, and fir'd long shots at one another for about ¾ of an hour, while I was at breakfast a little before 9. The Spaniards got up a Company in support; and Jack rattled the French very boldly off their ground, and pursued them to the next rise, but the French had then got up a Company also, & attack'd and drove the Spaniards entirely off the hill, and back within their own lines; which they had advanced the day before, when the French General sent in to say they should fire upon them if they advanc'd – The Spaniards lost 3 Officers wounded, one since dead. I have not heard the numbers lost on either side; but they behaved extremely well and it was one of the prettiest sights I ever saw; – being close to our Piquet –
Wed 26th	The Spanish & French Piquets engaged about 8 A M, firing pretty sharp. Each reinforced by a Company a little before 9 – A sharp attack for about half an hour, when the Spaniards were driven back. Relieved at ½ past 9. Rode up again with Colonel Kerrison
Thu 27th	John went on Piquet, A Subaltern being order'd for the future to the Main Piquet – Settl'd Troop Accounts with the Men – Colonel rode out to the Advanced Posts – Verners din'd & slept at our house –

Fri 28th   *To Chas. Gardiner To my Mother No 14*

Hitchin of my Troop taken on Patrol – Wrote Letters – A. Stanhope call'd – Nothing Extraordinary – Weather much the Same, as of late, Wet & Rainy – Din'd with Robbins, Fraser Din'd there –

Sat 29th   *Rainy bad weather – Nothing Extraordinary. Shirly return'd from St Jean de Luz Robbins & Stanhope Din'd with Colonel Kerrison. Stanhope slept here –*

Sun 30th   *Rain'd hard – Rode to Colonel Vivian's quarters with Major Horridge – Lowther much better – Remain'd there All Day – Return'd in the evening – John on Piquet with Robbins –*

Mon 31st   *Mounted the Main Piquet with O'Grady – Raining & heavy Storms of Hail all Day. Visited by Sir Stapleton Cotton & Lord Edward Somerset – All Quiet – No Fires on the Enemy's Hills during the night*

February 1814

Life at the outposts was fairly quiet during the first fortnight of February, but further behind the front line preparations were being made for the expected offensive. The main body of the army was leaving the cantonments and moving into the forward areas. Life at the picquets remained uneventful. On the 8th, Hamlyn came over from Villefranche and spent two days with Tom. During this visit he reported that the Allies were said to be within eight leagues of Paris. He was a trifle optimistic for they were still about forty or fifty miles away, and within the next few days Napoleon almost annihilated a Russian corps, followed this up by inflicting 17,000 casualties on the Prussians, and three days later defeated the Austrians at Montereau and re-entered Troyes. It seems likely that it was Hamlyn who taught Tom the verse he noted in his diary, which can be translated as:

> *Giving up his marshes*
> *The Cossack*
> *Who Sleeps in the open*
> *Believes, on the word of the English*
> *He will be lodging in your Palaces etc.*

When Tom added, 'Many a true word said in jest', he was nearer the mark than he realised. Captain Gronow of the Guards, later recalled that the Russian and Austrian emperors entering Paris after Waterloo 'refused to quarter their soldiers in the large and wholesome barracks which were in readiness for them; no; they preferred billeting them with peaceable merchants and tradespeople, whom they plundered and bullied in the most outrageous manner.'

The following week the advance began. Wellington intended to complete the investment of Bayonne by crossing the Adour, but to do this he had to draw Soult and his forces further to the east. By the middle of January, Napoleon had taken 14,000 men from the Marshal's army to reinforce his own hard-pressed forces, and when General Hill's corps began to advance thirty miles to the south the Marshal had little option but to withdraw his divisions from the north bank of the river to avoid being outflanked on his left. The British army now moved north-east on a front of some twenty miles, with the Adour and the Gave de Pau on the left flank and St-Jean-de-Pied-de-Port and the Pyrenees on the right. The Joyeuse, which had separated the British and French outposts, was crossed with little resistance.

There was stiff opposition along the Bidouze, which flowed across the front about twenty miles further east. Benjamin Badcock of the 14th Light Dragoons, whose brigade formed the advance guard of General Hill's corps, described their march in a letter to his father:

On the 15th we arrived near St. Palais and General Pringle's Brigade took some formidable Heights in great style. We got possession of St. Palais which gave us the Bidous river. On the 17th we drove the Enemy into Sauveterre and gained the Gave de Mauleon, a small river which runs into the other Gave. We were on the Gave d'Oleron till the 24th when we crossed it at a deep and rapid ford without loss at Verres Naves near Navarrens. On the 25th we were on the Gave de Pau, a river equally broad and rapid. On the 27th we crossed the River a little above Orthes at a ford without much loss, and the Dispatches will inform you of that day's Battle.

The 3rd Division under Sir Thomas Picton had followed on the General's left, accompanied by the Hussar Brigade. The 7th Hussars marched on the 16th to Isturits passing through Banloc, the scene of so much skirmishing. By the 19th they had reached Arraute-Charitte where Tom spent a comfortable night in the Mayor's chateau where Soult had recently stayed. Much to Tom's disgust he was ordered to move on the next day to Charette where they remained for a couple of days. While there Tom took the opportunity to visit St-Palais some eight miles to the right, which General Hill's corps had recently taken. On the 23rd the 7th Hussars moved on again to Bergouey, about three or four miles from the Gave de Oleron, 'a miserable village, as bad as any in Spain'. On the 24th they moved up to La Bastide-Villefranche close to this river. The French were holding the far bank of the river, and the Hussars now moved to the right along their side of the river towards Sauveterre. General Morillo, whose Spanish division had advanced on the right of General Hill's corps, had reached the small fortress of Navarrenx on the far side of the Gave. Hill was now ready to cross the Gave.

General Picton's 3rd Division and the Hussar Brigade were now ordered to create a diversion and threaten the river crossing by a weir close to a mill, but not to cross over. Captain Verner recalled that 'the shot and shells began to fly about in numbers'. Tom was also under heavy artillery fire. At this point Sir Stapleton Cotton arrived on the scene. He ordered a squadron of the 7th and a light company of Keane's Brigade to cross the river. As Cotton was senior to Picton, the order had to be obeyed, albeit with some hesitation.

The Gave flowing down from the Pyrenees was bitterly cold, swollen with melted snow and with a swift current. The ground beyond ascended upwards for half a mile, and it was not possible to see what lay beyond. Cotton then called for a subaltern and six men to lead the way. There was not one available, and the General commented on the slowness of the hussars. Captain Fraser (who, with Captain Hamlyn, had obtained special leave to come out to Spain) now stepped forward and called out: 'Subaltern or captain, it is no matter which, I will take the six men over and lead the way across.' In the face of severe fire he got them across and was the first to land. Verner then followed with his squadron, later writing:

> Just as I commenced passing this ford, if it may be so considered, Sir E. Kerrison said, 'Good-bye Pat.' I knew perfectly well what he meant; he knew the danger as he told me afterwards, and felt he was taking leave of me for ever. I had got nearly one half of my squadron across, when the French observing from the heights (to which I had been ordered to advance) what we were doing, sent down as fast as they could run, a number of skirmishers. Upon seeing them, the word 'Files about' was passed across the river. We were not long in going about, bringing with us as many of the infantry as we could, several of whom had waded through the river up to their middle, holding their firelocks with one hand above their heads. The French were not long reaching the edge of the river and commenced a heavy fire.

The infantry, finding themselves without support, had no choice but to retreat; Picton brought up a battery of artillery to cover them. Verner said that he lost the best horse he ever had – staked going across the the weir. The infantry lost five officers and forty men killed or wounded. Tom may not have witnessed this incident from close quarters for he may have been further back along the riverbank.

There was no love lost between Sir Thomas Picton and Sir Stapleton Cotton and a furious row ensued between them. William Bragge had written home a month before saying: 'Sir S. Cotton has got a pretty considerable command in the Front with Genl. Picton under his orders, therefore you may expect to hear of more Bloodshed shortly; one fights for Spite, the other for a Title ... ' The encounter between the dandified cavalry general and the elderly thickset veteran with his round hat and umbrella, whom Wellington had called 'a rough foul-mouthed devil as ever lived', must have held the hussars spellbound.

The regiment remained by the river while the French maintained their fire until the evening. Dr Irwin, the regimental surgeon, who had come along not thinking there was any likelihood of an attack, made his way down to the riverbank. When bullets began to fly around him, hitting the ground and hedges, he took shelter behind a house:

> but some of the officers observing his fright kept throwing stones over the house. The poor Doctor, who was not expected and never intended to fight, did not take time to consider how a ball could turn an angle to get at him, fancied they were balls falling about him and kept blinking like an owl and hugging close to the house, and by this means fancied he had come safe out of action.

While this engagement was taking place, General Hill's corps was able to cross the Gave about eight miles further up stream at Villenave de Navarrenx. The left wing of the French army was now outflanked. They evacuated Sauveterre that night, blowing up the bridge and withdrawing to the Gave de Pau by Orthez. On 25 February, Marshal Beresford and the left wing of the army crossed the Gave de Pau a few miles upstream from Peyrehorade and moved along the 'chausée' towards Orthez, led by Colonel Vivian's Hussar Brigade. They made contact with the enemy at Puyoo where Vivian led a charge of the 18th Hussars against the 15th Chasseurs. Somerset's Hussar brigade, meanwhile, passed through Sauveterre and Salies de Bearn, fording the Gave de Pau at Berenx, the bridge having been destroyed. Here they joined up with Marshal Beresford's forces. A pontoon train now came up and re-established a bridge, enabling the infantry of the Centre to cross the Gave.

The French were deployed along a ridge that stretched north from Orthez for about a mile, and then extended west for a further three miles. Three minor ridges ran down from this long ridge, like extended fingers pointing towards the Gave. The valleys in between were waterlogged and almost impassable. These three ridges were overlooked by French artillery – forty-eight guns in all – ranged along the top.

At 9 a.m. on 27 February, Wellington launched his attack on the left at St-Boes. The 3rd Division (to which the Hussar Brigade was attached), and the 6th Division then advanced to attack up the extended fingers of land. Captain Verner described the scene:

The day was lovely, perfectly calm with a bright sun more like Summer than the month of February. The appearance was more that of a review than the moment of battle. Our infantry advanced in line … the colours flying in the centre and the bands playing, it was not long before we received a salute from the enemy, which soon let us know that we had music of a different kind to attend to.

One of the first shots struck an Infantry Regiment near us, advancing, and made an opening which was soon filled up, leaving 3 or 4 men on the field. The band was ordered to the rear, and the Regiment advanced to take revenge for the loss of its comrades. The ground was open, well adapted for cavalry, and we could distinguish the movements of the troops at a considerable distance. The Cavalry, at least our regiment, was ordered to proceed by Squadrons, and the officers commanding told to act wherever their services were required … The French Cavalry charged some of our artillery not far from where I was, and drove the men from their guns. I hastened with my Squadron to their relief, but before I could reach them they had recovered their guns and the French suffered severely. Captain O'Grady was in my Squadron; about this time a round shot, a cannon shot, passed in front of my body, so close to my thigh that O'Grady, who saw it coming, felt so convinced that it must have struck me that he clapped his hand to his eyes, and told me afterwards he expected when he took it down to have seen me knocked to pieces.

The attack up the ridge on the left at St-Boes was unsuccessful. Then Picton's advance up the forward ridges was held up because his men were swept by the fire from the French guns on the ridge behind. There was now a lull while Wellington reorganised the disposition of his troops. When the attack was resumed the British began to made headway. General Hill, on the right now, forced a crossing of the Gave above Orthez, and advanced parallel to the main road north from the town through Sallespisse to Sault-de-Navailles and Mont de Marsan.

Picton's final attack up the ridge was described by Private Anton of the 42nd Royal Highlanders:

The hill rises rather abruptly on the East side of the road, and slopes gradually towards the North side, to which our advance was directed, in order to turn the enemy's right which had fallen back as we advanced. There is a small village of one street on that brow of the hill towards the North, upon which the enemy was driven back, and from which they kept up a destructive fire of musketry from garden walls, windows, and loopholes. Our regiment was ordered to drive him from that annoying post, which I may say had now become the right of his position ... The word of command to advance at the charge was received with loud animating cheers ... In an instant the village was in our possession, and the fugitives were partly intercepted by the advance of the second division of the army under Lord Hill which had passed the Pau above Orthez, and was now appearing round the east end of the heights.

The enemy thus dispossessed of his last position of any importance, commenced a hasty retreat through some enclosed fields and young plantations through which his columns directed their course until impeded by intersecting ditches which induced them to take the main road; there the ranks were broken, confusion ensued and a complete rout was the consequence.

By the afternoon the right wing of the French army had given way; Soult's reserve division helped maintain the line for a time, but the French gradually retreated north-east to gain the high road to Sault-de-Navailles, which is about eight miles from Orthez. Two battalions of conscripts from Toulouse now came up unexpectedly to join Soult's forces. They were mostly boys who had only been in the army for about a month; many lacked ammunition or did not know how to load their muskets, adding to the confusion.

In the general retreat across cultivated fields, surrounded by walls and intersected by ditches, the hussars had few opportunities to charge the fleeing French. Not until the 7th Hussars were within three miles of Sault-de-Navailles did they have an opportunity to charge. Sir Stapleton and Lord Edward Somerset were up leading the brigade. It is impossible to say what part, if any, Tom played, for all he says in his diary is 'the Seventh got amongst them, and took about 700 prisoners.' If he had taken an active part in this final action it is hard to believe that he would not have described what actually occurred. However, he has left us his views on the way a charge should be carried out, which he set down in a pamphlet some fifteen years later. In this he advises that the officer leading the charge must fix his eyes on certain points which indicate the line of the advance and not lose sight of them for one moment. He alone should be out in front of the formation and the men's attention must be focused upon him to ensure that they ride in a direct line. Troop officers should be stationed on either flank to restrain any tendency to rush forward or veer away from the centre. As it would be impossible, he said, in the actual charge to preserve the strict line of dressing (even it were desirable to do so), it had always been the custom to caution the men to keep back the flanks of the squadron in the form of a small segment of a circle, strictly following the squadron officer, and the whole attention of every man to be fixed upon him to preserve the dressing.

We know from the accounts of Vivian, Verner and Tom himself that Colonel Kerrison, Major Thornhill, Captain Heyliger and Captain Robbins all took part – that is to say the Right, the Right Centre and Left Centre squadrons. As the squadrons had been operating independently during the early part of the battle, Pipon's Left Squadron may have been in another part of the field. Alternatively this squadron may have been held in reserve. General Orders provided that cavalry should charge in three lines; the first and second deployed and the third behind in column, but ready to deploy. When charging infantry, the second line should be about 200 yards behind the first. The first line would receive the initial volley, but the second should be able to press home the attack before the enemy had time to reload.

The time was now about five o'clock and Verner takes up the story:

Towards the termination they retreated at a rapid pace across the extensive plain before they came to the river, the Luy de Bearn which flows through Sault-de-Navailles, which they had to pass, and a rush was made to the bridge to prevent their being intercepted. We were ordered forward as fast as possible to prevent their reaching the bridge and we were successful in cutting off and making prisoners a large body amounting to at least 2000.

Having thrown away their arms, the greater part of them later retrieved their weapons and escaped across the river. Verner goes on:

Major Thornhill commanded the Right Squadron which went first. As I passed on at full gallop with my squadron he was standing with a long pole with a spike on the top in one hand, and holding his horse by the bridle with the other. As I galloped past I cried out, 'I Congratulate you upon having taken that.' His reply was, and I must give it in his own words, 'Yes, but the d— fellow has run it into my

114

guts'. (For some time before the French had given up carrying colours because they did not like its appearing in Dispatches the number of Colours that had been taken, and in lieu they carried a pole with an eagle on the top, which when pressed, they unscrewed and put in their pockets, or else a long pole such as the one Thornhill had taken which served as a rallying standard). It appears that the person who carried the pole had placed himself on the back of a ditch with his feet in it. When Major Thornhill saw him he rode at him and cut at him with his sword; the forelegs of his horse got in the ditch, and he fell over. Whether the fellow ran the lance into him when he made the cut at him, or when he fell from his horse is not certain, nor is it certain what became of the man who carried the staff; one of our trumpeters said he shot him when he was running away – but Thornhill thinks his statement much to be doubted.

Verner was probably mistaken about the 'Colour'. It was more likely that this belonged to one of the French Provisional Regiments who in lieu of colours carried a pike with a spike and a miniature axe head to which a regimental guidon was attached.

At Sault-de-Navailles, General Tarbet in command of the French artillery managed to restore some sort of order. He placed twelve guns to cover the bridge and these were backed up by the sapper companies of the army together with two more battalions of conscripts which had come up. None of the latter had any cartridges but nevertheless stood there under fire while a mass of panic stricken veterans with ammunition pouches full rushed past them across the bridge. Verner's narrative concludes:

It was now getting late, and by attempting to follow the nearer the river we should have been exposing ourselves to the fire of the enemy without doing any good; as it was, we might have suffered severely had not the enemy, probably supposing we would have followed them across sent their artillery to the rear.

In retreating from the plain we had to ascend a hill, upon either side of which was a bank; when we reached it we came up with the infantry and the road became so jammed that for a length of time neither were able to move. By this time the enemy had got up their guns on the heights beyond the river, and commenced firing at us. I do not recollect ever to have seen a more miraculous, I may say, providential escape than we had. Had one shot fallen upon the road I do not think that less than a dozen men must have suffered from it, closely packed as we were. The ground upon either side of the road was ploughed up by the shots and shells, yet not one took effect.

If the pursuit had been pressed, the hussars and the rest of the cavalry might have captured the whole of the French rearguard instead of only two battalions. The lack of central direction has been put down to the fact that Wellington himself had been incapacitated; a spent ball had hit his sword hilt driving it against his thigh causing a cut and severe bruising. This did not prevent him expressing his pleasure when, at the end of the day, he met Thornhill walking back with his trophy.

As it was, the French struggled on through the night; many threw away their arms and large numbers deserted. Early the following day the Hussar Brigade crossed the river but do not appear to have pursued the enemy very far. Private Anton of the 42nd Highlanders recalled:

On the 28th we advanced on the road to St. Sever, our cavalry in front pursuing and harassing the enemy's rear, and making a number of his stragglers prisoners. Many of these were deeply gashed by sabre wounds, and being unable to get on so fast as the escorts urged, they fell down by the roadside faint from loss of blood, or panting with thirst soliciting a little water to wet their parched tongues.

Needless to say the gallant Highlanders came to their aid.

Anton's comment about sabre wounds is interesting. Although the sabre could inflict fearful wounds, they were not often lethal. It is hard to understand why this weapon remained in favour for so long. The straight-bladed sword with its slightly angled hilt adopted in 1908 was far more likely to cause a fatal wound when held with arm outstretched and elbow joint locked. Of course, by that time the cavalry charge was almost a thing of the past!

Journal

Tue
Feb 1st

Spaniards & French skirmishing again a little before 8 – Firing continued till ½ past 9. Reliev'd by Fraser – Call'd on Colonel Vivian who rode home with me – Nothing extraordinary General Murillo had persisted in posting a Vedette on a small Eminence far advanced on his front, where he had no sort of business and could be of no use; This the French certainly resisted; and some <u>very</u> <u>long</u>

Barkin Great or Barkin Yeat.

Looking over Roeburndale from the property.

Thomas Wildman M.P. from a painting
by George Romney.
Print in possession of Graham Brown Esq.

William Beckford.

James Wildman
(Relief from his tomb by
Sir Francis Chantry in
Chilham Church).

Turnham Green Hall, demolished about 1840, taken from an old print.

Edward Wildman.

Lord Byron by
Tomas Phillips
1813.
Courtesy of
Newstead Abbey.

Cavalry Review on Wimbledon Common by Thomas Rowlandson.

Newstead Abbey. Courtesy of Newstead Abbey.

Colonel Thomas Wildman
7th Hussars.
Courtesy of Newstead Abbey.

Colonel Edward Kerrison 7th Hussars.   Colonel Richard Vivian 7th Hussars.

The village of Waterloo copied by Colonel Thomas Wildman from a print.

Mrs Thomas Wildman
(née Louisa Preisig)
Courtesy of Newstead Abbey.

Chilham Castle (Kent)
A drawing believed to be by
Colonel Thomas Wildman.

Matilda Wildman, second cousin of Colonel Thomas Wildman, at the time of her visit to Newstead Abbey in 1857, aged about 17.

Colonel Thomas Wildman in old age.
Courtesy of Newstead Abbey.

shooting it generally ended in his being driven in. They are perpetually creating Alarms, which give us as much trouble to their Friends as to their Enemies and usually ends in smoke –

Wed 2nd — *John went on Piquet – Weather much the same – Nothing extraordinary – Rode round the Troop – & to see Heyliger & Chirmside. Major Thornhill Keane Verner & Robbins din'd with Colonel Kerrison; A Splendid Affair –*

Thu 3rd — *Bad Weather – Nothing extraordinary – Horses starving – Flogg'd a Muleteer – Gordon din'd with Us –*

Fri 4th — *Maj. Hodge Maria No 15*

Bad Weather as usual – Wrote letters – Nothing Extraordinary – Din'd at home

Sat 5th — *The 10th Hussars were to have taken the Out Post Duty, but some alteration having taken place I was order'd – Mann'd the Main Piquet at 9 – All quiet during the Day – Din'd with the Field Officer –*

Sun 6th — *Relieved at 9 – Edward & Mr Johnson of the 3rd arriv'd about 3 – Rode with them to Hasparren & down the Piquet at Banloc. Din'd at Home*

Mon 7th — *Rode with Edward & Mr Johnson to call on Colonel Vivian, Colonel Keane, Colonel Elley &cc. Wet cold weather – Grenfell arriv'd – Grenfell & Lascelles of the Guards din'd with us –*

Tue 8th — *Rode round with E & J to the Main Piquet, and along the Line of the Posts on the Right of the Position, return'd by Hasparren & Din'd at home – 8th Hamlyn came over from Villefranche and staid two days with Us – The Allies said to be within eight leagues of Paris! –*

*Renoncant à ses marais
Le Cosaque*

117

Qui bivouaque
Croit, sur le foi des Anglais
Se loger dans vos Palais &c &c

Many a true word said in Jest!!!

Wed 9th	Rode into Hasparren to buy meat &c from thence to call on Major Hughes, Bourke &c of the 18th – return'd late – Din'd at Home –
Thu 10th	Rode to Hasparren – Nothing Extraordinary – Weather clearing up – Din'd at Home –
Fri 11th	Joint letter to Maria
	Inspection in Watering Order by Sir Stapleton Cotton Rode with Edward to call on Colonel Keane – Newland, O'Grady, Fraser &cc Din'd with us –
Sat 12th	Colonel Kerrison went to St Jean de Luz – Rode out with Edward – Captain Luard, Light, & Darville Din'd with us –
Sun 13th	Rode out with Edward – Inspection of Cast Horses at ¹/₂ past 2. Edward & I Din'd with Sir Stapleton Cotton at Hasparren –
Mon 14th	An advance took place on the right – Rode wih Edward to the Main Piquet at Day Break; Went on with the Infantry till Evening – Din'd at Home. Colonel Kerrison return'd from St Jean de Luz – Having heard there would be a Movement on the right this morning Edward & I rode to the Main Piquet. About ¹/₂ past 9 the Columns were form'd in rear of that & Greciette and the Advance Order issued: The Spanish Division under General Murillo advancing at the same time along the Ridge from Macaye. The Enemy made no stand, merely occupying the Heights in succession to cover their Retreat; some fire of Artillery latterly on the right near Hellette – We rode with Sir Stapleton Cotton all the Fore part of the Day, and afterwards went with Colonel Keane's Brigade – The whole was as regular as a Field Day:

Lord Wellington arriv'd about Eleven, and return'd afterwards to Dine & Sleep at Hasparren. Fraser who went as an Amateur, had his Horse shot in the leg –

Tue 15th   *March'd at 9 into Quarters at Hasparren. Our infantry continued to Advance and the Enemy to retire in Front –*

Wed 16th   *March'd about 2 P M to Isturits thro' Bonlac a small straggly village. Badly put up – Lord Wellington and his staff were in the village –*

Thu 17th   *March'd at 1 P M to Oregue and Adjouet [?] – More Room than yesterday but less Forage – Edward & Johnson left on their return to Vittoria –*

Fri 18th   *Received an Order at 12 at night to March at 6. Counter-ordered at $^1\!/_2$ past 5 – Heavy fire of Artillery in Front; Rode out to the front to gain information – Lord Wellington drove the French a considerable way, and took our Posts over the Bidouze – General Sir Rowland Hill's Horse kill'd by a Cannon Shot*

Sat 19th   *Parade at 9 very sharp Frost – Rode round my Quarters – Got Orders to March at $^1\!/_2$ past 4 – March'd at 5 – Very bad Roads – Dark as pitch; Put up in the Chateau of the Mayor of Arraute – The Best House we had seen – Stall'd Stables and plenty of forage for our Horses – Large Bed Rooms & Fire Places for ourselves like England. Supp'd with the family à la François, capital Wines. Marshal Soult had liv'd there a short time before*

Sun 20th   *Much vex'd at receiving an Order to leave our excellent Quarters in the morning. March'd to occupy some Farm Houses in the Commune of Charritte – Much trouble in getting Quarters –*

Mon 21st   *Very sharp Frost – Rode round the Quarters and to the Colonel's House &c with Shirly – Plenty of Forage, Horses improving – Nothing Extraordinary –*

Tue 22nd	*Rode with Shirly to St Palais, join'd Newland of the Artillery on the Road – Pass'd Charitte Lord Wellington's Head Quarters – Saw Freemantle, Lord Gordon Lennox, Bruce &c.*

22nd – Lord Wellington came over to the Right on the 14th and remain'd on this Flank till the 19th when he went back to St Jean de Luz. He return'd again and took up his Quarters at Charitte (?Charitte) in the evening of the 21st. On the 22nd saw several Divisions & many Pontoons Artillery &c moving towards St Palais –

Wed 23rd	*March'd at 12 to Bergouey, a miserable village, as bad as any in Spain and completely plunder'd by the French – <u>No more Basque</u> Sharp Frost. Nothing Extraordinary –*
Thu 24th	*Turn'd out & Form'd at 3 A M. March'd about 5. Pass'd La Bastide and along the Bank of the River in front of the French Piquets – Cross'd the Bidouze & got under a heavy fire of Artillery – Remain'd out all Day – We march'd before Day break, pass'd La Bastide and stopp'd in a Field near Auteville where we remain'd an hour, when Sir Stapleton Cotton order'd us to move across the Bidouze to Osserain – The Infantry & Artillery had already commenced the Attack and the Enemy fir'd some Shot & Shells from the Town en passant; We were mov'd towards the ford of the Gave de Oloron in support of the Guns & Infantry, where the Shot & Shells flew pretty thick, and we had one Man & three Horses wounded by musket shots – One Squadron of ours was nearly over the Ford when they were order'd back – The Light Companies cross'd but were driven back by superior fire with some loss about 12. The Firing was very sharp – It continued more or less all day*
Fri 25th	*Turn'd out from the houses where we had put in for the night at 9. The French all off in the night – Cross'd the Ford near the Bridge which the French had blown up – Pass'd Sauveterre & Salies (de Bearn) and put up in Farm Houses in Front*
Sat 26th	*Several Divisions & Artillery halted all the morning on the Road. Cross'd the Ford of the Gave de Pau about 4 in the*

Afternoon – Some little skirmishing on the Road (15th in Front) Some Troops got Quarters – Most pass'd the Night en Bivouaque

Sun 27th   *Mov'd from our Bivouaque at $^1/_2$ past 7. The Brigade form'd by the Road side, mov'd forward at 10 in support of the Guns. Lord Wellington attack'd & drove the Enemy from all his positions; and completely routed them, with great loss The French in position in Front on the heights above Orthez. They were said to have 40,000 Men and 20 Pieces of Artillery. Lord Wellington attack'd them about 10 a m They stood for some time and defended their position very boldly – But the Infantry advanced about 11 cover'd by the Hussar Brigade across the Valley, and drove them from the Main Height; We remain'd there a short time under a heavy Fire of Shot & Shells – They made very little stand after and were driven from Position to Position through into a Flat Country, where the Seventh got amongst them, and took about 700 Prisoners – Major Thornhill's Squadron charged them four times; He was wounded severely in taking a Colour, which he brought away – Captain Heyliger was severly wounded, Douglass slightly, and his horse kill'd; Robbins had a horse kill'd The Seventh lost 5 Men & a Corporal kill'd 28 Horses. I Major, 1 Captain 2 Lieutenants, Elevan Rank & File and 17 Horses wounded – The whole British Loss was estimated at 2,500 – That of the Enemy 10,000 & Pieces of Cannon taken & one found after the Action: Lord Wellington was slightly grazed by a Ball*

Mon 28th   *Turn'd out Soon after Day Break, the 10th in front of the Brigade came up with the Enemy's Rear, and made several Prisoners. Captain Harding wounded. Pass's the Luy by a Bridge at Sault de Navailles and put up in Farm Houses in Front*

<u>*Extract from Cavalry Orders*</u>   <u>*July 28th 1814*</u>

Lieut. General Sir Stapleton Cotton was highly satisfied with Conduct of the Cavalry engaged with the Enemy yesterday, particularly Lord Edward Somerset's Brigade; and He begs the Major General will accept his best thanks for the manner in which he conducted his Brigade.

The Lieut. General requests that his Lordship will be pleased to make known to Colonel Kerrison and the Officers & Men of the Seventh Hussars the Lieut. General's Admiration of their Gallant Sturdy, and Soldierlike Conduct –

March 1814

Having spent the last day of February at Sault-de-Navailles, the Hussar Brigade moved on again. The French in the meantime had crossed the Adour at St-Sever some twenty miles further on by midday on the 28th. At this point Marshal Soult turned south-east towards Tarbes. His intention was to join forces with Marshal Suchet who was expected to withdraw from Catalonia and cross into France at Narbonne. However, Marshal Suchet showed no signs of moving; apart from other considerations he had no wish to find himself under the command of Soult, who was senior to him. As well as wanting to consolidate his forces with those of Suchet, Soult was anxious to draw Wellington after him, and thus deter him from striking north towards Bordeaux. If Soult had retreated towards Bordeaux, he would have had insuperable supply difficulties, so in fact he had little option. Unlike the British who brought up their own supplies, the French had always lived off the country, and a withdrawal to Bordeaux would have entailed crossing Les Landes, a vast triangular tract of pine forest and sand dunes extending some sixty miles from its base at Mont de Marsan to its apex near Bordeaux.

The Hussar Brigade now accompanied General Hill's corps, which had been ordered to follow the French, and came up with them at Aire. The French made a feeble stand and then continued their retreat. The weather was awful, and Wellington broke off the pursuit for the time being. Although his main objective was Toulouse, as indeed was Soult's, he also wished to secure the important city and port of Bordeaux. Bordeaux's mayor, in secret correspondence, had promised to deliver the city into British hands. Marshal Beresford was ordered to move forward in that direction with the Seventh and Fourth divisions and a force of cavalry including Vivian's brigade. They crossed Les Landes from Villeneuve de Marsan, through Roquefort and Captien, to Bordeaux.

Tom and his regiment spent five days in villages just north of Aire before being ordered to move to the southern border of Les Landes along with a regiment of Portuguese cavalry, commanded by a Colonel Campbell who had formerly been a captain in the 7th Hussars. Their task was to maintain a line of communication between Beresford and army headquarters at St-Sever by means of letter parties. On 9 March they reached Villeneuve de Marsan in heavy snow. The squadrons were then posted to various towns in the area, but Thornhill's squadron was ordered to remain at Villeneuve about twelve miles to the east of Mont de Marsan. His task was to keep a lookout for any French troops who might still be in the neighbourhood.

After Orthez, Thornhill had remained behind on account of his wound. Colonel Vivian may have referred to him as 'old', but he was certainly tough; a week later, and after a fifty-mile ride, he was back with the regiment. In view of his health, Colonel Kerrison wanted him to remain with the main body of the regiment and ordered Verner's squadron to take over the duty at Villeneuve. However, Thornhill was so insistent that he should do his turn that the colonel agreed. It was unfortunate that he did so, but Kerrison, unlike Vivian, was always anxious to please. Thornhill accordingly took up his quarters in a house on the outskirts of Villeneuve, where the forest adjoined the town. Captain Heyliger who was severely wounded in the thigh at Orthez, only six weeks after being shot in the ambush, was now allowed four weeks' sick leave in Orthez. Meanwhile the other officers of the regiment were enjoying the comforts of Roquefort where Tom slept in a bed 'as good as any in England'.

The old Landais houses had a distinctive style. They were half-timbered, with the spaces in between filled with *torchis*, or cob, a mixture of straw and plaster. The low pitched roofs were covered with Roman tiles, and the timber at the front was often unfilled, forming a covered vestibule or balcony. A typical interior comprised a large room with windows to the front and rooms leading off the other three sides. Mont de Marsan and Roquefort were well placed on excellent supply routes. Provisions for the army could now be brought up from the mouth of the Midouze at Bayonne by barge or by the main road, along which droves of cattle and mule trains passed daily.

Accounts varied as to the attitude of the population towards the British. Tom thought the population of Mont de Marsan was well disposed. Benjamin Badcock, writing from Aire on 5 March, told his father that, 'The people in general do not fly from us, but remain and receive us well; but I imagine our reception proceeds more from Terror Than from Love.' At Mont de Marson Commissary Schauman found that, 'The general feeling of the inhabitants was altogether against the Bourbons, who were openly cursed in the streets, while Bonaparte was extolled.' Elsewhere there was clearly no great enthusiasm for the Bourbons, but most people wished to be rid of Napoleon.

The Allies were still undecided whether Napoleon should be allowed to keep his throne or whether the Bourbons should be restored. Until this question was resolved, it was probably wiser for Frenchmen not to come down openly on one side or the other. Now that the British army was firmly established in France, the French royal family, living in England, decided to promote their cause and sent over the young Duke of Angoulême. Wellington, meanwhile, was careful not to lend any encouragement to the Duke of Angoulême's claims on behalf of the monarchy. The duke was the son of the Count of Artois, brother of the executed Louis XVI and of the present claimant who was to become Louis XVIII. Angoulême had been in St-Jean-de-Luz since the beginning of February. Although incognito, the identity of this little man in his pea-green trousers was known generally. He was affable and good-tempered, but not very talented.

Throughout this month Tom and his regiment were preoccupied with brigands who were lurking in Les Landes where the forests provided ideal cover. There is some mystery about the brigands' leader, Captain Florian. According to one account he had been a Spanish collaborator in the service of King Joseph. William Verner, on the other hand, thought he was a French cavalry officer working for Marshal Soult. It is possible that there may be some truth in both these versions.

There was a large French army depot at Mont de Marsan, which would have been the one that is mentioned in the diary as having been plundered by the brigands. Here they could have obtained French army uniforms and equipment. Hitherto Tom had provided few details of his day-to-day activities, but that now changed, and he had quite a lot to say about Captain Florian. During the campaign Tom had been cold and wet; he had been involved in a few skirmishes, and he had been under fire. But nothing very memorable had occurred. Chasing bandits now provided him with action that was worth recording in some detail. We shall never know whether Florian was receiving active encouragement from Soult or merely acting on his own behalf, or possibly a bit of both. The Marshal had been issuing proclamations calling upon the countryside to rise up. Many of the bandits were wearing army uniforms, either because they were deserters or as a result of plundering the store at Mont de Marsan. French sources regarded them as mere highway robbers who were more dangerous to the peasantry than to British soldiers.

The first encounter the regiment had with Captain Florian occurred when he raided poor Thornhill's quarters on 9 March. According to William Verner, the major was in bed asleep when he was woken up at about midnight by the sound of a sabre rattling in its scabbard coming up the stairs. He thought the noise was caused by an orderly from headquarters and called out, but there was no reply. He felt a hand groping on his bed and touching his chest and arms. Then a voice said, 'Vous êtes mon prisonnier,' and told him to get up. Thornhill reached for the pistol under his pillow but realised he had forgotten to put it there. He took out his watch, and the rattle of the watch chain made the intruder jump. In the meantime his portmanteau was being ransacked. The intruder, who was in fact Captain Florian, kept calling out, 'Depêchez-vous'. When Thornhill had dressed he could not find his shako, but another man he had not noticed before, put a hussar's fur cap on his head and asked where his horses were. Thornhill said he did not know because he had been wounded and could not look after them.

He was then taken to the stables in a long building which normally housed 150 to 200 mules on the very edge of the forest. The intruder left Thornhill in the charge of the other man while he entered the stable. Florian came out with a horse which he gave to his companion to hold while he fetched another and saddled them. Thornhill then had the presence of mind to say that his captors had left the best horse behind, whereupon Florian foolishly returned to the stable leaving his companion holding the two horses. Thornhill waited until he reckoned that Florian had reached the far end of the stables, then hit the brigand holding the horses as hard as he could and escaped into the forest. The man let out a bellow but did not dare let go of the horses, which would have run off. Thornhill was now doubled up in pain from his wound and threw himself on the ground where he lay until the men had gone.

Florian and his companion had managed to slip into Villeneuve because it had been market day. Thornhill had placed a picquet comprising a corporal and five men in the nearest house to his quarters. The corporal had heard nothing, and when he had gone to relieve the sentry posted outside Thornhill's door he was nowhere to be seen. Thornhill had also posted a mounted picquet under a subaltern in a farmhouse a short way out of the town, which Florian had managed to evade. It was evident that the brigands had been keeping a careful watch.

News of Thornhill's discomfiture soon got around and must have been a source of grave embarrassment. His friend Vivian was not sympathetic. Writing to his wife he said:

Poor old Thornhill, he fancies [the brigands] took him for me, but they would not have caught me so. It is a bad business: very disgraceful to the regiment and not creditable to Thornhill – There was never a post so easily guarded as Villeneuve. At a bridge at the

126

entrance of the place which I had barricaded and had placed a picket, he had none. The old fool.

Embarrassment did not deter Thornhill from submitting a claim in the following November for the loss of his effects – two saddles and bridles, a pistol; two saddlebags and a small bag; two pelisses, two jackets, three pairs of boots, a sash, fifteen shirts, twenty handkerchiefs, six drawers and flannel waistcoats, a dressing case, ten stockings and a cloak. To add insult to injury, Captain Florian was seen in Thornhill's uniform a few days later on the main road from Bayonne. He could speak English quite well and was able to gain information about mule trains bringing supplies that were shortly expected.

Tom records the ambush of this mule train on 13 March, but Verner describes it in greater detail:

Two men had galloped into Roquefort saying they had been attacked on the road by a large body of cavalry and had only escaped with difficulty. These men had taken cattle, destroyed a drove of mules and captured several soldiers on the way to join the army. The trumpets sounded immediately and the men were soon on their horses ready to march, a few were left to protect the baggage etc. with orders to fasten the doors and windows, and if any persons came to the town to keep firing on them out of the upper windows, as some of the party had followed these two men close up to the town. We proceeded along the road and soon came up with the two droves of cattle. There was no danger of their running away – so we went on and came to the mules, at least 70 in number. It was a dreadful sight, the road was covered with them for a length of way. There was not one of them that had not been stabbed in the body. They were alive but suffering dreadfully. Some of them appeared in so great pain, that we jumped off our horses and shot them thro' the head to release them from their agony. The men were greatly irritated, and had we come up with the party I am sure that they would have met with no mercy. We found that they had turned off the road into the wood, the cover of which was so thick in places that altho' there might be 500 men within 100 yards of us we could not distinguish them, so great the danger was of passing them by. Had it not been for this we must have come up with them, but we were forced occasionally to halt to endeavour to ascertain which way they went.

After going on further they came upon twenty or thirty soldiers returning to their regiments with a Lieutenant Clarke of the 40th Foot, part of the 4th Division. He told Colonel Kerrison that he had been convinced that they would have been murdered. As it was, a Brunswicker who would not march as quickly as they wished was shot. With nightfall the search was called off.

The party that had pursued the brigands comprised ten men from each troop with the Colonel and Captain Verner. Tom does not appear to have gone on this expedition, but the following night he took out forty men on a search party. He did manage to capture one man, who according to Captain Verner had a British cavalry sabre buckled round his waist. He was identified by the soldiers rescued on 9 March. Kerrison made inquiries about him in Roquefort, and the mayor and principal men confirmed that he was a rogue. The colonel submitted a report on 18 March and sought leave to hang the man; Wellington readily agreed and the Adjutant General directed that he be executed 'with such publicity as may answer to discourage the continuance of the predatory hostility this band have commenced to wage'. Kerrison's cautious approach may have been due to uncertainty whether or not Florian's gang were part of the French army. He then sent for the sergeant of the Provost Guard whose duty it was to act as executioner. Kerrison was unwilling to ask him to carry out an execution without explaining what the man had done. He told him and said it was necessary to make an example to deter others. The sergeant, who was Irish, promptly replied, 'Your Honour is quite right, and I am sure he will never do it again.' 'Yes, Sergeant', replied the Colonel, who could not help smiling, 'I agree with you, I am sure he will never do it again.'

A rope was slung over the branch of a tree, and a table provided for the man to stand on. As the rope was new, Verner thought it might stretch and the man's feet would touch the ground. So a chair was placed on the table. Verner continues:

> When all was ready the unfortunate man was brought forth, attended by the priest who carried a small crucifix in his hand. The man advanced with a firm step and unaltered countenance and mounted upon the table and then upon the chair unassisted. I suggested that a handkerchief should be tied over his face, which was done. During the time these preparations were making, the little priest was instructing the miserable man to pray to different saints. Upon the table and chair being removed, from the newness of the rope the unfortunate man kept spinning round like a tee totem, the priest kept

128

running round all the time holding up the crucifix in order as it appeared to get opposite his face, his eyes being covered, and repeating the names of the saints to which he was to pray, when all at once as if recollecting that the man could neither see nor hear, he stopped short and said, 'Il est mort', and putting the crucifix in his pocket he hurried away from a sight which to him was no doubt, disgusting.

While Tom was trying to round up the bandits, the pace of events on the international scene was quickening. Until the 9 March the Allies were still prepared to negotiate the Treaty of Chaumont whereby the Allies agreed not to negotiate separately with Napoleon, and the following day the negotiations which had been going on with the French at Châtillon were broken off. No decision had yet been taken as to the future government of France, and Marshal Beresford was on his way to Bordeaux. He left the 4th Division halfway at Langon and reached Bordeaux on the 12th. To Beresford's surprise, the Duke of Angoulême suddenly appeared with some followers and was received enthusiastically by the mayor. However when the Duke drew up a proclamation saying that he had taken over the city in the name of the King, Beresford told the mayor that he was taking possession of the city in the name of Lord Wellington. Wellington was quick to inform the Duke that, although he had no objection to his raising royalist troops, he would have to find the money to pay for them. Until the Bourbons were restored to the French throne, Wellington was determined to ensure that any changes in government were made in his name. This explains Tom's account of the appointment of a new prefect at Mont de Marsan on 24 March. As a result of this action, the local people can hardly be blamed for thinking the British were minded to keep Gascony, which they had lost at the end of the Hundred Years War.

There was little military activity in this sector and the troops were in cantonments. Tom does not mention any regimental parades or inspections, in contrast to the weeks leading up to their advance into France when Colonel Vivian was in command. With frequent entries stating 'Nothing extraordinary', Tom was clearly becoming bored. Vivian may well have been right when he told his wife that Kerrison let the men do as they liked. The men did not have enough to do and discipline appears to have become lax. This lack of discipline incurred the displeasure of the Adjutant-General who had to intervene on two occasions. On 7 March he referred to 'abuses and outrages committed daily'. On this occasion his complaints were addressed to all the regiments in the Hussar Brigade:

The Commander of the Forces again desires that the Churches may not be used by the Troops without permission from the Inhabitants and Clergy, and that when they are used the utmost care should be taken of the sacred vessels and of every article that serves for religious purposes. Neither Horses nor Animals are to be put into the Churches on any account whatever.

A few days later, on 13 March, Colonel Kerrison received a copy of a letter from Colonel Campbell complaining that a patrol of hussars had released a party of infantrymen who had been confined by the mayor of Borgue near Mont de Marsan. He was to find out who was involved and send them to Borgue under the charge of an officer to see if the mayor could identify them. On the 20th Tom mentions sending 'A party, 1 Sergeant & 12' to cooperate with Colonel Campbell, and the next day he presided over a court martial, after which the prisoners were pardoned. It rather looks as if the foot soldiers should not have been confined by the mayor in the first place! Tom with his usual discretion does not say anything that might imply criticism of his regiment.

Fortunately this period of idleness was coming to an end and the last battle of the Peninsular was about to be fought. By the middle of March the Hussar Brigade was ordered to move east in the general direction of Toulouse. Pipon's Left Squadron marched from Roquefort to Villeneuve de Marson. Robbin's squadron moved on to Nogaro a few miles further to the south-east, while the other two, Thornhill's and Verner's, went to Plaisance immediately south of Nogaro. Beresford and the 4th Division had now returned from Bordeaux and Tom noted that they passed through Villeneuve on 16 March, reaching Plaisance on the 19th, where they joined Somerset's and Vivian's Hussar Brigades and the Light Division. This corps under Marshal Beresford now formed the left flank of the army. Wellington's intention was for them to turn the right flank of Soult's forces.

The Hussar Brigade was now out in front and drove the French flank guard out of Rabastens. Beresford's infantry following on behind soon cut off the first of Soult's escape routes from Tarbes to Toulouse. Wellington had hoped to pin him against the Pyrenees south of Tarbes, but Soult foiled this move and was able to make his escape east along the left bank of the Garonne to Toulouse. Wellington decided not to pursue Soult but to march directly on Toulouse along the more northerly of the two roads. The Hussar Brigade fanned out ahead of the army roving over a front of some thirty miles as far as Auch in the north. Only two squadrons of the 7th

Hussars, Thornhill's and Robbins's, took part in this advance. Verner's squadron was sent to Auch, while Pipon's squadron remained in Villeneuve where they covered the northern flank of the army.

Owing to the appalling state of the roads Wellington's progress was slow: four mules, four large horses and two oxen were needed to drag his small coach through the deep clay. Soult, anxious to reach the strongly fortified and well-stocked city of Toulouse, drove his starving, ragged army on and arrived there on 24 March, about forty miles ahead of the British. The city was strongly royalist in sentiment and Wellington was told that if he could take it the whole of the countryside would declare for the monarchy.

On 30 March the Allied armies in northern France reached Montmartre and the following day Paris capitulated. Two days later Prince Talleyrand formed a provisional government. Napoleon with his marshals and the remnants of his army were at Fontainebleau. On 4 April he abdicated. Two days later the Senate declared the restoration of King Louis XVIII, and a treaty was signed on 11 April. Rumours had been flying about since the end of March – on the 23rd Tom noted 'Many reports' and, again on 6 April, 'Various reports. All false' – but no reliable information reached army headquarters until after the assault on Toulouse on 10 April.

While the army was gradually assembling in front of Toulouse – the Hussar Brigade had reached the Garonne a few miles south of the city on 27 March – Tom was spending his time quietly in Villeneuve with his French friends playing the flute and playing billiards. Captain Florian was still proving a nuisance. Supplies and dispatches for the army from Bordeaux passed along the road through Villeneuve and Auch where Verner was stationed. Still wearing Thornhill's uniform, Florian was intercepting these supply convoys by deceiving the porters and terrorising the villagers into keeping watch for British troops. He commandeered all the ferry boats on the River Gers just west of Auch, which made it difficult for Verner to follow him.

Journal

Tue	*Turn'd out at ½ past 6. Cross'd the Adour by a Ford near St*
Mar 1st	*Sever, and moved on the Road to Mont de Marsan – Halted*
	there till 4 o'clock – March'd to Grenade & put up in the
	houses in front – Rain'd hard all Day–

131

Wed 2nd	*Turn'd out as usual. The 7th in Front – The Enemy made some stand to gain time before Cazeres. The Guns cut them up & drove them – towards Evening Sir Rowland Hill drove them on the other Bank & took the Town of Aire –*
Thu 3rd	*Weather very rainy & Bad. Did not turn out – Violent Thunder Storm in the afternoon – Darville came to our Quarters, Din'd with us & slept –*
Fri 4th	*The Army moving into Cantonments – Rode out to find better Quarters – Got one near the Chateau de Vigneau – Receiv'd an Order at 5 & March'd to some houses in front of Barcelonne*
Sat 5th	*Rode round the Quarters with Shirly to Barcelonne & St Germain in front, Head Quarters of Cavalry at St Germain – Various Reports on foot – Nothing Extraordinary –*
Sun 6th	*To Major Hodge To Maria No. 16*
	Wet, Cold, Miserable Weather – Remain'd in Quarters – Wrote Letters &C Nothing Extraordinary – Major Thornhill came up from the Rear – Moffat Din'd with us –
Mon 7th	*To Edward*
	Cold Frosty Weather. Rode out to see Major Thornhill, the Colonel &c – Three Troops moved on to St Germe to make room for Major Gardner's Troop of Artillery –
Tue 8th	*Weather much the same – Receiv'd a sudden Order to march at 2 o'clock – March'd to La Henga – The Regiment quarter'd in and about the Town. The Left Squadron in the Village of St Aubyn about 2 miles off the road –*
Wed 9th	*Heavy fall of Snow. March'd at 6 thro' Villeneuve de Marsan where the Right Squadron halted, to Roquefort about 8 or 9 leagues. My Troop about 2 miles out of the Town. The 4th Division in Camp there – The Head Quarters of the Regiment at Roquefort, an excellent Town with 4 large Inns,*

besides the Post House – We were order'd here to keep up the Communication with Marshall Beresford. Our Troop at Capsien, and the Right Squadron at Villeneuve de Marsan– The Enemy had no force within Ten Leagues of us – but there were a party of Bandits, who had cloth'd and arm'd themselves from a Store the French had order'd to be destroy'd, some soldiers, others Douaniers &c, some said 200, some 60 and some 30 strong, who plunder'd and committed every kind of excess in this neighbourhood – A party of them enter'd Villeneuve in the night, and made their way to Major Thornhill's Quarters whom they robb'd of his Baggage & two Horses. They also succeeded in stealing 7 Troop Horses from a detach'd Stable

Thu 10th   *The Infantry March'd – Still Snowing – My Troop order'd into Town – Accounts of the French having come into Villeneuve in the night. Verners & Captain Downs, 40th, Din'd with us My Troop order'd into Quarters in the Town of Roquefort. The Officers of the Left Squadron all in one Auberge (Chez Madame Lafitte) where I got an excellent Bed, as good as any in England. Being the first time I had enjoy'd that luxury since the 19th of February*

Fri 11th   *To Thos. Deakey*

            Parties sent out in search of the Brigands – Rode my little Mare to Exercise – Nothing Extraordinary – Colonel Kerrison Din'd with us –

Sat 12th   *More search for the Brigands with as little success – Nothing Extraordinary – All the Officers here (16) Din'd together at The Soleil d'or a là Française –*

Sun 13th   *The Brigands attack'd & plunder'd some Stores & Baggage on the High Road about 2 miles from the Town – Took some Prisoners & Destroy'd above 50 Mules – Ten Men per Troop of ours drove them off & Retook the Prisoners &c The Brigands fell upon a party of Muleteers whom they cut & wounded, kill'd a Peasant who knew one of them, Hamstrung & ripp'd up the Bellies of 58 Mules, took an*

Infantry Officer & some Men prisoners, two of whom they shot because they could not keep up – When they saw our Men on the road – They all despers'd & fled different ways into the forest –

Mon 14th   *Shirly sent out with a Party to enforce Requisitions. Receiv'd some intelligence of the Brigands – I went out with 3 Men to patrole after them – More Information towards Evening – I went off at 11 at night with 40 Men in search of them – Received some Information from a Peasant who had seen some of the Brigands that morning at 7 O'Clock, and knew the place where they had encamped the night before. Patroled with 3 Men about 2 leagues into the Forest, but only found the place where they had been – On our Return having dismiss'd the Peasant we saw a Fire among the Trees to our left; and having plac'd a Man to keep the track, we rode to it. It was still burning with fresh wood, and appear'd not to have been left 10 minutes; but tho' we search'd in all directions we could not find a trace of Man or Beast, and return'd. Went off again at 11 at night with 40 Men, upon more Information; The Night was so dark that you could not see the man in front of you and the Tracks so narrow the men forced to march in single file. About half past 1 we came upon an extensive Heath, where after wandering an hour, and getting several horses bogg'd, our Guide inform'd me he had completely lost his way. We in vain attempted to find it again, and I was oblig'd to dismount the Party and stand by our horses waiting for a Moon, which however did not appear; and it was not till the first dawn of Day (a little before 5) that we were able to proceed. The Sun was however hardly well up when we surrounded the House to which I had been Directed, a small, lonely Inn in the Wildest Country imaginable. But we Search'd the house & stables in vain! I however, by Threats & alarming the Landlord got every Information respecting this formidable Banditti which I found to consist of Fifteen, One calling himself Captain, one Officer and thirteen others well arm'd and mounted. They had supp'd here on the night of the 13th and divided their plunders. This was their general Rendezvous, but they only came about 8 or 9 in the*

Evening – and went off again into the Forest again at Midnight, never sleeping in a house. I proceeded from there to St Justin a small village some leagues away, where they had committed much depredation on the Inhabitants and there took One of the gang in a small Inn whom I brought away Prisoner, but lost all traces of the rest. I heard also of a Party of 40 Gens d'Armes towards Nogara –

Tue 15th   *Out in the Landes all night, got to the Inn soon after day light, All off – March'd to St Justin where I took one of the Gang, and return'd about 3 p m – Pipon & 60 Men went off at 7 on the same Duty –*

Wed 16th   *The 4th Division march'd through from Bordeaux. Bourke's Squadron of the 18th March in – Pipon return'd empty handed about 4 p m. Bourke of the 18th & a large Party Din'd with me*

Thu 17th   *To My Mother No 17*

    The Squadron of the 18th March'd thro' – Colonel Campbell's Regiment of Portuguese March in – The Brigand Prisoner hanged in the middle of the Town; The Spanish Commissary &c Din'd with us

Fri 18th   *March'd the Left Squadron to Villeneuve de Marsan – The 3rd to Nogaro – The Right & 2nd to Plaisance. Captain Kennedy's Squadron of the 18th Halted the Night at Villeneuve. Din'd with Dunkin & Luard*

Sat 19th   *To Shakespear*

    The Squadron of the 18th March'd – Robbins's Troop march'd through to Nogaro from Capsienne – Nothing Extraordinary – The Officers Din'd with me –

Sun 20th   *To W. Drury A Party 1 Sergeant & 12 Order'd to co-operate with Colonel Campbell – Rode out towards Mont de Marsan Play'd the Flute with Monsieur – All Din'd at Peter's Quarters –*

Mon 21st	*Parade at 10; Court Martial of which I was President – Prisoners pardon'd afterwards – Nothing Extraordinary, Rainy Bad Weather – All Din'd with me a là Français*
Tue 22nd	*Pipon, Shirly & Peters rode over to Mont de Marson – Moffit rode over to Nogaro – I play'd the Flute with Monsieur Montbell – No News -All Din'd at Peters's Quarters –*
Wed 23rd	*To Maria No 18*
	Market Day Villeneuve. Nothing Extraordinary. Many Reports – All Din'd with me; Monsieur Montbell came in the Evening –
Thur 24th	*Rode over with John & Shirly to Mont de Marsan – Rainy bad Day – The National Guard doing duty with the English in the Town – Din'd at Peters's – Monsieur Montbell & a German Officer Din'd there Mont de Marsan as good as an English Country Town – The Main Street very handsome. The Hall of the Prefecture a very fine Building, but not quite finish'd – The Inhabitants all well Dispos'd. We were saluted by the National Guard form'd by the Inhabitants, and doing Duty with the English – The Duke D'Angouleme had appointed a Prefect, which assumption of Authority was not approv'd by Lord Wellington, who displaced him, but re-appointed him the Day after – The People in this part of the Country all seem to think that the English mean to keep this part of France, and cite old times, when it belonged to us. They seem very well pleased with the idea; Any thing for a quiet Life!!*
Fri 25th	*Rainy Weather – Peters & John rode to Mont de Marsan; Many Deserters came in – Nothing Extraordinary – All Din'd with me –*
Sat 26th	*Nothing Extraordinary – Din'd with Peters*
Sun 27th	*Same as yesterday – Monsieur St Marc & Monsieur Monbell Din'd with Us at my Quarters –*

136

Mon 28th Fine Weather. No News. No Employment – Lounging about & playing Billiards. Monsieur St Marc very bad – All Din'd at Peters's –

Tue 29th The same as yesterday, except that all Din'd with me at Peters's – Horses improving! Some Consolation!!

Wed 30th All Quiet – Market Day – Din'd at Peters's – about half past 11 the Brigands paid us a visit & fir'd several shots at the Vedette & ran away Being Market Day the Town was extremely full of all sorts of people – About ½ past 10 at night, as I was going home to my Quarters, heard an Alarm, and the turning out – and soon after 5 or six shots down the road – Went down to the Piquet, who were out – The Brigands, a party of 9 had come down and fir'd upon our vedette (Foley of my Troop). His Carbine miss'd; he however fir'd both pistols at them, and then Charg'd them alone, when they broke off and dispers'd into the forest having probably heard the Piquet coming– Had he retir'd, and drawn them towards the Town, we must have had some of them –

Thu 31st Rode out with John. Court Martial – Pay Parade at 3 – Colonel Campbell & two Portuguese Officers came over – All Din'd with me – Took two suspicious Fellows –

137

April–May 1814

Tom Wildman's period of inaction at Villeneuve came to an end on the 8 April when he was relieved by a detachment of Portuguese troops. The squadron departed the next day marching to Nogaro and thence to Vic-Fezenzac, on the road to Auch, where they arrived on the 10th – the day upon which the battle of Toulouse was fought some sixty miles to the east.

At this point it is worth mentioning the Military General Service Medal 1793–1814, for it reveals an amusing insight into Tom's character. This medal was issued in 1848, too late for most of those entitled to the award to be able to receive their medals, though it may have been some slight consolation to their next of kin that they were allowed to apply for them. Bars were awarded for battles in which recipients had taken part and these were attached to the red-and-blue ribbon. It was up to the recipient to apply for those to which he felt he was entitled. Tom received three bars – Sahagun and Benevente, Orthes and Toulouse. There is no evidence that he was at Sahagun, though he was probably present at Benevente. He was certainly entitled to the bar for Orthes, but on his own admission, he was nowhere near Toulouse on the day of the battle. Tom's brother John received the bar for Orthes but did not apply for the one for Toulouse, although they were together at the time. However, Tom was not alone in claiming this bar, for his squadron leader Thomas Pipon and William Verner also claimed it. There was no denying that the other two squadrons of the 7th Hussars were present at Toulouse, and if these old soldiers, now well into their sixties, thought that no one would remember that they had not been there, they were right, for their claims do not appear to have been questioned. However, some claims were unsuccessful. For example Captain Heyliger's application for the Toulouse bar was disallowed. This was hardly surprising for the Adjutant General had only just granted him four weeks' sick leave at Orthes on 27 March! As this was the first general campaign medal to be authorised, perhaps the eagerness of these veterans to claim as much as they could was excusable.

At Vic, Tom relates how difficult it was to post picquets to guard the town against Captain Florian and his bandits. William Verner, whose squadron was already in Auch, had previously been ordered to place a corporal and three men at Vic. He had realised it would be of no use and that the men would be sacrificed. Before sending them he wrote:

I gave instructions to the corporal how to act in case of being attacked, and to a certain extent he followed my instructions, but without deriving any beneficial results from doing so. I pointed out to him that the probability was, an attempt would be made to make prisoners of his party; he must be constantly on the watch, and keep the door and lower windows of the house barred, and if attacked keeping firing out of the upper windows of the house.

What happened is recorded by Tom on 10 April. Whether the three hussars who were taken managed to escape, or indeed, what fate ultimately overtook Florian we do not know. Fortunately Tom had no trouble during the night he spent at Vic, and the following day he joined Verner in Auch.

Verner was staying at an inn, but Pipon, the two Wildman brothers and the other officers were put up in the local barracks. The inn was kept by a Monsieur Alexandre,

whose repute as a first rate 'restauranteur' had spread all over France and many parts of the Continent. Nothing in the shape of French cookery could exceed the dinner provided by Alexandre. His brother Abbé, resided in the same house; they were both portly, but the Abbé was in figure and appearance what we see represented on the stage as a jolly well fed monk. He was a good tempered jolly fellow. He had emigrated to England during the revolution, and from having resided near London he had learned English and become acquainted with the tastes of Englishmen, so he took care that in addition to the superb cooking of his brother we should have every day a joint or two a l'Anglaise.

It is small wonder that Tom commented, 'Capital Dinners and excellent wine'.

During the week Tom spent at Auch peace was confirmed, and he received news of the battle. He describes Colonel Vivian's wound but does not mention the circumstances. On the day in question Soult's Chasseurs à Cheval had been falling back along the River Ers north of Toulouse, destroying the bridges as they went. Wellington's columns were advancing along both sides of the river which was impassable without pontoons. Vivian leading the 18th Hussars drove the Chasseurs up to one of the bridges which was still intact. Both regiments halted facing one another. The opposite bank was lined by dismounted French dragoons. Some British infantry were following behind the hussars. Vivian gave the order to charge, but at that moment a musket ball smashed his right arm and he was forced to retire. Major Hughes and the hussars surged forward before the Chasseurs had time to move. The hussars forced them against the bridge, sabring the front ranks; the rest broke and fled across the river with the hussars in pursuit.

The French suffered many casualties and a hundred men were taken prisoner. French artillery coming up soon afterwards forced the 18th to withdraw. By this time the British infantry had secured the bridge. Although Vivian was unable to take part in the charge, he did receive the credit for this bold stroke which secured a vital bridge. The 18th were delighted at having this opportunity to restore their tarnished reputation and showed their appreciation by presenting Vivian with a sword, which was the way in which outstanding conduct was often privately acknowledged in the days before medals for gallantry were instituted.

Five days later Wellington attacked the French lines round Toulouse. In this last and useless battle of the Peninsular War the 7th Hussars took no part in the fighting. The adjutant, Lieutenant Arther Myer, writing afterwards to Major Hodge, regretted the proclamation of peace had not come sooner: 'the lives of many a brave Fellow would have been saved.' He went on: 'We had two squadrons there under command of Colonel Kerrison ready to act but had nothing to perform that day.'

Both sides suffered heavy casualties on the 10 April. On the following day Wellington could not resume the action until he had regrouped and had fresh supplies of shot and shell brought up from his ammunition park. However, Soult did not wait for a resumption of the battle. He decided to retreat south toward Carcassone before the road was cut, and evacuated the city that night. Wellington and his staff entered the city on 12 April. 'It is impossible for anything to exceed the Reception we met with in Toulouse,' wrote Benjamin Badcock to his father:

> We were received with the greatest Joy by all ranks and it was more a parade through a City in England than an entry into an Enemy town. The people wore the White Cockade, which we have all adopted, and threw the bust of Napoleon out of the window of the Capital.

Now that the war was over, all the local families were anxious to welcome the British army as their deliverers and to display their loyalty to the Bourbons. A continual stream of army units was passing through Auch towards Toulouse, but Tom had little to do, so spent his time with the local families. After a week the two squadrons of the 7th were moved further north to St-Clair, and then to St-Nicolas-de-la-Grave on the banks of the Garonne. Here again there was a further round of dinners and parties.

The Duke of Angoulême now decided to leave Bordeaux and travelled down to Toulouse along the main road running beside the north bank of the Garonne on the opposite side to St-Nicolas. On 21 April, Tom, Verner, O'Grady and Chirmside agreed to go to Toulouse to see the Duke arrive. They crossed the river to Castelsarrasin where they spent the night, and early next morning they took the diligence to Toulouse. These huge lumbering coaches, with large baskets for the luggage on the back, carried many more passengers both inside and on top than an English stagecoach. They were drawn by at least six horses on long traces so that they would range all over the road and travelled at little more than a walking pace. The distance to Toulouse was only about thirty miles and notwithstanding an early start they did not arrive until two in the afternoon.

Toulouse had gone wild when Wellington had entered the city. Now, a fortnight later, the inhabitants gave an equally enthusiastic welcome to the Duke of Angoulême. A ball was held in his honour and he, in turn, gave another at the Palais-Royal. In view of the number of British officers in the city, it seems hardly likely that an officer as junior as Tom would have attended these functions, but the hussars held their own celebration dinners at fashionable restaurants which have long since disappeared.

Marshal Soult, who had retired to Carcassonne, was reluctant to sign an armistice agreement until he received official confirmation of the change of government. Marshal Suchet had no such qualms, and when Soult was recalled he received the command of Soult's army in addition to his own, hence Tom's reference to a review of the two armies. When this review took place, Napoleon's dejected veterans were disgusted when the Duke of Angoulême arrived wearing what appeared to be an English uniform with his aides wearing English hussar uniforms.

By contrast, the girls of Toulouse were very happy. There were balls, theatre parties and fêtes every day, and the British officers, after months of campaigning, had a rapturous reception. Harry Smith of the 95th Rifles, who was accompanied by the pretty little Spaniard he had rescued during the sack of Badajos and married, recalled: 'most of our gallant fellows were really in love, or fancied themselves so, and such had been the drain by conscription of the male population you never saw a young Frenchman.' Captain Johnny Kincaid, another officer in the 95th Rifles, was having an equally pleasant time billeted in Castelsarrasin, 'where every officer found in his quarters a family home.' 'We there found,' he reported, 'both the time and the opportunity of exercising one of the agreeable professions to which we had long been strangers, that of making love to pretty little girls with which the place abounded.'

Edward Wildman now arrived in Toulouse. The heavy cavalry had been brought up from Spain in March, and then joined the advance on Toulouse. Edward's brigade was directed to maintain contact between the Spanish Division and the 6th Division, and although the Spaniards were repulsed in confusion during the battle, Edward does not appear to have been involved in the action. The brothers were able to meet in Toulouse, but Tom did not spend many days in the city, returning to St-Nicolas with Lieutenant Maddison on 1 May. They travelled by post horses to Fronton, where they spent the night and arrived back in St-Nicolas in the evening. Verner and O'Grady did not come back until a few days later.

Wellington left Toulouse on 30 May, having just been rewarded with a dukedom, and appointed British ambassador in Paris. With the establishment of peace the time had now come for the Peninsular army to be broken up after seven years of war. Wellington had already turned his attention to the problem of bringing home his army, and in particular their horses. In a letter to Earl Bathurst dated 19 April he wrote:

> Some, probably half of each regiment might be disposed of in this country or in Spain or to the Spanish or Portuguese cavalry with advantage; but I calculate that there will be not less than 9,000 horses belonging to the cavalry, the artillery and the staff and field officers of the infantry to be embarked.
>
> It might be possible to march the cavalry, at least, across France with the permission of the French Government which I beg leave to suggest for Your Lordship's consideration.

On 26 April all Portuguese and Spanish women attached to soldiers but not married were ordered to leave their men. Returning Spanish and Portuguese troops were to escort them, and there were heartbreaking scenes as these unfortunate women were packed off home. So far as we know, the 7th Hussars had not formed any attachments; unlike many units who had spent years in Spain they had been there only for a few months. Officers' servants, on the other hand, who wished to return home were provided with documents which entitled them to receive rations on their journey. No provision seems to have been made for their transport, so unless they had money they faced a long walk. Tom's personal servant, Antonio, had originally agreed to come to England with his master. Then, two days before the regiment marched, Antonio's courage failed him and he decided to return to Spain. The sight of his compatriots leaving, the prospect of a cold wet climate and the realisation that he would have no friends in England was too much for Antonio. And who could blame him? Tom was upset, and notwithstanding his liberal principles, he was clearly lacking in understanding of his servant's problems. Although Tom felt that he lacked gratitude, one cannot help having some sympathy with Antonio's discontent at not being provided with a mule to carry him on his journey home.

Infantry units were already marching towards Bordeaux for embark-ation, either to England or to America, where the war with the United States was still continuing. On receipt of Wellington's letter, Lord Bathurst had contacted the Foreign Secretary, Lord Castlereagh, who in turn got in touch with the French government. On 5 May, Lord Castlereagh wrote to Lord Bathurst:

> The Infantry will be marched towards the Western Coast. Lord Wellington calculates that 6 weeks will be required for the march to Boulogne and Calais, in which time he expects you will have your transports ready. He counts on 12,000 horses embarking. For how many will you have tonnage at one trip? You must give him some idea in what succession they should arrive.

Tom's diary shows that preparations for the regiment's departure were already under way. On 11 May, Tom inspected his troop thoroughly; two days later he inspected their saddles and equipment, and on the following day there was an inspection of the horses. On 22 May, eighty-seven unfit horses were sold, and the next day Colonel Kerrison inspected Pipon's and Verner's squadrons. In March, seventy-eight troop horses and five officers' horses had been brought out from England by Captain Schmieden, who had remained behind with the Headquarters Squadron. When he later inspected the horses that had previously been returned to the remount depot at Urragun, he described them as mere skeletons. Relatively few horses had been lost in action, but the weather and the terrain had taken its toll. A number of the men did not have mounts, and on 30 May Tom received orders for these men to march home on foot. Taking the Army as a whole, the monthly returns of sick horses between December 1813 and May 1814 show that sick horses averaged 368, or 1 in 17. A curious feature is that the sickness rate was greater in May than in December when horses were starving.

On 18 May, Tom wrote to his mother for the last time before his return home; however, he wrote two more letters to Maria during the course of the march. He had written twenty-one letters in all to his mother. Since 1795 proper arrangements had been made for sending the Forces' mail, although an Act of Parliament had been passed in the time of George II providing for cheap postage rates for soldiers' letters. During the Peninsular War the post office had been established at Lisbon, but after the army crossed into France it moved to Passajes. Considering the high rate of illiteracy a surprisingly large number of letters passed through this post office. A civilian sorter was employed, assisted by two or three non-commissioned officers. Every unit was supposed to provide a list of all letters forwarded to the post office, but the sorter's task was made more difficult because the units so often failed to supply these lists. Privates and NCOs were charged a penny a letter and officers had to pay sixpence. On arrival at Falmouth, letters were transferred to the Royal Mail for delivery. The Army postal service appears to have anticipated the reform of the Post Office, which Sir Rowland Hiil introduced in 1840 when he set up the pre-paid Penny Post. Until that time rates were calculated on the distance and were normally paid by the recipient and not the sender. Nearly all the letters written to Tom during the Corunna campaign bear a Turnham Green stamp marked 'unpaid'.

Fortunately for Tom's men, their pay arrived on 25 May. The only previous mention of their pay was on 27 January when he had settled the accounts with the men. Keeping account of pay was the responsibility of the troop leader. The pay sergeant was responsible for entering up the debt and credit roll. Tom's pay sergeant was probably the man named Thompson to whom he gave a draft for a hundred doubloons on 24 January. By May, Sergeant Major Ryter must have been short of money, for Tom advanced him twelve doubloons on the 15th. Both British and French soldiers normally carried their money on their persons. When in action soldiers on both sides helped themselves to any money they found on the dead or even wounded men. For example, Private Wheeler of the 51st Foot described how a French soldier robbed him after he had been wounded. Shortly afterwards he shot the Frenchman in the back, and having crawled over to him he recovered his own money and some more into the bargain.

Pipon's and Verner's squadrons left St-Nicolas on 20 May, moving to Grissolles and Poupignon further down the Garonne where the Hussar Brigade was assembling in preparation for the first stage of the march to Montauban. By the last week of May, preparations were complete and on the 23rd there was a farewell ball and supper given by the inhabitants of

Grissolles. Tom and John then paid a final visit to Toulouse where they went shopping. Toulouse had a substantial silk industry at this period, producing a variety of materials from damasks to stockings. Mrs Wildman and Maria would have certainly welcomed lengths of silk for making gowns, but the Wildman brothers were probably looking for more exciting gifts – shawls, gloves and bonnets perhaps. Back in Grissolles there were races with the officers of the 95th, whom they entertained to dinner. If Johnny Kincaid took part, he had forgotten by the time he came to write his memoirs – for him Castelsarrasin only conjured up memories of pretty little girls!

The final route for the Grand Movement, as it was called, was agreed in a letter from the French Minister of War to Sir George Murray, the Quartermaster General, when he made a few alterations to ensure that there would be adequate supplies and quarters for the troops. In addition to the cavalry, twenty-one battalions of infantry would be marching across France in two divisions which were to converge on Mantes. The Hussar Brigade was to lead the right division, which also included the Household Cavalry, the Heavy Cavalry and 300 draught horses for the baggage train. They were to march in four columns, setting off at twenty-four hourly intervals. This must be the only occasion when a British army has travelled right across France since the Hundred Years War, and in those days a substantial area of France belonged to the English Crown.

Journal

Fri April 1st   *Nothing Extraordinary – Rode out – Monsieur Monbell Din'd with us at Peter's –*

Sat 2nd   *Nothing Extraordinary – Receiv'd some letters from the Regiment – Monsieur Mathieu arrested by Order of Colonel Campbell –*

Sun 3rd   *A Grand Procession from the Church – The Town very gay & Ladies very smart – No News – Nothing Extraordinary*

Mon 4th   *Rainy Weather – Nothing Extraordinary – Rode out, Rode back again – Din'd & slept –*

Tue 5th   *Much the same as yesterday – Did nothing, John help'd me*

Wed 6th	*Various Reports, All False. Market Day. Brigands did not come –*
Thu 7th	*To Maj. Hodge Note to Mary*
	Rode out, Talk'd to the Women Pelted with Peters – Din'd at his Quarters & Drank Wine with Pipon –
Fri 8th	*An Officer with a Detachment of 25 Portuguese march'd in to Relieve us – The Officer Din'd with me –*
Sat 9th	*March'd at 8 to Nogaro – thro' La Honza – Monsieur Mathieu march'd with us to go to Head Quarters –*
Sun 10th	*March'd at 5 to Vic – Fezensac. Posted the Piquet & guard for the night, All Din'd at the Auberge We arriv'd at Vic where the Brigands had taken a Letter Party of our Regiment – On Monday 4th – Captain Florian dash'd in about 4 O'Clock in the day, with 26 Men; Our Corporal and three men defended themselves some time but one man was kill'd, and the rest taken. Two Inhabitants who were Spectators of the fight, were wounded – We were told that the Man who was kill'd fir'd two shots close to Florian's Head, who was so enrag'd that after he was disarm'd he ran his sword thro' him – The Town lies in a very exposed situation, that I had some difficulty in posting a Piquet for the night Lord Wellington attack'd the Enemy in Position above Toulouse; and as usual completely Routed them The French retreated from the Town the same evening*
Mon 11th	*March'd at 5 to Auch. Put our Squadron with Verners into Barracks, Officers in Quarters – Went to Vespers – All Din'd at Verners Auberge –*
Tue 12th	*To my Mother No.19*
	Beautiful Weather, The Heavy Guns march'd in – Nothing Extraordinary here – Din'd at Fraser's Auberge –
Wed 13th	*Several Reports Afloat – Some People arriv'd in the Evening from Toulouse, who told us Peace was made*

Thu 14th   Cessation of Hostilities confirm'd to the Great Joy of the Inhabitants. Newland Din'd with us –

Fri 15th   Fraser & Newland set off to Head Quarters – The White Flag Hoisted – Speech from the Mayor – Procession &c &c &c

Sat 16th   More Accounts of Proceedings in Paris to the 5th of April – Nothing Extraordinary – Concert in the Evening –

Sun 17th   Great Procession to the Cathedral. Te Deum chaunted in grand style – Address from the Vicar General &c

On the 8th Colonel Vivian had a brilliant Affair with the 18th Hussars; who charg'd and completely routed a considerable force of French Cavalry near Toulouse: Colonel Vivian was severely wounded by a Shot in the right Arm, which shattered the bone just above the elbow The 18th were delighted with his gallantry & conduct by which they totally wip'd off the slur which had been cast upon them. They wrote him an excellent & most handsome letter, and voted him a Sword of 200 Guineas value –

10th – At the latter end of the Day near Toulouse when the Battle was just over, Captain Gordon of the 10th Hussars, who commanded a Squadron was struck in the side by a Cannon Shot which pass'd thro' his body, carrying away part of the Back bone; He just said 'They have done for me' & expir'd in about ten minutes. A most Valuable Officer, and a serious loss to his Regiment & his Country

PEACE

Mon 18th   Maj. Hodge Maria, No 20

Nothing Extraordinary – Weather Beautiful

Tue 19th   Several Detachments Marching thro' Daily – Nothing Extraordinary – Capital Dinners & excellent Wine

Wed 20th   Went out about a league into the Country, a large Party to Dine with a Countess. Spent a very pleasant Day –

Thu 21st   Went with Colonel Reuben to call on some Ladies we had met at Dinner the Day before. Nothing Extraordinary

Fri 22nd	Read French & English and exchanged Books with Monsieur Lacluvine de Soupets – Received an Order to March
Sat 23rd	March'd at 8 to the great grief of the Inhabitants of Auch, in which we also participated: Arrived at the village of St Clair where Nothing could exceed the kindness we received
Sun 24th	March'd at 6, Arrived at St Nicholas de la Grave, a small Town on the Garonne where we were received with Acclamations and Dinners prepar'd at every house –
Mon 25th	Breakfasted with my Hosts à la François. Din'd in the same style – Colonel Kerrison, Myer & Uniache came over – Went to a Party at Pipon's Quarters in the Evening –
Tue 26th	Rode with Verners, O'Grady & Chirmside to the Ferry near Castel Sarazin, sent back our horses & walk'd to the Town where we din'd & slept, in order to start next morning <u>par diligence</u>
Wed 27th	Arrived in Toulouse about 2 P M – at Four the Duke D'Angouleme made his Entree – Heard Te Deum in the Cathedral. Din'd a large Party of Tenth & Seventh at the Hotel de Prince. The Duke went to the Play
Thu 28th	Soult expected, did not arrive – All Bustle and Parade – Sat with Colonel Vivian – Din'd a large Hussar Party at the Grand Soleil. Ball at the Capitoleum in honor of the Prince
Fri 29th	Much the same as yesterday – Colonel Vivian doing well; Din'd at the Grand Soleil – Went to the Play with Morrison – Suchet arrived – Ball at the Palais Royal given by the Prince
Sat 30th	Suchet had a very long audience with Lord Wellington – Edward & Captain McNeal arriv'd – Din'd at the Traiteurs & went to the Play – Lord Wellington set out for Paris –

Marshal Soult recall'd from his Command and order'd to

Paris. 29th – Marshal Suchet arriv'd, and threw himself at the feet of the Duke D'Angouleme, saying that 'If the past could be forgotten, He should reckon this the happiest Day of his life'; on being assured it was; he rose up saying 'Vive Louis XVIII' and requested a Day for Reviewing the two Armies under his command that he might hear the same from them –

Sun 1st May   *Started with Maddison on Post Horses at 3, Edward return'd to his Regiment – Shmiedern's Party arriv'd at Toulouse – Arriv'd at Fronton at $^1\!/_2$ past 6 – Slept at Lowther's –*

Mon 2nd   *Rode with Maddison from Fronton; call'd on Elphinstone at La Bastide de Pierre, pass'd close to Montaubon thro' Castel Sarazin cross'd the Garonne and arriv'd at St Nicholas at 7 P M*

Tue 3rd   *To George*

           Fine weather – Nothing Extraordinary

Wed 4th   *To Maj Hodge*

           Fine Weather, Fine Country – Stupid Town – Nothing Extraordinary, Moffit arriv'd from Toulouse – Din'd at ye Auberge

Thu 5th   *Verners & O'Grady return'd from Toulouse – Din'd with our Hosts – Nothing Extraordinary*

Fri 6th   *Nothing Extraordinary*

Sat 7th   *Rode over to Moissac to see the Duke D'Angouleme &c pass through – Din'd at Castel Sarazin; return'd in the Evening*

Sun 8th   *Nothing Extraordinary – Dinner & Ball at Castel Sarazin*

Mon 9th   *Hot Weather as usual – Verners, Pipon, John &c &c rode on to Montaubon, Moffit return'd Sick –*

Tue 10th	*To Edward*
	Nothing Extraordinary
Wed 11th	*Inspected my Troop thoroughly – Shirly return'd from Toulouse – Nothing Extraordinary –*
Thu 12th	*Went out with some People on a Fishing Party – Nothing Extraordinary*
Fri 13th	*Took a Rural Walk with our Hosts – Fraser & Peters return'd from Toulouse – Inspected the Saddles, Shabraques & Appointments*
Sat 14th	*Inspection of Horses in Watering Order – Nothing Extraordinary*
Sun 15th	*Being the Fête of St Nicholas a Great Crowd &c all day – The Horses & Men joined from Daniel's Party – A Ball in the Evening –*

Advanced Serj Major Ryter Twelve Dobloons

Mon 16th	*Nothing Extraordinary*

Lord Wellington said to have return'd to Toulouse –

Tue 17th	*Pipon, John & Monsieur Delfagette rode out to Dine in the Country – Din'd at Moffit's Quarters –*
Wed 18th	*To My Mother No. 21*
	Nothing Extraordinary – Paraded at 3 in the Afternoon Parting to the great dismay of the Town
Thu 19th	*Parade in Watering Order – Nothing Extraordinary – Much grief at Parting with our Friends in St Nicholas*
Fri 20th	*Breakfasted with the 52nd. March'd thro' Castel Sarazin to Grissoles & Poupignan – Pipon's Squadron at the Former, Verner's at the Latter –*

Sat 21st   *John went with Verners to Toulouse – Nothing Extraordinary – Din'd with the Officers of the 95th; 3rd Battalion*

Sun 22nd   *87 Cast Horses sold at Fronton – Rien d'Extraordinaire A Dance in the Evening at Colonel Ross's Quarters –*

Mon 23rd   *John return'd from Toulouse – Colonel Kerrison inspected the Two Squadrons in Marching Order – Ball & Supper given by the Inhabitants of Grisolles*

Tue 24th   *Rode over to Poupignan in the morning – Colone Kerrison & Lowther Din'd & Slept here to Start in the morning for Paris –*

Wed 25th   *Rode out with John – Douglass & Darville came over – Received Pay Troop Allowances &c –*

Thu 26th   *Rode with John to Toulouse. Met Pipon coming back – Found Colonel Vivian up & doing very well – Went to the Play*

Fri 27th   *Engaged all the morning in <u>Shopping</u> – Colonel Vivian better Din'd at the Traiteurs and went to the Play*

Sat 28th   *Set off at ½ past 7 & rode to Grisolles in an hour & 20 minutes – Nothing Extraordinary –*

Sun 29th   *Rain'd all Day*

Nothing Extraordinary

28th. All the Portuguese & Spanish servants and women who chose to return to their Country were provided with Certificates to procure Rations & regular Route &cc – My Spanish Boy Antonio, who had always professed himself particularly attach'd, and desirous of going with me to England, was not included; however on my return from Toulouse, he informed me that he did not choose to trust himself so far from Spain, and beg'd to return with the others; he took his Departure without the slightest symptom of Regret or Gratitude for past favours, and considerably discontented that I did not make him a present of a Mule in additon to the money I had given him, and a new suit of clothes the day before – But I was a fool to have exected better from a Spaniard –

Mon 30th   Some Races amongst the 95th Officers in the morning – 3 Din'd with us – Received the Route in the Evening and Orders for ye March of the Dismounted

Tue 31st   Several 95th Officers Din'd with us – Nothing Extraordinary Ball at Colonel Ross's Quarters The Spanish Commissary came to take leave of me. I really believe him an exception to his Nation in general –

<u>Route for the Hussar Brigade – 1814</u>

June 2nd Montauban
  3rd Causade
  4th Cahors
  5th — Halt

  6th Fresinet
  7th Souillac
  8th Brive
  9th — Halt
  10th Uzerche
  11th Pierre Buffiere
  12th Limoges
  13th — Halt
  14th Bessines
  15th St Benoit
  16th Argenton
  17th Chateauroux
  18th — Halt
  19th Vatan

19th Vatan
20th Vierzon
21st Salbris
22nd Laferte Senneterre

23rd Orleans
24th — Halt
25th Artenay
26th Angerville
27th Etampes
28th — Halt
29th St Arnauld
30th Monfort
July 1st Mantes, there to wait for further Orders

June 1814

On 1 June, the 7th Hussars left Grissolles and marched to a village near Montauban where they were to join the rest of the Hussar Brigade. Montauban was an attractive old town with a fine view of the snowcapped Pyrenees. The following day the Grand Movement started, with the Hussar Brigade leading the way through Montauban to Caussade. Tom remained behind to meet Edward, who was following with the Heavy Brigade.

The next day Tom and Edward set off by carriage. Edward may have been feeling unwell, for five days later Dr Moffit 'physic'd' him. In the meantime they drove along a well-made road through avenues of mulberry trees as far as Caussade. From here the road passes through mountainous country until it drops down into Cahors. Before descending the steep road down into the town they had their last glimpse of the Pyrenees, a hundred and fifty miles to the south. At Cahors they caught up with the Hussar Brigade.

It would seem that, instead of waiting for his own regiment, Edward continued the march with Tom and John. Edward was clearly attracted to the 7th Hussars, for within a couple of months of his promotion to captain at the end of 1814 he exchanged into the regiment. His motive probably had more to do with a wish to be with his brothers than his liking for the regiment. After Waterloo, when Tom and Edward realised that they had little prospect of promotion in the 7th Hussars, Tom transferred to the 9th Light Dragoons and Edward returned to the heavy cavalry, leaving John who was much younger, and who was eventually to command the regiment.

Cahors was not a very attractive town in Arthur Young's opinion. Their arrival here coincided with one of the regular halts. Apart from giving men and horses a rest, these halts enabled stragglers to catch up with their units. Two days later Tom and Edward arrived in Brive, which Tom describes as a 'dirty old Town with a cotton manufactory'. Arthur Young's condemnation was more forthright:

> The view of Brive from the hill is so fine that it gives the expectation
> of a beautiful little town and the gaiety of the environs encourages
> the idea; but on entering, such contrast is found that it disgusts

completely. Close ill-built crooked dirty stinking streets, exclude the sun and almost the air from every habitation.

Fortunately the 7th were put up in a village beyond the town. It was here that Dr Moffit took Edward in hand. Whatever the doctor prescribed seems to have worked, for Edward was able to continue the march, and they arrived in Limoges on 12 June. Here Tom and Edward got a 'capital billet'. Fortunately the day following their arrival was a 'halt' and they were able to go sightseeing. Their hosts evidently liked the young officers, whose ability to speak French would have encouraged friendly relations. They invited them to dinner and then took them to watch a procession. The following day the brothers had breakfast with their hosts and later dined with them. Afterwards they visited the porcelain factory and the bishop's garden.

Nearly thirty years earlier Arthur Young had described Limoges as 'ill built with narrow and crooked streets, the houses are high and disagreeable'. However, he conceded that the bishop had recently built a large handsome palace and 'his garden is the finest object to be seen at Limoges'. The porcelain factory had been established in 1770. In about 1785 the business was purchased by the King as a subsidiary to the Sèvres factory. At the time of Tom's visit the Limoges factory was still only making white porcelain. When Young was there in 1787 he thought their products were expensive.

After leaving Limoges, Tom was not so fortunate with his billets, and he found himself sleeping above the cow stalls in a stable. At St-Benoit no accommodation was available and the brigade had to bivouac. During the whole of the six-week march there were only two occasions when the troops had to bivouac – the other being at Vierzon. The country between Limoges and Argenton was sparsely populated and poor, with only small villages and no towns.

Between Argenton and Châteauroux they passed a 'beautiful Squadron of Dragons de la Garde'. One wonders what sort of impression the 7th Hussars made on the Chasseurs. After eleven months in the field the worn, patched uniforms of the hussars and their thin, tired horses must have been a rather sorry sight.

They were now riding across flat uninteresting heathland. At Châteauroux they halted for a couple of nights, and there was a horse inspection. Tom was invited to dine with General Fane, whose brigade had formerly comprised the 3rd Dragoon Guards and the First Dragoons. Early in 1814 Fane transferred to Vivian's 1st Brigade and by the end of the war he was commanding both brigades and working them as a division.

On 23 June the 7th Hussars marched into Orleans – 'singing in the rain'. Benjamin Badcock of the 14th Light Dragoons arrived the same day. He commented on the fine stone bridge with its nine arches – the first experiment with a flat arch in France according to Arthur Young. Badcock mentions the statue of Joan of Arc and the pictures of her to be seen on most of the houses. Tom did not waste any time looking at Orleans and set off immediately for Paris with his friend Lieutenant Osborne Barwell. They rode to Longjumeau, a distance of some sixty miles, where they put up for the night. In view of the speed at which they travelled, it is likely that they used post horses. Lord Blayney, who had been interned in France after being captured in Spain, had noted how little private traffic there was on the roads around Paris. This had little to do with the war, for even before the Revolution Arthur Young had described this road as 'a desert compared with those round London'. The French *pavés* were generally very good, for the monarchy had long been concerned to ensure that roads were well maintained to facilitate troop movements. Benjamin Badcock, who also set out for Paris on the same day, remarked that the roads in France were better than those in England. As they rode along, Tom and his friend passed the shafts of numerous quarries where huge 'lanthorn' (lantern) wheels brought up to the surface stone for road-making.

Presumably they stayed at an inn at Longjumeau, though Tom does not mention one. The food in French inns was more varied than in England, and the wine was generally good. The beds were better, and, unlike England, the sheets were properly aired. On the other hand, there was no parlour in which to eat; only a room with three or four beds in it. The walls were whitewashed or covered with paper of different patterns in the same room. The table was a board laid across trestles, and 'the furniture such that an English innkeeper would light his fire with it'. Windows leaked and doors were generally draughty; 'mops, brooms and scrubbing brushes are not in the catalogue of the necessaries of a French inn. Bells there are none; the fille must be bawled for; and when she comes, is neither neat, well dressed nor handsome.'

With little incentive to stay in bed in such conditions, Tom and Barwell set off again early next morning and completed the last ten miles to Paris by nine o'clock. The artist Benjamin Haydon who arrived in Paris in the same month, travelling from England, described the country around the capital as 'vast dreary and melancholy – old chateaux, delapidated.' This was the generally accepted view of English travellers, who found little evidence of trade and the streets of ancient crumbling buildings filthy, while Captain Mercer complained of an all-pervading smell. Tom, arriving in Paris from the south, would have had a more favourable impression, for he would have passed the great public buildings erected by Napoleon. Badcock considered these surpassed the public buildings in London. The palace and gardens of the Tuileries also surpassed his expectations, but 'the monument built by Buonaparte in place Vendôme in commemoration of his victories in Germany and of bronze from the artillery captured I consider one of the finest monuments in the World'.

Every British officer who was able to do so was taking this opportunity to see Paris. Colonel Kerrison and Captain Lowther had set off the previous month, and many others from the regiment followed Tom's example on his return. English visitors were pouring into Paris for the first time since 1802. Aristocratic families, young men anxious to make the Grand Tour, dandies, gamblers and all the world of fashion, not to mention those enterprising courtesans, Harriet Wilson and her sister Amy, were there. These, in addition to the Allied armies occupying Paris, made accommodation difficult for all but the rich. Lord Blayney complained that the city was 'so full there was no obtaining a seat at the theatres and the coffee houses were disagreeably crowded'.

Tom took a room at the Hotel Wagram, a fashionable and expensive hotel in rue des Capucines, comprising two buildings, numbers 14 and 16. This street is near place Vendôme, just off rue de la Paix. At the time the hotel may not have looked very impressive from the outside because there was a row of shops at street level.*

Samuel Rogers, the wealthy banker poet and habitué of Holland House, stayed at this hotel a month later on his way to Italy. (He, too, had been a friend of Byron, who had called him 'our Poetical Papa'; after Byron left his wife he turned against Rogers.) The Paris Tom saw was very different to the city transformed by Baron Haussman during the Second Empire. When he visited the Louvre the square in front adjoined 'stalls where squalid people offered for sale dogs birds, sweepings of bric à brac shops; spots infested by the lazzaroni of Paris, thieves and courtesans.' The museum had been opened in 1800 to display the works of art captured by Napoleon during his Italian campaigns, and subsequently the treasures looted by his armies all over Europe. Here was displayed the finest collection of paintings and sculpture ever seen under one roof, and even

---

* A few years later the hotel was demolished to make way for the government offices which occupy the site today.

though they may have disapproved of the way the collection had been assembled, English visitors were certainly full of admiration. Entry was free, and so long as they obeyed the notices telling them not to touch the exhibits, they could spend as much time there as they pleased. Badcock told his father:

> We went to the museum two successive days, and indeed 2 hours a day for a month would be well spent.
> The lower part of the Louvre is destined to the statuary and a gallery 600 yards long to the Pictures.

However, Benjamin Haydon thought it was too long and had 'too much the look as if one was looking in at the wrong end of a spy glass.'

The Arc de Triomphe was still being built and was adorned by the bronze horses looted in Venice. Tom was fortunate in seeing Paris when he did, for a year later the Austrians removed the horses and took away the lions looted from St Mark's, much to the fury of the French. The stolen paintings and sculpture in the Louvre were likewise being returned to their owners.

Tom does not tell us whom he heard at the Opéra, but Madame Grassini was then appearing there – and was enjoying the attentions of the Duke of Wellington, much to the delight of the gossip mongers. In the theatre the English were having their first opportunity of seeing Talma and Madame George, who for many years had been rivals in grand tragic roles. Tom would have noticed how French audiences differed from those in England, such as the one in Plymouth. The silent attention of French audiences compared with the noisy behaviour of London audiences impressed another visitor at the time. Badcock, who went to two or three theatres, considered 'the Performances and Scenery good, but the Houses not near so fine as those in London or at all brilliantly attended'. The audiences certainly did not come up to English standards – they had no style, they did not dress up and spat on the floor!

Badcock complained that there was no society at that time, but that was not to say that Paris was dull. On the contrary, the boulevards were thronged with people whose only aim in life seemed to be the pursuit of pleasure. To the English upper classes they looked an unprepossessing lot. The dandified Captain Gronow certainly disapproved of their dress:

> The ladies wore very scanty and short skirts, which left little or no waist; their bonnets were of exaggerated proportions, and protruded

157

at least a foot from their faces; and they generally carried a fan! The men wore blue or black coats, which were baggily made, and reached down to their ankles; their hats were enormously large, and spread out at the top.

Amid the throngs of pleasure seekers the Russian Emperor's cossacks were still patrolling the streets, a reminder to Tom of the verse he had copied in his diary.

On Sunday 26th Tom and Badcock both watched the King review his troops in front of his palace. The fat, good-natured old King in his blue coat and cocked hat was so crippled by gout that he could barely walk. Badcock thought 'the troops were in good order, particularly the cavalry and there was a good deal of "Vive le Roi"'. His final comment on Paris was 'I do not think the English are much liked in Paris, and less here than in any other part of France.'

After a further visit to the Louvre, more sightseeing, and second night at the Opéra, Tom returned to his regiment having 'breakfasted en Prince'. He found the regiment at Etampes, which he had passed through on his way to Paris. Here he found his barrister brother, George, who had come out from England to meet him. 'Din'd en cochon and should have ceased to exist had I not found George to meet me.' However disparaging English visitors may have been about Paris, it was exciting and had fired Tom's imagination. His enthusiasm infected his brother officers, and the following day several of them, including Major Thornhill and Edward, set off to Paris. On the last day of June the squadrons marched separately to Montfort, but Tom's squadron was sent to Les Menules on the northern edge of the Forest of Rambouillet. Here Tom, George, Robbins, Peters and Moffit spent the night in the chateau which lies within a large estate.

The Hussar Brigade had now been on the march for just over four weeks and had covered three quarters of the distance from Toulouse to Boulogne.

Journal

Wed Jun 1st   *March'd to a small village between Grisolles & Montauban on the right – put up somewhat a l'Espagnole*

Thur 2nd   *The Grand Movement commenced – The Hussar Brigade right in front march'd into Montauban –*

Fri 3rd	*Brigade march'd in the morning to Causade: I remain'd behind to meet Edward. The Heavy Brigade march'd in*
Sat 4th	*Brigade march'd to Cahors, Edward & I set out at 10 O'Clock en Voiture, and arrived at Cahors about 7 –*

Halt

Sun 5th	*Watering Order at 10, Parade for Divine Service 7th & 10th Hussars at 3. 15th March'd to some village in front –*
Mon 6th	*Brigade March'd to Fresinet – Edward & myself set out at 10 O'Clock en voiture – breakfasted at Fresinet with Woodhouse of the 15th and arrived at Brives at 12 at night –*
Tue 7th	*Spent the Day very stupidly – raining hard. Shirly arrived in the evening. Din'd together. A dirty old Town with a cotton manufactury –*
Wed 8th	*The Brigade march'd in – Seventh order'd forward to the Village of Malmort about $^1/_2$ a league from Brive – Edward went on with us –*
Thu 9th	*To Maria*
	Halt – Moffit took Edward in hand and physic'd him – A beautiful Country, but a miserable village –
Fri 10th	*March'd to Uzerche, where we had scarcely begun billetting off when we were ordered forward to some little place on the road –*
Sat 11th	*March'd to Pierre Buffiere. The Left Squadron order'd to Bivouaque but afterwards put up with Verners, two leagues further on*
Sun 12th	*March'd into Limoges, where Edward & I got a capital Billet – It being a Jour de Fête, we din'd with our Hosts and afterwards went to see the Procession –*

Mon 13th	Inspection of Horses. Breakfasted with our Hosts. Bath'd, Din'd with them and afterwards walk'd out to see the Porcelain manufactury, the Bishop's Gardens &c
Tue 14th	March'd to Bessines – The Seventh put up in miserable Villages, as bad as Spain. After much trouble in getting any Quarters slept in the Stable over some Cows –
Wed 15th	Turn'd out at $\frac{1}{2}$ past 2 – Hussar Brigade form'd in the high road before 5. March'd to St Benoit. All the three Regiments in Bivouaque –
Thu 16th	March'd to Argenton a tolerable good town – Bath'd in the Creuse. Edward & I Din'd with Lord Edward Somerset.
Fri 17th	March'd to Chateauroux – Met a beautiful Squadron of Dragons de la Garde on the Road; Din'd at the Mess
Sat 18th	Halt. – Inspection of Horses at 9 A M. Din'd with General Fane. Play'd whist till late at night
Sun 19th	March'd to Vatan. John went forward for Billets – My Troop about a league out of the Town; Edward & I at a Chateau –
Mon 20th	March'd to Vinzon. Most of the Troops in Bivouaque. Din'd with General Fane
Tue 21st	March'd to Salbris – The 7th sent ? leagues further – General & Staff came on also, ask'd to play there in the evening –
Wed 22nd	March'd to Laferte St Aubin – All the Generals went on to Orleans. Wilkinson & I Din'd with the Staff
Thu 23rd	March'd into Orleans singing in the rain – Met Barwell and started with him for Paris, slept at Longjumeau
Fri 24th	To Maria
	Arrived in Paris at 9 A M, took Appartements at the Hotel de Wagram, and began to Levé

160

Sat 25th	*Le Palais des Tuileries Le Louvre L'Opera Italien &c &c &c*
Sun 26th	*Le Revue des Troupes par le Roi; La Galerie de Luxembourg &c &c &c &c &c &c &c &c &c L'Opera au Soir –*
Mon 27th	*Le Louvre &c &c &c &c & Notre Dame &c &c &c Le Loge a L'Opera*
Tue 28th	*Breakfasted en Prince – Left Paris, return'd to the Regiment at Etampes. Din'd en cochon, and should have ceas'd to exist had I not found George there to meet me*
Wed 29th	*March'd to St Arnauld [? St-Arnoux]. The Regiment all separate several Officers set off for Paris in the Morning*
Thu 30th	*March'd to Montfort – my Squadron detach'd to Les Menusles – Robbins Peters, Moffit George & myself in the Chateau –*

July–August 1814

The Hussar Brigade arrived at Mantes-La-Jolie on 1 July, the day appointed by the route issued on 30 May, a distance of over 400 miles. This was no mean achievement, but one feels that the credit for this logistical exercise was largely due to the French, who organised the route and made the arrangements for accommodation and rations. They were as anxious to get rid of their unwelcome guests as the latter were to get home!

Tom only stopped long enough in Mantes to give his men breakfast and to receive the route for the final stage of their march to Boulogne. His troop was then ordered to cross the Seine and go to St-Cyr about ten miles further on. Here Tom and George were put up in the attractive little chateau with an entrance in the centre of the village with a farm close by. It was, and still is, approached by an avenue of trees leading to a courtyard in front of the house.

Leaving St-Cyr early on Sunday 3 July they reached Gisors, twenty-five miles away by breakfast time. On their way they passed through Aincourt which Tom came to know in later years. The small chateau there was later acquired by Charles Tennyson d'Aincourt, the uncle of Alfred Lord Tennyson. He and Tom met a few years after the war and became close friends. Charles Tennyson d'Aincourt was a radical and for many years represented Lambeth in Parliament. Nicknamed the 'Lambeth Spouter', he was later called 'The Father of Reform' and, no doubt, influenced Tom's own radical views. The reference to Monsieur Nugent, whom Tom appears to have met at St-Cyr, is intriguing, for the 2nd Baron Nugent played an important part in d'Aincourt's later life.

The pace of the march had now quickened, for there were no more halts until they reached Abbeville. At Gournay the 7th and 10th Hussars resumed their custom of dining together where possible. A row must have occurred at the inn, for Tom relates that 'O'Grady licked the landlord'. On the face of it Lieutenant Standish O'Grady might appear to have been a rather unruly young man, for it was he who got into trouble the previous January for commandeering three mules for the conveyance of baggage contrary to orders. The unfortunate owner had turned up at army headquarters in St-Jean-de-Luz with two of them 'in a most miserable condition', the other one having died on the road. However, his great friend William Verner later recalled, 'I never knew him say an illnatured thing of anybody, and I never knew him do an unkind one.' So maybe the landlord deserved what he got.

Three days later the brigade arrived in Abbeville. Tom describes it as a 'Capital Town'. They all dined at the Hôtel de l'Europe, where the champagne was also 'capital'. (At this period champagne would have cost them about a shilling a bottle!) Tom's opinion of Abbeville was very different from that of Arthur Young who, when he passed through in 1787, described it as 'old and disagreeably built with many of the houses made of wood'. Maybe the town had achieved a measure of prosperity when the Grande Armée was encamped along the north coast of France between 1803 and 1805 while Napoleon was awaiting an opportunity to invade England.

The final three days' march to Boulogne was uneventful, save that George was thrown by Tom's bay horse. This was probably a six-year-old bay mare named Miranda, purchased in London in July 1813. She was the only horse that would remain with him throughout her life, dying at Newstead in 1834, aged twenty-nine years. Two days after their arrival in Boulogne, Pipon's squadron went on board a large brig. Owing to her size, she could only tie up at the jetty at high water. Two more days elapsed before high tide coincided with a favourable wind, enabling the brig to put to sea.

While waiting, Tom bought a five-year-old grey mare named Adèle from Captain Bradshaw of the 5th Dragoon Guards. At 14.3 hands she was a remarkably small animal for anyone in the heavy cavalry, whose chargers were over fifteen hands. Bradshaw had probably acquired her for hacking, but she was an ideal size for Tom, who gave her to John that October.

Sailing at 9 a.m. on 15 July they made Dover in five hours. With a westerly wind they scudded across on a broad reach, but were unable to enter Dover harbour. With so many ships bringing troops home, they could not berth until 8 p.m. Tom spent the night ashore almost certainly at Weight's celebrated house The Ship, where two years later he met Byron for the last time.

As soon as it was light, the troops disembarked and at 5 a.m. marched off to Canterbury. Here Tom left his troop and rode over to Chilham Castle to visit his Uncle James and his cousins. The village of Chilham lies about five or six miles along the road from Canterbury to Ashford. The entrance to the castle is in the little village square. The castle, said to have been designed by Inigo Jones, was built in 1616. Built round four sides of a hexagon, it is a rather inconvenient building, though impressive from the outside. Uncle James purchased the castle in 1794 and filled it with furniture and pictures calculated to give the house the impression of ancestral tradition. Fortunately for him there were plenty of works of art coming onto the market as a result of the French Revolution. Unfortunately not all of them were genuine, but Uncle James was not to know about that.

Despite their wealth, the Wildmans led a fairly quiet life at Chilham, with occasional trips to Bath to take the waters. Cousin James was a year younger than Tom and had been educated at Winchester. On leaving school, he joined his cousin at Christ Church, Oxford. They remained on friendly, if not on intimate, terms throughout their lives. Three years after this visit Tom presented his cousin with a horse whose name, incidentally, was Miss Peggy. James had no particular interest in military matters, but they were both to become absorbed in the restoration and improvement of their properties. They had a common interest in their Jamaican estates. There is no evidence that Tom ever visited his plantations, but his cousin went out there on a number of occasions. In character Cousin James was rather different. He was a friend of William Wilberforce and favoured emancipation of the slaves.* Robert Raikes, the founder of the Sunday Schools movement, was a friend of the family and had a profound influence on Cousin James who was drawn to the Evangelical movement and later set up a school on his estate where he taught for forty years. So far as women were concerned he seems to have been rather a prig.

A few years later Fanny Knight, the daughter of the Wildmans' neighbour Edward Knight, lent him her Aunt Jane's books to read. He evidently did not care for less-than-perfect heroines, for he wished to 'think well of all young ladies'. Jane Austen knew the Wildman family quite well, meeting them when visiting her brother Edward at Godmersham Park. She had dined at Chilham in November 1813 and left this vignette of the family at home:

We met only the Brittons at Chilham Castle, besides a Mr. and Mrs. Osborn and a Miss Lee staying in the house, and were only 14 together. My brother and Fanny thought it the pleasantest party they had ever known there and I was very well entertained by bits and scraps – I had long wanted to see Dr. Britton, and his wife amuses me

---

* In 1818 he entered Parliament as the Member for Colchester, holding the seat until 1826.

very much with her affected refinement and elegance – Miss Lee I found very conversible; she admires Crabbe as she ought – she is at an age of reason, ten years older than myself at least. She was at the famous ball at Chilham, so of course you remember her. Bye the bye I must leave off being young, I find many Douceurs in being a sort of Chaperone for I am put on the sofa by the fire and can drink as much wine as I like. We had music in the Evening, Fanny and Miss Wildman played, and Mr. James Wildman sat close by and listened or pretended to listen.

On the Sunday morning Tom accompanied the family to the little church on the other side of the village square, and after staying for dinner, which would have been at about four o'clock, he rejoined the regiment at Faversham. The next morning they marched to Rochester where they were put up at the new barracks. They were ordered to halt here for a day. The officers held their mess first at the Crown and then at the Bull. They reached Gravesend on 20 July where they received a new route to Romford. The troops had to be ferried across the Thames to Tilbury, where they resumed their march to Romford, some ten to twelve miles away. Getting all the horses on board the ferries and disembarking them on the other side would have been a slow business. The three Wildman brothers therefore took the opportunity to ride to Turnham Green to see their mother.

They rode through Dartford along the Old Kent Road, skirted Greenwich and crossed Deptford Common, before continuing through open country as far as Bermondsey, where they turned into the New Kent Road and found themselves coming into the London suburbs. The area between Dartford was

> poor, and the surface ugly by nature, to which ugliness there has been made, just before we came to the latter place, a considerable addition by the inclosure of a common, and by the sticking up of some shabby-genteel houses, surrounded with dead fences and things called gardens, in all manner of ridiculous forms, making, all together, the bricks, hurdle-rods and earth say, as plainly as they can speak, 'Here dwell <u>vanity</u> and <u>poverty</u>'.

Crossing the river at Westminster, they probably reached Turnham Green in a little more than three hours. Mrs Wildman could not have seen her sons for very long, for they arrived in Romford soon after the troops and in time for dinner in the mess. To achieve this within that time they would have changed horses at Turnham Green, where Tom had about ten horses of his own in the stables.

The barracks at Romford had been built in 1795; the buildings, constructed of wood, were situated on the London road. They were intended to accommodate six troops of cavalry, but as the whole regiment, including the Headquarters Squadron under Major Hodge, appears to have been quartered there, more buildings must have been added in the course of time. They were demolished in about 1825. With his arrival in Romford, Tom's diary begins to peter out. For the next ten days there are no entries. Having spent a year abroad in conditions that had taken a heavy toll of arms and equipment, not to mention the horses, the regiment had to be re-equipped. Obviously it took longer than a week to replace uniforms. Their shakos had not even been replaced by the time they were ordered abroad again when the war was renewed the following year, and they reverted to their fur caps.

The next entry in the diary, on Sunday 21 July – 'din'd at Mrs P' – introduces the mystery of Tom's marriage, which even aroused the curiosity of his contemporaries and has never been solved. In 1816 he married a Swiss girl, Louisa Preisig, daughter of F. Preisig of Appenzell in Switzerland. She had a sister, Caroline, who came to live with them at Newstead Abbey, but otherwise nothing is known of her family. She was only fourteen years old at the date of her marriage; according to the census returns she was born in London in 1802. Possibly her parents came to England during the Peace of Amiens. There is no record of her father among the officers of the Kings German Legion, nor in the Commissaries Department.

Under canon law a girl could marry at the age of twelve, but this was most unusual at that period. Lady Elizabeth Spencer-Stanhope, who visited Newstead in 1851, recalled:

Mrs Wildman sang extremely well in the evening, evidently quite professionally. I was amused when looking at a miniature painting of her when very young, she said 'That was painted of me at 17 when I had been a wife of two years'.

Both ladies evidently regarded fifteen as unusually young for marriage, let alone fourteen. An earlier visitor to Newstead in the 1820s remarked:

Colonel Wildman was a West Indian and very rich. He had made one

166

of those queer marriages some queer men make – educated a child for his wife. She turned out neither pretty nor clever, but she satisfied him and was well liked.

She may not have been clever, but the album she kept shows that besides being able to sing well, she could draw and could write verse quite competently in French.

The only other evidence comes from James Beckford Wildman's niece Matilda, who visited Newstead in 1857 and would have had an intimate knowledge of Tom's family. In a note written in her own hand in 1913, she wrote: 'Colonel Wildman, 7th Hussars, became acquainted with Miss Preisig during the war in the Peninsular, she was very young at the time he paid for her education and married her at the close of the war.' In 1813–14 Louisa would have been twelve years old. If he met her in Spain or France, he kept the meeting very quiet, but there is nothing in the diary to suggest such a meeting. Until January 1813 he was in Ireland, so it is possible that he met her there, or during the few months he spent in London before leaving for Spain. If this was the case, one might have expected him to write to her or to her parents, but if he did he was careful not to record the fact.

Returning now to the diary entry, could it be that 'Mrs P' refers to Mrs Preisig? This is the only entry that refers to anyone merely by an initial, which would be consistent with secrecy. If the child had no father and was poor, Mrs Wildman does not seem to have been the sort of woman who would have approved of such a match. If she had, one might have expected her to have undertaken the marriage arrangements and wedding in her parish church in Chiswick, where Maria was married in 1822. There is, however, no record of any such marriage in the parish register. Unfortunately it seems unlikely that the mystery will ever be solved.

Tom could not have had any sleep that night after his visit to 'Mrs P'. Returning to the barracks at 2 a.m., the regiment turned out an hour later. The occasion was the celebration of the Centenary of the Hanoverian succession to the English throne. The 7th Hussars, along with other regiments, had the duty of patrolling the streets during the celebrations. The Prince Regent, throwing open the Royal Parks, had arranged a splendid display. Commissary Schauman, being a loyal Hanoverian, had come up to London to join the festivities – and to settle his accounts with the Treasury before returning home:

At about three o'clock I went to St. James's and Kensington Gardens to look at all the splendid things with which, by the King's command, the Peace Festival was to be celebrated. The preparations were on a grand scale. Everywhere I saw artillery detachments standing ready with large supplies of rockets and other fireworks. There were pagodas, Chinese towers (one of which on the canal bridge in St. James's Park, was exceedingly high), triumphal arches, stars rosettes, globes, illuminated names, and suitable devices formed with coloured Chinese lanterns, such as 'Peace and Plenty', 'Rule Britannia', etc. All trees and avenues were hung with coloured paper Chinese lanterns. On a small lake, either in Kensington Gardens or the Green Park, there were two fleets of miniature men-o'-war, one English and the other French, properly manned and mounted with guns, which were to fight a naval battle; and on the water of St. James's Park there was a regatta of beautiful boats, rowed by sailors in bright-coloured silk jerseys and caps, who were going to have a boat race. To the North of St. James's Park there stood a huge Temple of Peace, which was still concealed from view by a large screen of grey canvas; in front of it there was a battery of fifty guns, and close by an enormous pavilion with boxes and benches, all covered with red cloth, for the King and the nobility, the ambassadors and foreign princes. Row upon row of huts and booths – some offering refreshments, others sheltering brass bands – covered the ground. It was interesting to see the people of London streaming in at all the park gates; 500,000 people are said to have been present ... The moment the naval battle began in the Green Park and the roar of the guns was heard, everybody rushed to the spot; then the regatta started, followed by the fireworks, which lasted a long time. The finest sight of all was to see the so-called Congreve rockets; they were immediately followed by the fifty guns, which fired as rapidly as possible. They fired 500 rounds, making an uproar that almost deafened me, and while they were thus engaged the screen of grey canvas was suddenly lifted and the Temple of Peace was revealed, all glittering with its beautiful illumination of lamps. Water flowed from the jaws of lions into golden basins and on the roof of the temple there stood a detachment of the Foot Guards with the Royal Standard, who gave three loud hurrahs. Then the people began to wander among the tents and booths, and the eating and drinking began. A noteworthy feature of the celebrations was the fact that there was no disorder, no fighting, no pickpockets, and no importunate fast women.

The celebrating continued well into the night, and the hussars must have been kept fully occupied even if the crowds were well behaved. As the evening wore on the crowds, by now somewhat the worse for drink, were becoming harder to control. By 2 a.m. Schauman had had enough and went back to his lodgings in the Strand, but 'the stream of people that poured down the Strand with me was so great that every time I stopped to find the number of the house where I had put up it dragged me along with it'. Not surprisingly, Tom and his men were only able to return to Romford the following evening.

During the next seven days there is a gap in the diary – he was clearly engaged in regimental duties not worth recording. The following week he went to the races and to the theatre and attended a ball. After this he went on leave. Having taken on a manservant and hired a coachman, he and his friend Edward Hodge drove down to Norfolk to stay with the Hodges in Yarmouth. Mrs Hodge was the daughter of Sir Edward Bacon, baronet, of Raveningham Hall, Norwich. A round of parties and excursions followed. On 24 August he returned to Romford, completing the journey in a day. He must have been driving at an average speed of 10 mph, which would have involved hiring post horses.

The diary now comes to an end. After that fleeting visit to his mother on 20 July, he now found time to visit her again, and the last entry on 29 August concludes the diary in a truly English way with a cricket match at Hornchurch.

Journal

Fri Jul 1st   *March'd to Mantes where we stopp'd to Breakfast my Troop at St Cyr, George & myself in a Capital Chateau*

Sat 2nd   *Halt. – Spent the Day very pleasantly with Monsieur de Slade and his Family – Practis'd with Carbines*

Sun 3rd   *March'd thro' Gisors where we Breakfasted; My Squadron, at Eragui and two other Villages – A Jour de Fete; George & I almost kill'd with kindness –*

169

July		*Lieus de Poste*	
	3rd - - - - - - - -	Gisors - - - - - - - - -	6$^{1}/_{2}$
	4th.- - - - - - - -	Gournay - - - - - - -	6
	5th - - - - - - - -	Neufchatel - - - - - -	9
	6th - - - - - - - -	Blangy - - - - - - - -	6$^{1}/_{2}$
	7th - - - - - - - -	Abbeville - - - - - - -	6
	8th - - - - - - - -	Halt	
	9th - - - - - - - -	Rue - - - - - - - - - -	6
	10th - - - - - - -	Montreuil - - - - - -	6
	11th - - - - - - -	Boulogne - - - - - -	9

Le Chateau de Menusles, Madame de Camie; – L'Addresse de Monsieur Nugent
Rue de Faubourg St Honore
Madame Risler   N 94 a Paris
Rue Chanchat No. G   5 or 9
Monsieur de Slade
en son Chateau, a St Cyr pres de Mantes

Mon 4th	March'd to Gournay – Tenth & Seventh Din'd together as usual. O'Grady lick'd the Landlord. Major Thornhill & Edward return'd from Paris
Tue 5th	March'd to a small village on the right of the High Road – George & John went to Neufchatel – Moffit Gordon & I together Moffit slept in the Chateau –
Wed 6th	Pass's thro' Neufchatel at 5 AM – March'd to Blangy, where we foraged and then proceded to a Village 2 leagues further – 10th at Blangy –
Thu 7th	March'd to Abbeville a Capital Town, Tenth & Seventh Din'd together, a very large Party as usual
Fri 8th	Halt – Breakfasted at the Hotel de l'Europe. Bath'd & din'd together as usual – Capital Champagne

Sat 9th	*March'd to Rue & Adjacent villages – Nothing Extraordinary*
Sun 10th	*March'd thro Montreuil a beautifully situated and fortified Town – Breakfasted there & put up in villages in front – George got upset by the Bay Horse*
Mon 11th	*My Squadron 3 leagues from the Road – a long March; Began to pour with rain just as the Brigade Assembled – March'd to Boulogne – I was Captain of the Day*
Tue 12th	*Selection of Horses for the King – My Troop in a village 3 miles off. Some of the right Troops embark'd. Some talk of bringing mine into Town*
Wed 13th	*Embark'd the Squadron at 4 O'Clock – Some small vessels sail'd at high water. Mine being a large Brig could not move; went on shore, came back for the evening tide Bought a Grey Mare of Captain Bradshaw of the 5th D. G. – and got her embark'd –*
Thu 14th	*Went on board by 6 O'Clock, no chance of sailing, return'd on shore. Din'd and went on board for the Evening Tide with as little success –*
Fri 15th	*Went on board at 7, and sail'd about nine – Beautiful Passage, made Dover in 5 hours, but could not get in – I went on shore in a boat – the Ship got into Harbour about 8 at night –*
Sat 16th	*Disembark'd the Troops at Day Break & March'd off at 5 AM – to Canterbury. Rode over to Chilham Castle*
Sun 17th	*<u>Went to Church</u>, Din'd at Chilham and rode over in the Evening to Faversham –*
Mon 18th	*March'd to Rochester where we found an Order to Halt the 19th. Din'd together at the Crown –*
Tue 19th	*Halt – Walk'd about the new Barracks &c &c Din'd together at the Bull*

Wed 20th	*March'd to Gravesend, where we found a fresh Rout for Romford. All 3 went to Turnham Green*
Thu 21st	*Went to Romford, arrived there soon after the Troops – and Din'd together at the Mess –*
Sun 31st	*Din'd at Mrs P*
Mon 1st Aug	*Arriv'd at Romford at 2 A M – Turn'd out at 3 – March'd to London at first in Southwark &c Afterwards in Finsbury Square, Russell Square &c Grand Fete – Fireworks &c &c in the Parks –*
Tue 2nd	*March'd back to Romford at 6 O'Clock in the evening*
Mon 8th	*Went down to Romford with Major Thornhill & O'Hagerty*
Tue 9th	*Set out with Majors Hodge & Thornhill to Chelmsford Races – Din'd at the Ordinary & went to the Play –*
Wed 10th	*Rainy morning – Went to the Course – Din'd at the Ordinary – Went to the Play & Ball*
Thu 11th	*Return'd to Romford*
Sat 13th	*Engaged Smith – Hir'd a Coachman*
Sun 14th	*Started with Major Hodge for Yarmouth – Slept at Saxmundham*
Mon 15th	*Arrived at Yarmouth Din'd with Mrs Hodge*
Tue 16th	*Races – Rain'd hard – Din'd at the Ordinary Ball in the Evening*
Wed 17th	*Races – Good Weather – Din'd at the Ordinary Ball at night –*

172

Thu 18th   *Public Breakfast*
Din'd with Mrs Hodge
Play in the Evening

Fri 19th   *Boat Races &c &c*
Din'd with Captain Beauchamp
Call'd on Mrs Bagwell

Sat 20th   *Went over to Raveningham Park*
Sir Edward Bacon's

Sun 21st   *Major H drove me over to Langley Park – Went to Church A large Party Din'd at Raveningham*

Mon 22nd   *A large Water Party at Langley – Din'd in the Boat House Return'd To Raveningham at night*

Tue 23rd   *Went to Bungay, Beccles & to call on Captain & Mrs Beauchamp at Broom. Din'd at Raveningham*

Wed 24th   *Set out on our Return to Romford at 8 A M, and arriv'd at the Barracks $^{1}/_{4}$ before 8 P M the same Evening –*

Fri 26th   *Went home to Dinner*

Sat 27th   *Return'd to Romford*

Sun 28th   *Rode Home to Dinner & back to Romford at night*

Mon 29th   *Cricket Match near Hornchurch*

EPILOGUE

Waterloo

When hostilities were resumed after Napoleon's escape from Elba on 1 March 1815, Tom once more found himself on active service. Unfortunately he did not keep a daily record of the Waterloo campaign, but he has left a description of the battle in a letter he wrote to his mother on the following day, 19 June. Elation is mingled with the shock caused by the terrible scenes of carnage he had witnessed. Although he says he will not spare his mother's feelings, he says little about the part he and his brothers played in the battle, and one must look elsewhere to try and find out what they were doing that day.

At the beginning of the year the 7th Hussars were stationed at Brighton. Here their duties brought them into contact with the Prince Regent's court at the Pavillion. With the world of fashion cutting a dash along the promenade, visits to the theatre, invitations to balls and with London only half a day's journey away, this was a most desirable posting. However, during that winter the regiment was ordered up to London to help control civil unrest, which had been stirred up by the introduction of the Corn Law Bill to restrict the import of foreign corn. They set up their mess at the British Hotel in Cockspur Street, but as soon as the news of Napoleon's return to France came through the unrest ceased immediately. The regiment returned to Brighton, but within a few weeks they were on the move again.

When preparations began for sending an army back to the Continent, the delicate problem of choosing a commander for the cavalry came up for consideration. Lord Paget, who was now the Earl of Uxbridge, had been unemployed since 1809. His maxim for a cavalry leader was that he should inspire his men as early as possible with the most perfect confidence in his personal gallantry: 'Let him but lead, they are sure to follow, and I believe hardly anything will stop them.' This attitude did not appeal to Wellington, who preferred Sir Stapleton Cotton (now Lord Combermere), whom he considered sound but mediocre and who could be trusted to obey orders without question. He would have chosen Lord Combermere, but the Commander-in-Chief, the Duke of York, and Lord Uxbridge's friend, the Prince Regent, thought otherwise, and Uxbridge was given the command on 15 April.

The Earl lost no time in selecting his staff, and he turned to his own regiment whose officers were all known to him personally. So 'old' Thornhill, who had been appointed lieutenant colonel on 8 April, Captains Seymour, Fraser and Wildman, and Captain Steerwitz of the 2nd Hussars (King's German Legion) were appointed to be his aides-de-camp. Within a week they sailed to Ostend along with another small ship 'appointed exclusively for the conveyance of the horses belonging to His Lordship and staff' – in number forty – arriving on 25 April.

Shortly afterwards the 7th Hussars followed and set off on the four-day march to Dover where the men and horses were put on board the transports immediately. A storm blew up and the transports could not put out to sea, so the officers remained on shore at the Ship Inn. After one unsuccessful attempt to set sail, the storm abated and ten days later they were able to leave harbour. Arriving in Ostend, they marched to the Plains of Grammont where the cavalry were quartered along the line of the River Delder. Lord Uxbridge had set up his headquarters at Ninove, and three times a week he assembled the whole of the cavalry on the plain for exercise.

The British and Dutch–Belgian forces lay west and north of the road from Charleroi to Brussels, while Field-Marshal Blucher and his Prussians were encamped to the east of this road with his headquarters in Namur. On 7 May, Colonel Vivian, who was still in command of his old brigade, joined Lord Uxbridge on a visit to the forward area of the army. Tom and Captain Steerwitz went along too in the General's carriage. They travelled as far as Tournai, where they dined and walked round the fortifications, spending the night at an inn called Le Singe d'Or – 'a very tolerable one' in Vivian's opinion.

On 29 May there was a splendid review of the fifteen British cavalry regiments, followed by a dinner attended by Wellington, Blucher and all the commanding officers. It seems unlikely that the aides-de-camp would have found themselves left out!

Standish O'Grady and William Verner soon afterwards got leave to stay with the Duke and Duchess of Richmond, who were now residing in Brussels. Verner had served on the Duke's staff when the 7th were in Ireland and the Duke had been Lord Lieutenant. On leaving Brussels the Duchess handed Verner the invitations for her famous ball to distribute among the British cavalry officers.

The French, meanwhile, were moving up towards the Belgian frontier. Napoleon, reckoning that the British would not risk their lines of communication with the Channel ports, planned to strike first at the Prussians. Tom can now take up the story in his letter to Mrs Wildman.

178

June 19th 1815

My dearest Mother will I trust have received the hasty note I wrote by Lord Uxbridge's bedside last night, merely to say that all her three sons are safe and well after the most tremendous battle that ever yet was fought.

The Affair of yesterday was however complete and decisive and we may truly say of the Force opposed to us 'L'Armée Francoise n'existe plus'!!! ... I will now send you an account of a victory so splended and important that you may search the annals of history in vain for the parallel. Nor is it only extraordinary in the effect it must produce upon the present state of Europe and the blow it has given to all Napoleon's expectations, but as a grand military affair it will probably for ever stand unrivalled and alone.

And, you are, my dearest Mother, an instance of very few indeed, who may enjoy the whole Pride and Glory of the Day without a cloud to darken or diminish the Splendour. But, one only serious misfortune prevents me from saying that it was the proudest happiest day I ever knew – but the loss the British Army will sustain in the services of Lord Uxbridge must be felt by all and you may conceive how much more strongly by me, who always admired and looked up to him as an Officer and have lately learned to respect, esteem and love him as a man. His conduct the whole day beggars all description. His arrangement, firmness and intrepidity surpassed what had been expected of him, and not in Cavalry movements and attacks only, but he frequently rendered the most judicious and timely assistance in affairs of Infantry when any sudden danger was to be apprehended. The Field was literally three times lost and won. The fate of the battle seemed to hang upon a thread, both parties being well aware that defeat and destruction were almost synonymous, there being but one road to retreat and that, of course, blocked up with baggage, ammunition, wounded etc.

The French fought to desperation, charging frequently to the very mouths of our cannon – three times they forced their way, both Cavalry and infantry, into our position and were three times repulsed with immense slaughter by sword and bayonet alone. They commenced the attack about 11 o'clock and the battle lasted without intermission till past 9 at night. It was no action of manoeuvre, of turning a flank etc. The whole was sheer fighting and almost hand to hand.

179

Buonaparte commanded in person and had animated his troops by going down the ranks of the different Corps and addressing them during the morning. He headed the last attack in person, placing himself in front of his Imperial Guard and leading up to the very mouth of our guns. They did him ample justice and I firmly believe that, under any other man but the Duke of Wellington, even British valour would have been unavailing. It was 'Vaincre ou Mourir' on both sides and Wellington and England prevailed.

When the advantage was once gained, Vittoria was nothing to it. They fled in such disorder that all their cannon, ammunition, baggage and even Buonaparte's carriage, plate etc. fell into our hands and, it is said, he had himself a narrow escape. Jerome Buonaparte and Murat are reported to be killed and Bertrand to have lost his thigh. I am sorry to say we must set against these, Sir Thomas Picton and Sir William Ponsonby killed and our noble General's right leg amputated; – far more valuable characters.

But I will commence my despatch regularly and shall not attempt to soften down for you, as I do not expect that I shall have many more battles to record.

It was always expected that the first affair would be desperate and sanguinary:– The French have done their worst and if there should be more fighting, I do not think he would ever get them to stand again in the same manner.

Bounaparte had 160,000 men in the field, including 22,000 cavalry. The Duke of Wellington about 67,000 of which 30,000 only were British and Bulow's Prussian Corps, of about 40,000 on our left, which did not get into action until very late in the evening.

On Thursday the 15th, we rode over from Ninove to Brussels to a ball at the Duchess of Richmond's and were just dressed when news arrived that the Prussians had been attacked in the morning, their outposts driven in and that the enemy had occupied the frontier town of Binch. We went to the ball, where the Duke of Wellington and Lord Uxbridge had a long conversation, after which we mounted and rode back to Ninove. From thence orders were sent to assemble the whole of the cavalry and Royal Horse Artillery near Enghien. There I met Lord Uxbridge, who immediately sent me on to Brain-le-Comte and, not finding the Duke there, I proceeded to Nivelles. It was then about four 0'clock and I heard a considerable firing in front, to which point I made accordingly, and found Belgian and Dutch troops engaged in a village called Quatre Bras about five miles on the road to Namur.

Two English Divisions had been sent for and I was immediately despatched again to bring up all the cavalry and another British Division from Braine-le-Comte. There I met Lord Uxbridge and returned with him to the scene of action which was beginning to get very warm. Our infantry had arrived and the action lasted till dark, when the French were repulsed at all points and retired, leaving us master of the field. This affair was obstinately contested and the Lanciers charged our solid squares of infantry several times and, when repulsed with loss by one, wheeled about and attacked another. The Guards suffered considerably and the Highlanders received a charge of the Cuirassiers – repulsed them and destroyed the whole squadron. Our Cavalry did not arrive till after the action was over which was not until 10 o'clock at night, except for Sir John O. Vandeleur's Brigade of Light Dragoons with which Lord Uxbridge showed a front and kept the enemy's Cavalry in check. In this affair, the gallant Duke of Brunswick was killed by a grape shot, in whom the Army has sustained a severe loss. They made some show of attack about 3 a.m. on the 17th, which is soon after day-break, but again all was quiet till 11 when the Duke of Wellington received intelligence that the Prussians had repulsed the attack made upon them the day before, but that during the night, the enemy had made a dash upon their centre with a large Division of Cavalry and taken or destroyed an immense number and 24 pieces of cannon. In consequence of which Marshal Blucher found it expedient to retire. This of course rendered the same movement necessary on our part, in order to form the junction and act in concert with the Prussians. All our Cavalry had come up during the night and when the arrangement was made to retire, the cavalry were ordered to cover the retreat. This movement commenced about 2 p.m. with the infantry and artillery and lastly the Cavalry moving off towards the left, so that the 7th being the right regiment covered the whole. When the infantry were all gone, the French began to move and soon after advanced with an immense column of Cavalry – the Lancers and Cuirassiers in front – three regiments of each. We skirmished with them till we had passed the village of Genappe, when they advanced so strong that it was thought necessary to charge them. This fell to the 7th and Major Hodge moved down with his squadron supported by the two others. The Lanciers were however so wedged in the street of Genappe and, with so large a column in their rear, that they were obliged to stand at all events and our squadron not making any impression was repulsed. When we retired, they pursued. Some men were killed and wounded. Major Hodge, Elphinstone and Myers were made prisoners. John Wildman and Peters were also taken and stripped of their pelisses belts money etc. Just at that moment the 1st Life Guards made a most gallant charge and drove the Lanciers in confusion in which time the two young gents caught a couple of spare French horses and made their escape. Elphinstone got away last night and has arrived here and Lord Uxbridge sent to the enemy's advanced post to enquire about the Major and Myers (whom report had good naturedly killed) and was informed that they were both prisoners, the Major slightly and Myers severely wounded but both doing well. I have no doubt but that both will be exchanged very shortly.

We manoeuvred and cannonaded with this cavalry all the way to our position in front of Waterloo and at about dark, they retired. I sent John, who was bruised by his horse falling, to Brussels, by which he missed being in the action yesterday but is now perfectly well and gone this morning to join the remains of the 7th in front ...

Pausing here, William Verner has left an account of the 7th Hussars at Genappe which amplifies Tom's description of this action:

We had proceeded a short way when we observed the French cavalry coming on. They commenced skirmishing and Major Hodge's Squadron was ordered to oppose them. We had to pass through the Village of Genappe, which we did at a good pace followed by the enemy's Cavalry. When we had cleared the town we halted and fronted; by this time the cavalry were close upon us. The Road, or Causeway upon which we were was elevated above the ground on both sides, which prevented the possibility of getting into the Fields on either side, except where a passage had been made for Carts. The enemy's cavalry formed a dense body, extending into the town of Genappe, and how much further we could not tell. About this time there came a tremendous storm of lightning and rain. The road was one mass of liquid mud and when we were halted and fronted, the men were so covered with mud that it was utterly impossible to distinguish a feature in their faces or the colour of the lace on the dress. The French Cavalry had a great advantage over ours. They had Lancers, which were at that time unknown in our army, and which they placed in the front rank in a line with the other men; they kept poking at us with their lances, and our men were unable to reach them with their sabres.

About this time Lord Uxbridge rode up and placed himself upon a rising on the left of the Regiment, as it faced Genappe. As Commander of the Cavalry the command then devolved upon him. A parley then took place in the hearing of the men, as to the propriety of charging, and a difference of opinion was expressed upon the subject, as it is always to be regretted when such conversations take place within the hearing of the men. My belief is that the order to charge was given, but we might as well have charged a house, as the front of the enemy's line presenting a Cheveux de Frise of lances supported by a body consisting of some thousands of mounted Cavalry.

In this dilemma we were ordered to file off into the field. Captain Fraser with a troop of my Squadron was ordered to skirmish in addition to the Right Squadron commanded by Major Hodge. After a short time we were informed that Major Hodge and the Adjutant were killed and others of the officers wounded and taken prisoners, amongst them Captain Elphinstone who was taken prisoner, and Mr Peters who was dragged a length of way by his Pouch Belt, but escaped and joined the Regiment. Captain Fraser came in to report to me that unless some Infantry were sent to protect our men not one of them would be left alive, as the enemy's Skirmishers were coming forward each man having a sharpshooter on the horse behind him, who got off, took deliberate aim, and when he was pursued jumped upon the horse, cantered away, and had any of our men attempted to follow them, they must have rode into the Enemy's lines. I told Captain Fraser that it was not possible for me to render him any assistance. I could not leave my position to go in search of Infantry, and if every man was destroyed I could not Prevent it.

At this moment, seeing the dangerous position the Regiment was placed, a party of Life Guards was ordered to advance who charged along the road and drove the Enemy back into the town of Genappe, and two guns being placed upon the rising ground in our rear, and the remains of the Regiment was withdrawn and no further attack was made that afternoon. My Squadron suffered considerably being reduced nearly one half.

The 7th, having rejoined the army, spent the night before the battle on the forward slope of the ridge of Mont St Jean, which formed the British front line. 'There we remained all night,' wrote William Verner, 'the horses up to their knees in mud and the rain pouring and raining into our boots.' Wellington had retired to his headquarters in the village of Waterloo. Here Lord Uxbridge joined him, so Tom did at least have a roof over his head in one of the little whitewashed houses in the village.

Tom's letter continues:

> *... Yesterday morning the 18th, all appeared quiet till about 11 when the enemy was perceived advancing in full force.*
>
> *Buonaparte had reconnoitred our position himself and harangued his troops telling them that in spite of 'ce Villaintonet cet orange' he would be in Brussels by night. You may imagine the spirit and confidence he felt when such a person would condescend to a pun.*
>
> *General Count Cambron, who commanded his Guard in Elba (one of the new peers) and his own personal orderly officer are among our prisoners and they gave the account to Sir Neil Campbell, their old acquaintance, who told me of it.*
>
> *His plan was to force the centre of our position and so cut off the communication between our Army and the Prussians, thus (as the Brussels Gazette expresses it) 'to carry out one of those decisive blows which have made his military reputation'. Our Armies were in position – the British in front of Waterloo – the right towards Braine and the left towards Wavre, where General Bulow's corps was posted which lately arrived from Liege – Marshal Prince Blucher being at Geniblowx. A Cannonade commenced about 11 and the French fought hard to carry a small village and wood on our right, but failed. About half past 12, the action became general ...*

William Verner now provides a glimpse of Tom in this opening stage of the battle.

At the commencement of the action we were mostly exposed to the fire of artillery, consisting chiefly of shots which were aimed at Troops in front of us, but from their being directed too high, many passed over us, or fell amongst us. A battalion of the Coldstream Guards was on our left in close column, sitting down, as also a Troop of Artillery on our right drew upon us a heavy fire of Artillery; in addition to which the Duke, passing backwards and forwards upon elevated ground in our front, with an immense Staff, attracted the notice of the Enemy. A heavy fire was directed upon him and his staff, so much so, that whenever his party came in a line with us the shots which were directed at him poured upon us in quick succession.

Captain Wildman belonging to the Regiment was serving on the Staff of Ld. Uxbridge; seeing the danger of our position, he rode up to Colonel Kerrison and said he thought we would be less exposed to the fire by moving a little to the right. This advice was acted upon by the Colonel. I have entertained a strong feeling that where I was placed was the proper place, there I was willing to remain and take my chance as to the result, and so it proved in this instance. We were then formed in half Squadrons at quarter distance – a position which enabled us to form line at any moment.

Hardly had we taken up the new ground, when a shot came, went thro' the Breast of the man beside me, passed thro' the knee of a Sergeant close behind, and broke the leg of a horse in his rear, all of which took place in less time than it takes to write it. The Sergeant was lifted off his horse, and there being no assistance at hand and no means of taking him to the rear, he bled to death. The death of the soldier was instantaneous, the poor horse's sufferings were soon put to an end by shooting him thro' the head. I could not help wishing that Wildman had left us where we were.

Returning now to Tom's letter:

... Our ground was high but open and our infantry was obliged to form squares and receive the charge of French cavalry, who attacked them in the heart of our position. But their firmness and courage were unshaken and everywhere prevailed.

The Life Guards and Blues distinguished themselves particularly and charged and overthrew the French Cuirassiers several times. Our Light Cavalry was frequently engaged with the Lanciers and I believe there was no part of the Army which was not perpetually under fire and, such a terrific fire, as the oldest officers declared they never before experienced.

Three separate times, I believe, all hopes were given over by everyone, except the Duke of Wellington, who only said, 'We will beat them yet, before night'.

Their Cavalry and infantry were in mélee with our people, some of our guns in the midst of them and in our own position but were driven back again with enormous slaughter.

In the preceding paragraphs Tom is clearly describing events as they were reported to him, or of which he only had a hazy recollection. When he spoke to Colonel Kerrison, the 7th Hussars were on the right of the British line behind the ridge above the Chateau of Hougoumont. The next stage of the battle, following the bombardment described by Verner, was the massed infantry attack by General d'Erlon against the left centre of the line. Tramping up to the ridge with drums beating, the massed columns supported by cuirassiers pushed back the Dutch–Belgians and a Hanoverian regiment, who eventually turned tail, leaving the centre dangerously exposed. Seeing the danger, Lord Uxbridge immediately ordered the Household Brigade and the Union Brigade to charge the advancing columns. Unfortunately he failed to ensure that there was a second line in support to meet an eventual counter-attack. Following his own precept he led the charge in person, but as the 'Heavies' crashed through the French and swept down the valley he lost control of them. They almost reached the muzzles of the French guns before they rallied. By now they had lost all formation, and when the French counter-attacked they suffered heavy casualties. One would have expected Uxbridge to have been accompanied by at least one aide-de-camp, and one can only assume that Tom did not take part in what was one of the most spectacular charges ever made by British cavalry; otherwise he would have said so! Nevertheless he would have been continually under fire.

The aide-de-camp's job was to convey the general's orders to the regiments under his command, to locate these units and report their situation. He was continually under fire, galloping from one unit to another, directing where cavalry was needed in support of the infantry. Avoiding French cuirassiers swirling round the British squares, watching out for cannonballs ricocheting and bouncing over the ground whenever the French resumed their bombardment each time their cavalry were repulsed, an aide-de-camp was in constant danger. During this stage of the battle the British infantry had been withdrawn behind the skyline, so apart from seeing the helmets of the cuirassiers as they appeared over the brow of the ridge, there was little to be seen of the enemy. Thornhill wrote later that he had been so occupied with the 'prompt and direct transmission of the orders he had little time to contemplate passing events irrelevant thereto'. During the cavalry attacks the squares were enveloped in smoke which Vivian later described as 'literally so thick we could not see ten yards off'. During the day Tom had at least one horse shot under him – Uxbridge lost eight horses! Being on that general's staff was a dangerous business, as Tom relates later on in his letter.

Resuming Tom's narrative, he now describes what he actually saw:

... Just about sunset, they were preparing a last effort of attack when Lord Uxbridge brought up Sir H. Vivian's Brigade supported by Sir O. Vandeleur's Brigade in a second line. They moved immediately from the front of the position and formed a line on the brow of the hill whence they charged down upon the enemy, taking two squares of infantry and a column of cavalry on their way. Our infantry rushed down also; the Prussians closed in on the left.

General Vandeleur's Brigade cut up those that were dispersed and the rout became general.

A panic seized the enemy in every direction and they fled on all sides, deserting their artillery, throwing down their arms and each man thinking only for his own preservation. Our cavalry and the Prussians joined in the pursuit, the latter continued it the whole night, giving no quarter.

It is said the British have taken 150 pieces of cannon and the Prussians 60, making 210 in all. All their material, ammunition, stores, baggage, even Buonaparte's carriage. The slaughter was terrific. I have heard that the Duke of Wellington was affected to tears and said that he never again wished to see a field of battle.

I must now again revert to that which throws a damper upon what would otherwise have been the most glorious, most satisfactory moment of our lives. Just as Sir H. Vivian's Brigade were going down to the charge, Lord Uxbridge was struck by a grape-shot from the enemy's guns on the right knee, which shattered the joint all to pieces. I did not see him fall and went on in the charge and soon missed him and found Seymour taking him to the rear. Lord Uxbridge told me immediately that he must lose his leg and then began conversing about the action and seemed to forget his wound in the exultation for the victory. Then the surgeons examined it they all agreed that it would be at the imminent danger of his life to attempt to save the limb. Lord Uxbridge only said 'well gentlemen, I thought so myself. I have put myself in your hands and if it is to be taken off the sooner it is done the better'. He wrote a short note to Lady Uxbridge saying that if he had been a young single man he would have probably run the risk but that he would preserve his life for her and his children, if possible. During the operation he never moved or complained: no one even held his hand. He said once, perfectly calmly, that he thought the instrument was not very sharp. When it

187

was over, his nerves did not appear the least shaken and the surgeons said his pulse even was not altered.

He said, smiling 'I have had a pretty long run, I have been a beau these 47 years and it would not be fair to cut the young men out any longer' and then asked us if we did not admire his vanity.

I have seen many operations but neither Lord Greenock nor myself could bear this, we were obliged to go to the other end of the room.

Thank God he is doing as well as possible. He had had no fever and the surgeons say nothing could be more favourable.

I began this on the 19th the evening we brought Lord Uxbridge here on a litter. This is the morning of the 21st. He has had it dressed for the first time and the surgeons report is as favourable as ever. His steady firmness and the calm courage of his disposition will assist his recovery more than anything. The regret of the Army is beyond bounds. Infantry and cavalry all saw him – all admired him. How he escaped with his life I can scarcely imagine. He was everywhere in the hottest fire. When the day was doubtful, he cheered and assisted the infantry and I saw him, and was by him, when he put himself at the head of a Squadron of Cavalry and charged a solid mass of their infantry. The fire was terrific and destroyed many – the rest would not go on and he rode on and struck their bayonets before he turned and yet escaped. It was hard to have him wounded at the last, after so many escapes.

Sir John Elley, one of the bravest soldiers and as good an officer as ever lived, is here with three stabs and a sabre cut. When I went to see him, he cried like a child in speaking of Lord Uxbridge and said that though he rejoiced that his valuable life had been preserved yet the loss to the British Army was irreparable. His emotion was so great that I was obliged to leave him for his own sake after trying in vain to change the subject.

The loss on our side has been immense but the enemy's army is annihilated. There never was yet known such a battle and probably never will again. At least, much as I rejoice at having shared in this, I hope I never may see such another.

I must again remind you of your own singular good fortune who have three sons in a regiment which was particularly engaged and as you will see by the Gazette has suffered pretty considerably and yet all safe.

John was not in the great action. Edward was everywhere and has been remarked for his conduct.

He had three horses killed under him, yet escaped without a wound. I was slightly hit by a musket shot in the foot early in the day but no bone broke and so trifling that it did not take one a minute from the field.

I long to see the Gazette.

Adieux – you had better enclose your next to the Earl of Uxbridge at Brussels.

With best love to Mary, Believe me,
Your ever truly affectionate son

THOMAS WILDMAN

Three eagles are amongst the spoils. Elphinstone saw Buonaparte before the great action, who spoke to him for some time very civilly, and, on going away, said to an officer 'I desire you will treat these officers well in every respect – as British Officers deserve'.

On receipt of Tom's letter his sister Maria wrote to Mrs Hodge to say that her husband had been taken prisoner. Eventually news came through that Arthur Myer and Edward Hodge had both died of wounds. In great distress Mrs Hodge came out to Brussels and searched the battlefield for her husband and even had one grave dug up thinking it might contain his body. Eventually she was convinced that he had died.

Apart from Tom's brief mention of Edward towards the end of his letter there is no record of the part he played in the battle. However, some of his brother officers left accounts of the 7th Hussars in action during the battle. Edward's experiences would have been broadly similar. After Tom left the regiment in the morning, as described by William Verner, the regiment did not get into action until about four o'clock that afternoon when Marshal Ney began a succession of attacks by massed squadrons of cavalry against the British squares.

During the morning the officers' servants had arrived from Brussels with cold pies, other eatables and a plentiful supply of brandy. The sun had come out and their uniforms gradually dried out. After being exposed to fire for some time, Colonel Kerrison moved the regiment into a narrow lane with high banks which gave some protection. Here they dismounted. Verner lay down on his back and watched the round shot passing overhead until he fell asleep. He was wakened by the order: 'Stand to your horses – Prepare to mount.'

Up to this time Edward would have seen little or nothing of the battle, as they were behind the ridge that ran along the front. Writing many years later, Captain Robbins said that when the alarm was given the French were advancing up the side of the valley on the left of the Chateau of Hougoumont. The regiment moved rapidly to the left and wheeled into line. The enemy lancers were advancing in echelon as steadily as on a field day, and the hussars then charged. Up to this time Robbins had not seen any of the enemy that day. Robbins was then hit and had no further recollection of the action until he came to some time later.

The cuirassiers now came on at their traditional trot, but as they reached the squares the volleys of the infantry brought down the leading ranks into a struggling mass of men and horses. Those following swerved and passed down either side of the squares, where they were met by the hussars who charged and threw them back. The pattern of these attacks was repeated again and again as the Marshal attempted to break the squares. He then tried attacking with a mixed force of infantry and cavalry. Verner now found himself under heavy fire from infantry among some trees to his right:

The officers kept moving their horses backwards and forwards in front, to prevent as far as they could the infantry taking deliberate aim. I had just turned my horse for this purpose when I was struck by a Bullet on the right side of my head. I became completely stunned and only wonder I did not fall off my horse.

His head was bleeding but fortunately the bullet had been deflected by the overlapping plates of his chin strap.

Throughout the action the 7th Hussars had remained more or less in their original position on the right of the line. By about seven o'clock the losses sustained by the brigade (the 7th, 13th and 15th Hussars), were so great that they formed up in a single line. The 7th and 13th had been reduced to one squadron each. By now the Imperial Guard had been repulsed and were in retreat, and Field Marshal Blucher's Prussians were in action on the right of the French line.

When the final Grand Advance was ordered, Lieutenant Standish O'Grady recalled the hussars swept down past Hougoumont, 'entered the enemy's lines on his left and charged down his line until we met Sir Hussey Vivian at the head of his brigade,' with whom they now joined forces.

Edward was fortunate to come through that day unscathed. Some of his brother officers were not so lucky. Lieutenant Peters was struck in the chest by a grapeshot about the size of a pigeon's egg, taking with it part of his jacket and some of the buttons. The unfortunate Peter Heyliger was again wounded in the arm by a musket ball that lodged in his elbow joint, while the ball that struck Lord Uxbridge also wounded Colonel Kerrison and killed his horse.

Newstead

The end of the Napoleonic Wars left Tom with little prospect of promotion in the 7th Hussars. He therefore started to look round for an opportunity to purchase a majority in another regiment. In the meantime he married, but we do not know where he was living. During 1816 he was in London, though he appears to have visited the Continent again, for it was on his return from Ostend in April 1816 that he met Lord Byron for the last time.

Byron's disastrous marriage to Annabella Milbanke broke up finally when she left their house in Piccadilly Terrace in January 1816, never to return. By March a deed of separation had been settled, and Byron decided to go abroad. The deed was executed on 21 April and two days later, he left for Dover with his friends John Cam Hobhouse and Scrope Davies, who came to see him off. Travelling in Byron's huge coach for which he had paid £500, they put it on board the packet as soon as they arrived in Dover in case the bailiffs had been following them.

Byron then took rooms at the Ship, where Tom had, by coincidence, already arrived. Writing to Augusta on the 24th Byron told her:

We sail to-night for Ostend, & I seize this moment to say two or three words. I met last night an old Schoolfellow (Wildman by name) Aid de Camp of Lord Uxbridge. He tells me poor Fred Howard was not mangled, nor in the hands of the French; he was shot through the body charging with a party of infantry, & died (not on the field) half an hour afterwards at some farmhouse not far off, & in no great pain I thought this might make his friends easier, as they had heard he was a sufferer by falling into the enemy's hands. Capt. Wildman was near him at the time, & I believe saw him again shortly before his death, and after his wound.

What else they talked about is not recorded, but it is unlikely that Newstead entered into the conversation. Nevertheless it is possible that this encounter may have later suggested to Tom the possibility of the abbey as a home.

In August 1812, while Tom was still in Ireland, Newstead had been put up for auction. The property was withdrawn, but then sold to a Lancashire lawyer for £140,000. The lawyer soon changed his mind and did all he could to delay completion of his purchase. Eventually in August 1814 he decided to call off the deal and forfeited his £25,000 deposit. The property was again put up for auction the following July, while Tom would have been in Brussels after Waterloo. It failed to reach the reserve price of £95,000, and was withdrawn once more. When Byron left England the following year the need to sell was no longer pressing and Byron had other things to think about.

On his arrival in Brussels he visited the field of Waterloo. He was now beginning the Third Canto of *Childe Harold* with its well-known evocation of the Duchess of Richmond's ball – 'There was a sound of revelry by night...' As he described the battle, no doubt he recalled his recent meeting with his former schoolfellow:

Their praise is hymn'd by loftier harps than mine;
Yet one I would select from that proud throng,
Partly because they blend me with his line,
And partly that I did his sire some wrong,
And partly that bright names will hallow song;
And his was of the bravest, and when shower'd
The death-bolts deadliest the thinn'd files along,
Even where the thickest of war's tempest lower'd,
They reach'd no nobler breast than thine, young, gallant Howard!

On 31 October, Tom exchanged into the 9th Light Dragoons (Lancers) with the rank of major. Now that he was married he started to look round for a permanent home. In the summer of 1817 Byron wrote to his friend Douglas Kinnaird saying only absolute necessity would bring him back to England and expressing his intention to dispose of Newstead in the course of that summer 'at any price which it will bring'. By the following December, Tom had agreed to buy the property for £94,500. Writing to his solicitor, John Hanson, who had evidently inquired what his client knew about Major Wildman, Byron said, 'I am unaquainted with his means or his property:– but I recollect him as my old schoolfellow and a man of honour – and would rather as my personal feelings are concerned that he should be the purchaser than another –'

For some reason or other completion of the purchase was delayed. The following July, Byron was beginning to be worried, and in a letter to Kinnaird dated 15 July 1818 he said, 'If I didn't know of old – Wildman to be a man of honour – and Spooney (Hanson) a damned tortoise in all his proceedings – I should expect foul play – in this delay of the man & papers –'. The delay is rather surprising because Tom could not have been short of funds, nor should he have had to raise money on his Jamaican estates. During the years that elapsed between his father's death and his coming of age in 1808 the income from these estates would have been accumulating, and there is nothing to suggest he had been enjoying an extravagant way of life; on the contrary he seems to have been quite frugal in his day-to-day life. He must have had enough money to buy Newstead twice over!

By September, Hanson was hinting at further delays, and Byron told Hobhouse, 'I gave him ample time – it is no fault of mine – and if we don't complete – I presume that I shall at least have the property again.' Fortunately, whatever it was that caused the delay – possibly a problem relating to the title to the property which had been in the family since Tudor times – was soon overcome, and the sale was completed by the end of the year.

Now that Tom was the owner of a landed estate with endless possibilities for improvement the attractions of army life soon began to wane, especially as there was no likelihood of further promotion in the 9th Lancers for years to come. So in 1819 he retired on half-pay with the rank of brevet lieutenant colonel. While still in the army he had become a Freemason, and about this time he had met and became a close friend of the Prince Regent's brother, the Duke of Sussex, who appointed him to be his equerry. The 'little Colonel' must have made an amusing contrast beside the burly Duke, who was six feet three inches tall, and whom that political gossip, Thomas Creevey, usually referred to as 'Little Sussex'. The Duke was Grand Master of the United Lodge of England, and it may have been through this common interest that Tom was introduced to the Duke.

At about this time he met Charles Tennyson d'Eyncourt, already mentioned, a recently elected Member of Parliament and also a friend of the Duke of Sussex. He, too, was a Freemason. Both Tom and Tennyson belonged to a small group of Romantics and Radicals, and became lifelong friends. The Radicals were now forcing the pace for parliamentary reform, and calling for the enlargement of the franchise and the abolition of the pocket boroughs, such as Tom's father had held on behalf of William Beckford. Supported by the Whigs and the industrial classes, these reforms were not generally welcome to the squirearchy among whom Tom had come to live. However, he lost no time in entering into the life of the county, becoming High Sheriff in 1822 and later a deputy lieutenant. As befitted his position he also became a Justice of the Peace.

Tom's entry into county society appears to have been received with mixed feelings. Regarded as a parvenu by some, his great wealth attracted envy among other landowners, and he was sometimes referred to as the 'West Indian'. Some of the county families were unflattering about his pseudo-Tudor interiors. One such lady, Leah Fortrie Gossip, wrote in 1828:

> I have been to-day to chapel at Newstead and seen the little Colonel at the summit of his happiness and the height of his pride, surrounded by all his new-bought dependants and looking more like the West Indian than the desparate Radical – I could not help fancying one of its late possessors and seeing this original Chapter House which was for centuries their Chapel, and now painted and gilded and overdone with modern innovations and luxuries and the owner not priding himself on ancestry and titles, but on the richness of his carpet and the costliness of his chairs...

Having spent years in the company of young men for whom the ownership of landed estates was an accepted part of life, one can well understand Tom's pleasure at finding himself the owner of some 3,000 acres and a mansion with such a romantic past. As soon as he had entered into occupation, he threw himself into the task of restoring the abbey, an undertaking that was to last the rest of his life. Besides being a competent artist, he was also interested in architecture, and two of his designs for additions to the property survive. To carry out the work of restoration he employed John Shaw (1776–1832), and it is said that he spent over £100,000 on renovations and improvements, of which he had already spent £80,000 by 1832. In addition to the building work, Tom began to furnish the house in a manner he considered fitting to what today would be called a 'stately home'. Even the Duke of Sussex kept a lookout for likely 'antiques'. Writing to his 'Dear Tom' in 1830 he said:

> Before I left Town Mr Morant brought me some beautiful imitations of armour made in Paris of papier mache which I think would much assist you in filling up the hall and would have a happy effect as really, at a certain distance one can not distinguish them from the original ... they are so light that they would not occasion any additional weight to put up.

Another visitor to Newstead commented that he had bought the house when in a ruinous state, but ... has saved it from destruction and when his present projects are complete it will be one of the most magnificent and interesting seats in England ... I was ushered through various galleries to a noble room, 80ft long and most beautifully furnished ... where my hostess, Mrs. Wildman, received me very courteously ... on Sunday evening ... evening prayers in the Chapel, the original Chapter-house of ye monks it has a very curious roof and the painted glass is exceedingly beautiful. All the domestics attended ...

Those who could see behind the desire of this man with a somewhat dubious social background to be what he clearly was not could appreciate Tom for what he really was, and this same visitor described him as 'a kind and hospitable little man and a complete gentleman. Never was hospitality, attention and gentlemanly benevolence like the Colonel's.' Many years later in 1850, Byron's daughter Ada, Countess of Lovelace, visited the abbey, but the melancholy effect its associations had upon her were dispelled by the 'kindly Colonel's sympathetic attentions and conversation about her father.'

This courtesy and a rather formal manner seem to have been displayed in Tom's domestic life. When he and Louisa moved to Newstead she brought her sister Caroline to live with them. Then, in 1825, old Mrs Wildman, who was now seventy-four, sold Turnham Green Hall and came to live at Newstead where she died in November 1830. Caroline remained at Newstead and the three of them seem to have lived quite happily together. Tom, in keeping with romantic notions of the past and his medieval surroundings, treated Louisa with a courtly love worthy of a troubadour. His quaint formality may have, subconsciously, struck the Duke of Sussex who stayed with them in 1827. Writing a contribution to Caroline's album, he referred to 'my excellent friends the Abbott & Lady Abbess of Newstead'. Tom and Louisa did not have any children, and they must have been disappointed not to have had an heir. In contrast to Cousin James's large brood at Chilham, there were no children's voices to disturb the decorum of Newstead.

Each year on 21 April Tom composed a birthday ode for Louisa. In 1828 his poem begins:

So soon again! How swiftly fly
The hours and days thus pass'd with thee;
Twelve blissful years have now gone by
Since heart and hand were given me.

Two years later in 1831, he is anxious to show that he is still in mourning for his mother:

> *I cannot sing in mirthful strain*
> *Nor wake my lyre to festive numbers.*
> *I court the silent muse in vain*
> *To rouse her from her mournful slumbers.*
>
> *Yet still my spirit hails the day*
> *As fondly true, as warm as ever,*
> *Bound by a tie which mocks decay*
> *And Death has not pow'r to sever.*

Each of these poems contains five or six verses, and a rather curious feature of these birthday offerings is that he wrote them in Caroline's album along with other verses she collected from visitors to Newstead. It would seem that he wrote them as much for the benefit of their friends as for the pleasure of his wife!

This apparent desire to make a public display of his feelings is demonstrated by another poem he wrote in November 1831, the anniversary of his mother's death, which begins:

> *Tis now the time when o'er my soul,*
> *Sad thoughts arise and darkly roll ...*

All the same, Tom was capable of less self-conscious efforts and on 20 February 1847 he wrote in Caroline's album:

> *It is thy birthday Carry dear!*
> *And I've no gift to bring:*
> *No chance was left me to prepare*
> *The very simplest thing –*

In the fourth verse he concludes:

> *For Birth Day Present on my part*
> *I can but offer <u>This</u>*
> *But I will give it from my heart*
> *A loving Brother's Kiss.*

As for Caroline herself, we know even less about her than we do about Louisa. The only description of her comes from an admirer who in the course of a poem he wrote for her says:

Let us say her flaxen hair,
Her light blue eyes, her neck so fair;
Tell we of her gentle manners,
Knights might range beneath her banners.

Notwithstanding such charms she never married, and the explanation may lie in a letter addressed to the Revd G.B. she copied into her album containing a long and damning indictment of the 'insolent superiority which your sex has assumed over ours'. Her arguments for equal educational opportunities for men and women were, in all likelihood, influenced by Mary Wollstonecraft. This letter was probably written between 1835–40. Unfortunately for her such views were fifty years ahead of her time, though they may have been shared by her radical brother-in-law.

Turning now to Tom's public life, the arch-Tory Duke of Newcastle, as Lord Lieutenant of the county appointed Tom in 1828 to be colonel of the Sherwood Rangers, the local yeomanry regiment. The whole country was now preoccupied by the question of reform. There was unrest on all sides, with riots and rick burning. (The Wildmans of Chilham Castle were receiving threats.) Having evicted some of his tenants in Newark for expressing political views contrary to his own, the Duke of Newcastle was vilified for saying in Parliament: 'Have I not the right to do what I like with mine own?' Tenants who had the right to vote in the days before the secret ballot were expected to conform to the views of their landlord. As it was, the Duke controlled nine pocket boroughs, whose members were known as his 'ninepins'! Trouble broke out in Nottingham, and in October 1831 the mob burned down the Duke's home, Nottingham Castle. The Sherwood Rangers were called out to help put down trouble round Mansfield, for which Tom was commended by the Home Secretary, Lord Melbourne.

Notwithstanding all this unrest, Tom was publicly supporting the Reform Bill then before Parliament. The fury of the Duke was, perhaps, understandable. As a result of all the unpleasantness Tom decided to resign his command 'with feelings of extreme regret and reluctance'. In a letter to the regiment he spoke of 'the misunderstandings and differences of opinion which occur between the Lord Lieutenant of the County and myself and the unpleasant circumstances arising therefrom'. It may have given him some satisfaction when, in 1839, the Duke, having resisted the appointment of two prospective magistrates because he disagreed with their politics, was told that the Queen had no further occasion for his services as Lord Lieutenant.

In 1832 the Whigs succeeded in passing their second Reform Bill. When the reformed Parliament met, the question of slavery soon came up. The days of Tom's prosperity were now numbered. W.E. Gladstone had been invited to enter Parliament as a Tory candidate for Newark by the Duke of Newcastle, with the support of his father, Sir John Gladstone Bart. The latter owned extensive estates in Jamaica and, like the Wildmans, he owed his fortune to slavery. Gladstone, who could be relied upon to do the unexpected, then startled the Duke by issuing an election address in which he supported the extinction of slavery. In his maiden speech in 1833, he welcomed a safe and gradual emancipation, but said that emancipation before the slaves were ripe for freedom would be 'ruinous to the colonies, to the country, and to the slaves themselves'. The Act abolishing slavery became law in 1835, and substituted a compulsory system of apprenticeship for an interim period. However, in 1838 apprenticeship was abolished in favour of immediate freedom. This spelt ruin for plantation owners such as Tom, his cousin and Gladstone's father. The owners received compensation, but James Beckford Wildman, who as an Evangelical, had been in favour of emancipation, considered it 'perfectly inadequate'. How much the cousins received we do not know, but Sir John Gladstone got over £70,000.

Having gained their freedom, the slaves showed an understandable reluctance to work for their former owners. Living was cheap, the climate was warm and many had small plots of land, so they could manage on very little. Even if Tom did not visit his estates, Cousin James used to go out to Jamaica. He tried to make his plantations pay by installing steam machinery, and Chilham Castle was heavily mortgaged to provide the capital. In all likelihood Tom was forced to follow his example. It was all to no avail. The planters had never done much to maintain the fertility of the soil, preferring to develop new plantations when the land was exhausted. Their virgin land was diminishing, and by the middle of the century the Wildman plantations were becoming worked out and were being abandoned. To make matters worse, the price of sugar had been falling since before the end of the war. To try and remedy the situation James sent his son-in-law, William Augustus Munn, the husband of his eldest daughter, Marianne, out to Jamaica to manage his estates. It is quite likely that Munn cooperated in the management of Tom's plantations for the properties were not far apart.

These financial problems do not seem to have altered Tom's way of life. He continued with his building works, and during the 1830s and 1840s they entertained a great deal and exchanged visits over a wide area. The Reverend Reaton Rodes of Barlborough Hall, an Elizabethen house near Chesterfield, seems to have been a frequent guest at Newstead and contributed a number of verses to Caroline's album. On one occasion a fancy dress fête he held at Barlborough so inspired Tom that he composed some stanzas in honour of his host and hostess ending,

And long may such spells and such sounds of delight
Drive care from this Hall, and its inmates beguile;
And may she, this Titania, fair Queen of to-night
Bind them fast by the majic which dwells in her smile

Thus Tom concludes what, in his desire to compete with his host's high-flown verse, must be one of his less happy compositions! On other occasions they stayed with Charles Tennyson d'Eyncourt at Bayons, his Gothic pile at Tealby in Lincolnshire. Here Tom threw himself enthusiastically into amateur theatricals. As time passed, Tom devoted more of his time to farming some four hundred or so acres of his estate. His political views were changing or, more probably, the political realities were no longer in conflict with his early radical ideas, and in his later years he was described as a Liberal Conservative. Visiting also took up a great deal of his time, for such visits usually involved staying the night, or probably several nights, when they had to drive quite considerable distances. As the years went by they travelled less, but a small pocket diary that survives records that during the last year of his life he usually 'accompanied the ladies' to Nottingham or to friends' houses once or twice a week. These words conjure up a pleasing picture of the 'little Colonel' in a stovepipe hat, frock coat and sponge-bag 'inexpressibles',* with his ladies in their crinolines, visiting shops and paying calls.

During the 1850s Tom's thoughts seem to have reverted to the past, which is so often the way with old men. He was now well into his sixties, a fair age at this period. The Duke of Wellington died in 1852, putting an end to the Waterloo commemoration dinners at Apsley House. Lord

---

* Trousers, considered by some Victorians to be too impolite to be mentioned in society.

Edward Somerset, Hussey Vivian and Edward Kerrison had already died and the Marquess of Anglesey (Lord Uxbridge) followed in 1854. Tom's brother Edward had died in 1846 and, although John was to survive him, neither had any sons to carry on his name. By now his fortune was almost exhausted and he must have realised that he could not maintain Newstead for much longer. How then was his family to be remembered?

The wish to be remembered seems to be the most likely explanation for the decision of this childless man approaching seventy to put up the stained-glass windows in the great hall of the abbey. One window is devoted to himself, Edward and John, setting out the battles in which they had all taken part over forty years earlier. Other windows display the arms of his brother George, his mother and his sister Maria. Perhaps it was a sense of history or a wish not to appear egotistical that caused him to put up another window devoted to other worthies who had had somewhat tenuous associations with the abbey. The exact date of these windows is not known, but they must have been installed between 1850 and 1857 when Cousin James's daughter Matilda saw them:

I went there on a visit with Leila [her sister] when I left the schoolroom in 1857 … in July a large dinner party of 30 people was held in the Refectory. After dinner we walked round the Abbey to see the moonlight streaming thro' the famous window shown in the left side of the engraving. Col. W. put up in the Refectory 3 stained glass windows to himself and his two brothers all of whom were present at Waterloo, fought all day and came out unwounded.

Although Tom had transferred to the 9th Lancers, his heart remained with the 7th Hussars. Shortly before he died, his portrait was painted for the last time. For this the 'little Colonel' unpacked his old hussar uniform. He had not put on much weight over the years, he still had the drooping hussar moustache, but his moustache and whiskers were now grizzled and he may have been wearing a wig. However, he remained quite active, but in the early part of 1859 his health was not very good. On 9 January he recorded in his pocket diary, 'Very bad night. Took some of my Boulogne Prescription. Kept to my bed all day.' He got better but was ill again on the 12th. By 15 January he noted, 'Rather weak but better generally.'

He was soon getting about again and even riding his pony. On 23 May he records, 'Drove with the Ladies to Linby Station to meet Col John Wildman.' The next day he finished loading oats and walked with John. In September, John had again come down from London and they went out shooting. His normal routine continued until 10 September but thereafter the diary entries cease. Tom died quite suddenly on 20 September.

In one respect Tom was more fortunate than his cousin James, for he had been able to live out his days at his beloved Newstead. Two years later James was forced to sell Chilham Castle which had been mortgaged to the hilt to maintain his Jamaican estates, as must have been the case with Newstead. The sugar plantations had been abandoned and the land was almost worthless.

Tom left all his property to Louisa, who lost no time in selling Newstead lock, stock and barrel, retaining only a few possessions of sentimental value. Shortly afterwards she and Caroline moved south and went to live at 33 Palmeira Square, Hove in Sussex, a terrace of recently built houses within sight of the sea. When she died on 1 August 1879 her personal estate was valued at less than £35,000.

Principal Sources

Manuscripts and Private Letters

Attorney's Roll, Court of Kings Bench, Public Record Office
Solicitors Admission Book, Court of Chancery, Law Society
Barracks in Sussex, Chichester Record Office
Major-General Benjamin Lovell Badcock, Copy Letters, Chichester Record Office
Edward Hodge, Diary, National Army Museum
J.B. Wildman's Marriage Settlement, M. Birks
Matilda Wildman (Lady Fraser) Family Notes, M. Birks
Paget Papers, National Army Museum
Caroline Preisig's Album, Mrs Hilary Sweet-Escott
Wellington (General Orders, Adjutant-General's letters), Southampton University Library
Wildman Papers, Newstead Abbey
Richard's Roll, Law Society
Fonds de Domaines, Archives de la Seine, Archives de Paris

Works of Reference

Army Lists, National Army Museum
Black Books of Lincoln's Inn
British Battles and Medals (Spink, London, 1981)
Burke's Landed Gentry
Dictionary of National Biography
History of Parliament
Lloyd's List (1810)
Lloyd's Register of Shipping (1808–1813)
Military Service Roll, 1793–1814
Report on the Slave Trade by the Legislative Council of Jamaica, 1789
Royal Military Calendar
Victoria County History of Middlesex

Newspapers

Hampshire Telegraph, 1813

Published Letters, Diaries and Memoirs

Waterloo Letters, edited by Major-General H.T. Siborne (1891)
James Anton, *A Retrospect of Military Life* (1841)
Jane Austen's Letters, edited by Guy Chapman (OUP)
A Peninsular Portrait: Letters of William Bragg (OUP, 1959)
Captain Gronow, Reminiscences, edited by John Rougement (1964)
Benjamin Haydon, *Autobiography* (Harvard, 1927)
Memoirs of William Hickey, edited Alfred Spencer (Hurst & Blacket Ltd, 1919)
Captain J. Kincaid, *Adventures in the Rifle Brigade*
L.A. Marchand, *Byron: A Biography* (New York, 1957)
Cavalie Mercer, *Journal of the Waterloo Campaign* (Peter Davies, 1927)
Captain David O'Brien, *My Adventures During the Late War* (London, 1902)
Sir Harry Smith, *Autobiography, 1787–1814* (John Murray, 1910)
On the Road with Wellington: The Diary of a War Commissary August Schauman, edited by A. Ludovici (London, 1924)
Reminiscences of William Verner, 1782–1871, Special publication of *S.A.H.R.* (1965 No. 8)
Letters of a Young Diplomat and Soldier, Ralph Heathcote (edited by Grober, 1907)
Hon. Claud Vivian, *Richard Hussey Vivian: Memoirs & Letters* (London, 1897)
William Cobbett, *Rural Rides* (A. Cobbett, 1853)
Arthur Young, *Travels in France* (Cambridge University Press, 1950)
The English Traveller in France (Routledge, 1932)

Biographies, Historical and General Works

Boyd Alexander, *England's Wealthiest Son*
C.R.P. Barrett, *History of the 7th. Hussars*
P.B. Boyden, *Thomas Atkin's Letters* (National Army Museum)
Michael Brown, *South to Gascony* (Hamish Hamilton, 1969)
Rosalys Coope, *The Wildman Family and Col. Thomas Wildman* (Thoroton Society, 1991)

Melinda Elder, *Lancaster and the African Slave Trade* (Lancaster Museums)

Sir John Fortescue, *History of The British Army*, Vols IX & XV

Bryan Fosten, *Wellington's Light Cavalry* (Osprey Pub. Ltd)

David Glover, *Wellington's Army in the Peninsular* (1977)

Douglas Hall, *In Miserable Slavery* (Macmillan)

T.W. Horsfield, *Histories and Antiquities of Sussex* (1835)

John Keagan, *The Face of Battle* (Penguin)

Elizabeth Longford, *Wellington: The Years of the Sword* (Weidenfeld & Nicholson, 1969)

Philip Magnus, *Gladstone* (John Murray, 1954)

Marquess of Anglesey, *History of the British Cavalry*, Vol. I (Leo Cooper)

Marquess of Anglesey, *One Leg* (Jonathan Cape, 1961)

T.H. McGuffie, 'Life in a Light Cavalry Regiment Regiment', *J.A.H.R.*, Vols 38 & 39

T.H. McGuffie, 'The 7th. Hussars in 1813', *J.A.H.R.*, Vol. 42

David Miller, *The Duchess of Richmond's Ball in June 1815* (Spellmount, 2005)

C.D. O'Doll, *Annals of the New York Stage* (Columbia University Press)

Sir Charles Oman, *History of the Peninsular War*, Vol. VII (OUP)

Sir Charles Oman, *Wellington's Army* (Edward Arnold, 1912)

Panorama of Falmouth (Philp, 1822)

The Portsmouth Guide (1822)

Louis Perouas Privat, *L'Histoire de Limoges*

Christopher Robinson, *Victorian Plymouth*

Alexander Scrivens, *Life of John Horne Tooke* (1824)

Captain William Siborne, *The Waterloo Campaign* (London, 1904)

Stately Homes around Truro (1980)

Philip Warner, *The British Cavalry* (J.M. Dent & Co)

Wellington's Dispatches, Vols VIII–XIV

Lt. Col. Wildman, *Remarks on the New Instructions for the New Movements of Cavalry* (1830)

'William Playfair's British Family', *Antiquity*, Vol. 7 (British Museum Press)